The Complete SAVing Source Catalog

A Guide to Saving the Earth and Money

Michelle A. Potter

RIMA WORLD PRESS
COLUMBIA, MARYLAND

This book is dedicated to all those who love the beauty and spirit of the earth

ACKNOWLEDGMENTS

First, I want to thank my husband whose persistent encouragement convinced me to do this book. I want to thank my mother and my aunt, Romy, for being the first subscribers to *The SAVing Source.* And I want to thank each and every subscriber who encouraged me, through their interest and letters, to continue with the newsletter. Thanks must go to subscribers for their ideas and suggestions, and the many people from organizations, companies and government agencies who provided me with information and documentation I needed to complete many articles. And fondly, I thank Jasmin and Simba, my Siamese cats, for the lighter moments during the preparation of this book.

Acknowledgment goes to *Bloomsbury Treasury of Quotations* edited by John Daintith and published by Bloomsbury Publishing Plc for the quotes used at the beginning of each chapter in this book.

Publisher's Cataloging in Publication
(Prepared by Quality Books Inc.)

Potter, Michelle A.
The complete saving source catalog : a guide to saving the earth and money / Michelle A. Potter. – 1st ed.
p. cm.
Includes index.
LCCN: 96-92197
ISBN 0-9652196-0-7

1. Environmental protection—Citizen participation. 2. Human ecology. 3. Finance, Personal. 4. Saving and thrift. I. Title.

TD171.7.P68 1996 363.7'0525
QBI96-1025

This book is printed on recycled paper with soy-based inks.

Printed and bound by McNaughton & Gunn, Inc., Saline, MI.

The Complete SAVing Source Catalog

A Guide to Saving the Earth and Money

CONTENTS

INTRODUCTION

As a child, I would often take long walks after school in the beautiful woods adjacent to my house. Those walks among the trees and birds regenerated my soul and taught me to appreciate the earth's beauty. However, like many people, I took this beauty for granted—until I bought my first house and began a vegetable garden. I was determined to garden organically, without chemicals. Through my mother, the local extension service, and lots of research, I learned how to work with nature to improve the soil, compost, prevent disease, and deter pests. Frequently, I was amazed at how adept nature is in solving seemingly difficult problems with a little help from me and my homemade concoctions. I love gardening. Better yet, I love eating vegetables and herbs from my garden, knowing they are free of chemicals. I no longer take nature for granted. Instead, I feel a deep reverence for nature's adaptability, tenacity and vigor.

A few years after I began gardening, Earth Day 1990 reared its magnificently loud head. I was moved to act, and yet I did not know what *I* could do to help. In previous years, I had been writing and editing newsletters for communities and other groups. Hence, it occurred to me to begin a newsletter which addressed environmental issues. On the other hand, numerous environmental publications had sprouted or become more visible since Earth Day 1990. There would be no use in being redundant. But then one day as I was discussing our budget with my husband, I realized we had saved lots of money since I had been gardening, using herbs to make homemade foods and products, and reusing items for other purposes. I realized there is an obvious connection between saving the earth and saving money. Reducing, recycling, reusing and renewing are not only environmental gains, but financial ones as well. Thus, *The SAVing Source* newsletter was born.

My goal when I began the newsletter was to share what I had learned and to learn what others had to share about saving the earth and money. It worked out well. I explored ideas and issues in the newsletter and readers sent me letters with new ideas and more information. And sometimes, readers would send letters asking for solutions to problems—which challenged me to research some areas I would not have originally thought topics for the newsletter. All in all, I believe the newsletter addressed environmental questions with honest and simple solutions which usually saved money. Needless to say, saving the earth and saving money are related subjects since both suggest less waste.

This book is a compilation of most of the material covered in the newsletter for the first four years. Although the newsletter provided a source of information to readers, it, in no way, was designed to be an authority or to encompass all subjects or all areas of subjects. *The SAVing Source*, and therefore, this book, are an exploration of subjects which may offer readers a distinctive view of environmental matters within the context of the individual. Indeed, choices we make as individuals at home or in our backyard can make a difference in our lives and to the environment. The cherry on top is the additional money in our pocket. Therefore, the book offers numerous resources for additional information in various areas. Many companies and products are mentioned throughout, not as personal endorsements, but as sources of environmental products. In my opinion, there are not enough companies producing environmental products.

Theoretically, this book is for anyone who is interested in saving the earth and money. However, I would say this book is also for anyone who is interested in exploring new ideas on old subjects. For instance, you can make a window quilt to insulate windows or use autumn leaves to decorate your house.

Or you can color your hair with strawberries. This book suggests using elements from nature to substitute commercial products with the idea—to use what is from nature is to give back to nature. We have taken a lot from this earth, and we need to give some back.

And finally, this book is a source of fun, creativity and ideas. Saving the earth and saving money are serious subjects, but as in most things, a lighter side exists. It can be fun to throw an Earth Day party! It can be fun to whip up your own bug sprays! It can be fun to create a budget! And it can be exciting to start your own recycling business! My hope is that this book will at times make you laugh, make you think, and make you conjure up ideas of your own. Enjoy!

Michelle A. Potter

Chapter 1

HOME ON THE GREEN

How doth the little busy bee
Improve each shining hour,
And gather honey all the day
From every opening flower!

- Isaac Watts, *Divine Songs for Children*

INSIDE

Tips for a NONTOXIC House

- **Avoid carpeting floors. Opt for wood or tile flooring.**
- **Use plants, such as the Spider Plant to purify indoor air.**
- **Use untreated cotton or flannel sheets.**
- **Avoid furniture made with adhesives instead of nails and made with pressed wood. Opt for solid wood furniture which is nailed together.**
- **Use cedar, redwood or cypress wood to build decks, flower gardens or sheds.**
- **Use natural cleaners as much as possible.**
- **Control pests with natural concoctions.**
- **Keep the house ventilated as much as possible.**

The Nontoxic House

In this day and age most things in our house have been processed with some chemical for one reason or another. Although we, as a society, are becoming more aware of the chemicals which possess dangers for us and our environment, we still have a long way to go. After all, if we know of no substitute, what can we do! Of course, we can do without in some cases, but in others, more research is needed to alert us to chemical dangers and the alternatives to using chemicals.

Lead Paint

Because some of us still live and work in older buildings, we come in contact with lead paint. Besides the hazards of peeling paint being eaten by young children, tiny particles of peeling paint can be inhaled by anyone in the building. To remove lead paint, scrape it off with a sharp blade. Do not use heat guns or power

sanders because the result is a vapor or a fine dust which can be inhaled. Wear protective clothing and face filters.

Pesticides

Pesticides have been blamed for many illnesses among humans. Scientists say pesticides are stored in human body fat and over time can accumulate to levels of severe toxicity which can cause many illnesses, including cancer. The best way to avoid pesticides is to not use them. Use alternatives instead.

ANTS - Check all around the outside of the house for nests and small openings around windows and doors. To remove the nest, dig it out and pour lemon juice inside. Caulk openings.

COCKROACHES - Search out damp areas where cockroaches nest and dry the area. Boric acid is an excellent control for cockroaches.

Sprinkle some behind the refrigerator, under the stove, and in areas where pets cannot reach. Place bay leaves in cabinets.

MOTHS - Avoid using mothballs. Instead, use cedar chips or blocks. Some herbal moth repellents are now available in stores.

Outside Building Materials

Pressure-treated wood is often used to build outside decks, flower gardens and sheds to avoid rotting and pest damage. However, pressure-treated wood contains chemicals, such as arsenic and creosote. Alternative woods are cedar, redwood and cypress which will last for years and resist insects.

Indoor Air

Pollution occurs in the house as well as outside the house because of chemicals trapped inside.

RADON - Kits available to check for radon in your home. If you find radon is entering your home, seal cracks in the foundation. If radon is entering from a dirt crawl space, cover the area with concrete.

FORMALDEHYDE - Formaldehyde is used in processing many items we use in our homes, such as furniture, wood products, carpets and insulation. Unless you are willing to replace these items, it would probably be better to ensure your home has adequate ventilation. When the weather permits, open the windows. Use plants to help purify the air. Invest in a chemical filter system.

Plastics

We have become so accustomed to using plastic. However, there is research that foods stored in some plastic containers will be contaminated with chemicals leached from the plastic. Furthermore, plastic is not biodegradable and quite toxic when burned. Start using glass or earthenware products for storing food. Avoid buying food products in plastic containers.

Home Heating

Studies have shown heating methods which use gas, oil or coal pollute the indoor air of homes. The best method of heating the home is to use solar methods or heat pumps or electricity.

Hotlines

Indoor Air Quality
Information Clearinghouse
(800) 438-4318

Safe Drinking Water Hotline
(800) 426-4791

National Lead Information
Center (800) LEAD-FYI

National Radon Hotline
(800) SOS-RADON

Air RISC Hotline
(919) 541-0888

The Healthy Household: A Complete Guide for Creating a Healthy Indoor Environment by Lynn Marie Bower is available from the Healthy House Institute at (812) 332-5073.

Write the Consumer Information Center at P. O. Box 100, Pueblo, CO 81002 and ask for their catalog of publications to order the following pamphlets and booklets:

Asbestos in Your Home - Household Hazardous Waste: Steps to Safe Management - Home Buyer's Guide to Environmental Hazards - A Citizens Guide to Radon - A Guide to Radon: How to Protect Yourself and Your Family - Lead Poisoning and Your Child - How Healthy Is the Air in Your Home?

The Inside Story on Spiders

The scientific name for spiders is *Arachnoidea* which is derived from the Greek word, *arachne*. The origin of the Greek word comes from Greek mythology. A maiden, Arachne, challenged Athena, the goddess of wisdom, skills and warfare, to a weaving and spinning contest. Arachne's weaving and spinning was of such superior quality that Athena became enraged and turned Arachne into a spider with a life of spinning silk.

Spiders prey on other insects by constructing webs which catch the unsuspecting victims and hold them until their death. This is why they are excellent companions in the house. Many of us would like nothing better than to have no creepy, crawly thingy near us at all, however insects inevitably find ways into our homes—whether because they stray into it or are looking for a new dwelling.

In recent years, chemicals have been produced to rid our homes of every possible insect invader, but they are not foolproof and they are hazardous to our health and to the health of our children and our pets. They also cost a lot of money in the long run. Spiders cost nothing, are safe (except for a few), and are effective insect killers.

Spiders and their webs are better companions if they are kept out of sight. Even though I try to leave my house-dwelling spiders alone, I really do not want to see them. The best way to keep spiders out of sight is to tear down their webs where they are not wanted without killing the spider. Excellent places for spiders to dwell and not be seen are behind the washer in the basement, behind or under the refrigerator, behind the water heater, and inside the walls.

Some people may suffer from Arachnophobia, the fear of spiders, and therefore be unable to tolerate even the idea of spiders living with them in the house. Most are completely harmless and very small. They are the most effective weapon against houseflies, earwigs, cockroaches and other insects which are bothersome and spread disease.

Spicy Almonds

31/2 cups whole almonds
1/2 tsp. salt
1 tbsp. water
1 tbsp. oil
1 tsp. Cajun seasoning

Place almonds in a bowl. Dissolve the salt in the water. Mix the salt water with the almonds and let sit for 15 minutes. Place the almonds on a flat plate or microwave dish. Smooth them out flat. In the microwave cook on HIGH for seven minutes stirring every two minutes.

Sprinkle the almonds with the oil, mixing well. Sprinkle with Cajun seasoning. Mix well. In microwave, cook on HIGH for three minutes stirring after one minute.

Cool for 30 minutes before serving.

Two poisonous spiders to be on the watch for are--the black widow and the brown recluse. Large spiders, compared to most other varieties, they should be easy to spot. The black widow is

approximately 3/8 of an inch long with a shiny black body. An hourglass-shaped red marking is on the underside. Only the female bites. The brown recluse is mostly found in the western part of the United States. Grayish brown with an orange-yellow violin pattern on its back, it ranges from 1/4 to 3/8 of an inch long. Both of these spiders are not aggressive and will usually try to escape rather than bite. The black widow when guarding an egg mass, however, will defend it fiercely.

Just as spiders are valuable in the garden against disease-spreading and plant-devouring insects, they are also valuable in the house against disease-spreading and food-eating insects. They are an important part of balancing nature. Let them do their work and you will have less to do in the fight against household pests.

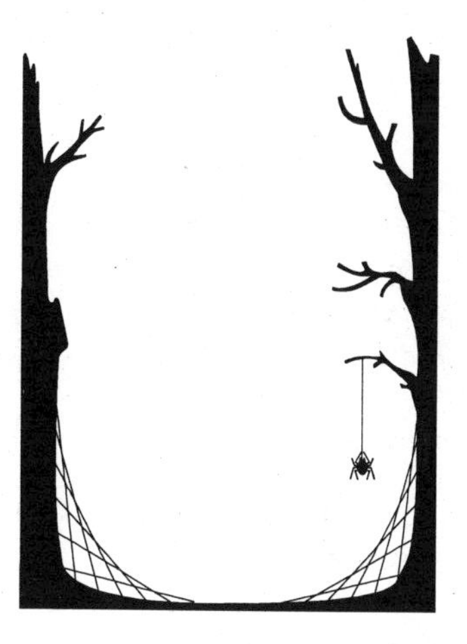

Make Your Own Spice Mixes

Taco Seasoning Mix
1 tablespoon cumin powder
1 tablespoon oregano powder
1/4 tablespoon cayenne pepper
1 tablespoon garlic salt
3 tablespoons onion powder
1/2 tablespoon dried basil

Mix all ingredients together. Store in an airtight container.

Curry Powder
1/2 cup coriander seeds
1 1/2 teaspoon cumin seeds
1 teaspoon ginger powder
1 teaspoon dry mustard seeds
1 teaspoon black peppercorns
1/4 teaspoon cloves
1/8 teaspoon cayenne pepper
1 teaspoon turmeric powder

Grind all ingredients in a spice mill. Store in a small jar or airtight container.

Salami Home Run

Salami can be very expensive, but here's a recipe to make it yourself for much less.

5 pounds hamburger
2 1/2 tsp. Liquid Smoke
2 1/2 tsp. mustard (gourmet)
4 tbsp. curing salt
1 tsp. garlic salt
2 1/2 tsp. coarsely ground pepper

Mix and knead all ingredients together well. Put mixture in a large bowl and cover. Store in the refrigerator, kneading for five minutes each day for four days. On the fourth day, roll into four long rolls. Place in a broiler pan. Bake for nine hours at 160°F. Turn the rolls a few times during baking. Freeze all but one roll.

A Mouse in the House

When the cold months begin, mice search for warm places to breed and have their young. Unfortunately, those warm places are often our homes. In my home, we use part of our closet under the stairs as a pantry, and this is where we have problems with mice. Only from late October through March or early April, however. During the warm months, the traps remain empty.

The best way to keep mice out of our houses is to search for openings all around the outside and close them up to prevent mice from entering, however in town houses the problem may be more complex. The mice may be entering from another home and finding their way through the inner walls to your house. Still, it would be a good idea to search for openings and plug them.

Mice are not only bothersome because they eat and contaminate our food, but because there never seems to be an end to them. Mice produce litters only 21 days after mating. Each litter could contain 4 to 6 young, maybe even 10 to 12. Young mice are ready to mate at 3 months of age. It may sound harsh, but killing them may be the single most effective thing to do to get them out of your house.

Many people set out poison for mice. Even though this is an effective method of controlling mice, the bad far outweighs the good. Once the mouse has eaten some of the poisoned bate, it may scurry back into the wall of your house or your neighbor's house and die. The ugly odor of a decomposing mouse somewhere in the walls where you cannot get to it is not only terrible, but embarrassing when you have company. If you have pets, especially cats, they could be poisoned by biting into the poisoned mouse. Furthermore, the dead poisoned mouse is not good for the environment. Poisons used to kill mice usually contain white phosphorus or arsenic trioxide which are highly toxic chemicals.

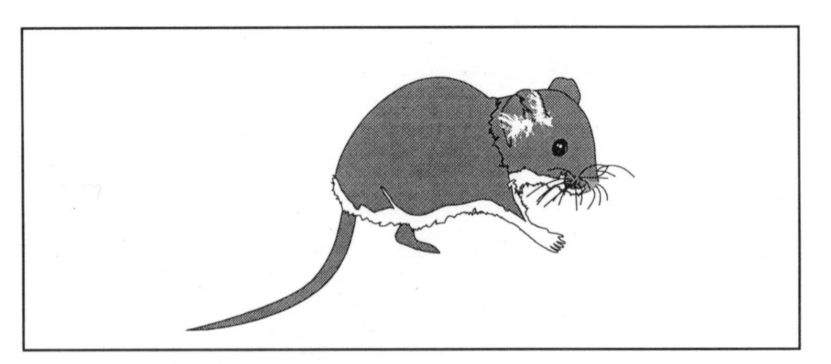

Natural deterrents work well for controlling mice. Pennyroyal or mint planted close to the house may deter them from entering. Some claim pet hamsters are good deterrents because mice and hamsters are enemies. When mice smell the odor of hamsters, they will resist entering that area. Dabbing cotton balls with mint oil bought in the grocery store and placing them where you have seen mice in the house will deter them.

Traps are excellent mice control tools. Available types are

humane traps, spring traps and sticky traps. Humane traps are helpful if you cannot bear to kill mice, however be sure to take the mice far away from your house to ensure they will not return. Some wildlife experts claim this is not truly humane because the animal is taken out of its familiar habitat and will die anyway. And there are those who claim mice will find their way back to your house no matter how far you take them.

Spring traps are the most effective tool for controlling mice in your house. They are inexpensive and easy to use. You buy them only once, and they work very well. Peanut butter is one of the easiest baits to use because it is easy to apply and mice love it.

Sticky traps are designed to make things easier than spring traps, because they trap mice and then can be thrown away. Two types of spring traps are the flat type and the box type. Dead mice are visible in the flat type, in the box type, they are not. In sticky traps, mice die from heart failure from the struggle or from starvation because they cannot get out of the trap. To some, this may sound cruel. At least with the spring traps, death is quick. Using sticky traps can be bothersome because you must replace them after each mouse. If you have a very serious problem, this can be costly as well. In any case, you have many choices for ridding your house of mice, and making it easier.

Trash Rehash

As much as we try to recycle newspaper, plastics and aluminum cans, there are some items which seem hard to fit into these categories. Below are a few of the tough ones with ideas on how to dispose of them or reuse them:

BOTTLE CORKS

⇒ When around the pool, tie a cork to little baby's toys, so they float on the water if they happen to fall in.

⇒ Make a coaster by cutting 1/8" slices off the cork. Glue these small circles on a piece of cardboard.

CANDLES

⇒ Rub the bottom tracks of wooden drawers with candle stubs to keep drawers opening smoothly.

⇒ Rub a white candle over the address on a package to protect it from wetness.

STEEL WOOL

⇒ Make a pin cushion with steel wool. An added bonus is the pins and needles will be sharpened each time they are stuck into the cushion.

EARTHSAVING WAYS TO INCREASE YOUR SAVINGS BY $1000 OR MORE THIS YEAR

- Instead of buying harsh chemicals to rid your house of ants, squeeze a lemon on the entrance trail and leave the peels. Other ant deterrents are talcum, chalk, damp coffee grounds, bone meal, charcoal ashes and cayenne pepper. ($10 - $50)

- Hand wash delicate items in cold water instead of dry-cleaning. ($100 - $200)

- Make your own gourmet coffee. Add cinnamon or cocoa to coffee before brewing. ($50 - $100)

- Instead of throwing away your floor mop once the sponge has worn out, replace the sponge only. ($10 - $25)

- Make your own jellies. ($10 - $50)

- Citrus fruit shells (after juicing) can be used as party serving containers for desserts. ($10 - $50)

- Make table centerpieces out of your pruning leftovers, such as juniper, azalea and tree branches. ($20 - $100)

- Clean oven racks without using caustic chemicals. Cover and soak in tub with hot water and baking soda. ($10 - $20)

- Make your own yogurt. Add yogurt culture to a cooking pot of milk. (Yogurt culture can be found at health food stores or substitute a tablespoon of plain yogurt.) Heat milk until it reaches a boil. Take off heat, cover and put in oven. By morning you will have yogurt. (This does not work in a cold house.) ($50 - $200)

- Make your own clothes. ($200 - $500)

- Instead of cooking lasagna noodles before baking, assemble lasagna with uncooked noodles and store in refrigerator overnight. The next day bake as usual. The noodles are just as soft as if you had boiled them before baking. ($10 - $20)

- Do not buy clothes requiring dry-cleaning. They cost more to maintain, and some of the chemicals used for dry-cleaning are harmful to the environment. ($100 - $200)

- Make your own confectioner's sugar. Grind granulated sugar in spice mill or food processor with blade attachment. ($10 - $25)

- Make your own bread. ($60 - $100)

- Instead of throwing out leftover mashed potatoes, make potato balls. In the center of a heaping tablespoon of potatoes place shredded cheddar cheese and roll into ball. Roll in bread crumbs. Broil in oven until brown on all sides. ($10 - $50)

- Reduce popcorn kernel waste. Store popcorn kernels in the refrigerator. Most or all the kernels will pop. ($5 - $25)

- Make your own placemats by purchasing a roll of inexpensive rubber at a home improvement store. Cut out placemat shapes and decorate with paint or fabric. ($10 - $25)

- Instead of throwing away faded and yellowed handkerchiefs, whiten them by soaking in cold water for 10 minutes with 1 teaspoon of cream of tartar. ($10 - $25)*

*Figures are estimated for a family of four. Your savings may be more or less.

Homemade Pest Control

Preventing insect and animal pests in our homes and yards is a constant chore. Many chemical products are available on the market, but most pest problems can be solved more inexpensively and more naturally.

- Fill bowls with sweet clover and set around the house to deter houseflies. Wash windows with vinegar or lemon juice. Flies hate the smell.
- To rid your house of cockroaches, mix flour, Plaster of Paris, powdered sugar and borax. Place in strategic places. Roaches will eat this and die. Be sure to place this mixture away from children and pets.
- Soak cotton balls in mint oil or citrus peel water and leave in strategic places to repel mice.
- Sprinkle crushed pennyroyal around the house to deter ants.
- To rid your house plants of destructive bugs, rinse them in the shower thoroughly. Spray them with environmentally safe insecticidal soap and keep them isolated until the problem is gone. Sometimes by simply isolating the plant and cleaning it thoroughly, you can rid the plant of insects. If there are insects or worms in the soil of your plant, place a cut potato on the surface of the soil. The pests will be attracted to the potato. If you place some of your house plants outdoors in the warmer months, be sure to check them periodically for pests. To repel pests spray with garlic solution.
- If mosquitoes get in the screened-in porch or in the house, set out pots or hang bunches of basil around the room or rooms.
- If you have a problem with bats in your roof, wildlife experts suggest sprinkling zinc naphthenate flakes because of its low toxicity. To keep bats out screen over areas 1/4" or larger. Try not to kill bats unnecessarily. Bats are beneficial animals because they assist nature in maintaining a balance by eating lots of insects.

One of the best ways to keep insect pests out of your home is to repair window screens.

Bengal Roach Chamber kills cockroaches with organic ingredients. For more information, call (800) 367-0394.

Sweet Potato Biscuits

4 cups flour
6 tsp. baking powder
1/2 tsp. cinnamon
1 cup butter, melted
1 1/4 cup buttermilk
1 tsp. baking soda
1 tsp. salt
1/2 cup brown sugar, firmly packed
2 cups sweet potatoes, cooked and mashed

Preheat oven to 450°F. Sift flour, baking soda, baking powder, salt and cinnamon together. Set aside. In a large bowl, beat brown sugar, butter and potatoes until smooth. Add a third of the dry mixture and mix thoroughly. Add a third of the buttermilk and mix thoroughly. Repeat the alternating with the dry mixture and the milk until thoroughly mixed.

Roll out dough on a floured surface. Cut into biscuit shapes. Bake on a lightly greased pan for 20 minutes.

Earthsaver

When you have a death in the family, ask the funeral home not to use a PVC (Polyvinyl chloride) wrap on the body. Whether the body is buried or cremated, the PVC emissions pollute the ground and the air.

Make Your Own Worcestershire Sauce

4 cups wine vinegar
2 cups sherry
2 tbsp. black pepper
2 tbsp. cloves, powdered
2 tbsp. ginger, powdered
2 tbsp. curry powder
2 tbsp. cayenne pepper
1/4 cup dry mustard
1/4 cup salt
1/3 cup Tamarind paste (found in Asian grocery stores)

Mix all the ingredients in large pot. Bring to a boil and simmer for 1 hour. Let stand in cool dark place for 1 week. Strain and fill bottles. Some of the ingredients will settle on bottom, however this is normal. Shake well prior to using.

Autumn Leaf Decorating

Autumnal color is so varied and beautiful. Use it to decorate your house for the Fall season.

Centerpieces

- Arrange large leaves in a circle in the center of your dining table. Place a pumpkin on top.
- Fill a bowl with small leaves, rust-colored ribbon and gold buttons.
- Place a small branch of fall leaves in a vase.
- To prevent fall leaves from drying out, paint them with school glue or iron them with wax paper.
- For a party table decoration, place leaves all around the table or place them all around the table under a clear tablecloth or glass top.
- Tuck leaves inside napkin holders with the napkin.
- Glue leaves on a cardboard paper towel roll. Slip the roll over a narrow vase and add dried flowers.
- Use leaves as table placemats by arranging leaves in a rectangle at each place setting.
- Stuff a few small leaves in a pretty and clear glass bottle. Fill with water to the top and cork or close the bottle. Shake. Add glitter or sequins in the bottle with the water.
- Completely cover table with leaves to create a leaf tablecloth or only cover part of the table as a table runner..
- Glue a leaf or leaves to ribbon and tie around napkins.
- Arrange leaves on a platter. Cover with saran wrap and place food on top.
- Fill a bowl 1/3 to 1/2 full with water. Place a heavy bowl inside the first bowl. The second bowl must be a bit smaller than the first bowl. In the area of water between the bowls, place some leaves. Freeze until the water is frozen. Take out the bowls and lift out the *ice bowl.*

Wreaths

- Cover a Styrofoam wreath entirely with leaves by gluing or pinning them to the wreath. Add a bow or some dried flowers.
- Glue a bunch of leaves in the center of the left side of a straw wreath. Place a bow in the center of the leaves.
- Make a square wreath out of wood or branches. Arrange a group of leaves in the bottom right corner. Add small figurines or dried flowers.
- Tie several branches with fall leaves together with ribbon and hang on front door.

Miscellaneous

- ♦ Decorate mums in outside pots by arranging leaves under the pot or around the mums at the top of the pot.
- ♦ Hang leaves with ribbon from indoor trees, large house plants or doorknobs.
- ♦ Hang a branch or branches of fall leaves on the wall.
- ♦ Pack gifts with leaves.
- ♦ Clean leaves and serve au d'oeuvres or dessert on them. (Check to ensure leaves are safe and not poisonous.)
- ♦ Fill empty flower pots with fall leaves.
- ♦ Tie bunches of leaves with ribbon and hang on edges of dining table chairs.
- ♦ Arrange several branches with fall leaves in a large flower pot.
- ♦ Arrange leaves under and around your doormat outside.
- ♦ Use clean leaves to wrap small gifts. Tie with ribbon or string or decorate with wood or branches.
- ♦ Tie together several branches of fall leaves with ribbon and hang on front door.

Homemade Applesauce

8 Granny Smith apples (or other tart apples), peeled and cored
1/4 cup water
1 tbsp. brown sugar
1 tsp. cinnamon
Dash of nutmeg

Cut apples in small pieces and put them in a pan with water, sugar, cinnamon and nutmeg. Bring water to a boil, then turn down heat to a simmer. Cover and let cook for 20 minutes. Stir, then puree.

Homemade Burritos

1 lb. dried pinto beans, soaked overnight
2 medium-sized onions, finely chopped and sautéed
1 to 11/2 cups brown rice, cooked
2 teaspoon cumin powder
1 teaspoon garlic powder
1/4 teaspoon cayenne pepper
1/2 teaspoon paprika
1/2 teaspoon salt
water
10 flour tortillas
1/2 to 1 cup cheddar cheese

Cook beans with enough water to cover beans. Cook for 1 to 2 hours or until beans are soft. Purée beans. Bean mixture should be thick not watery. Cook down if watery. Add rice, onions and spices and stir on medium-low heat for five minutes. Add salt to taste and stir in thoroughly. Remove from heat.

Soften flour tortillas by wrapping individually in thin wet towels and placing in warm oven for a few minutes. Place approximately 1/3 cup of the bean mixture in the center of each tortilla in a straight line, 1-inch from each end. Sprinkle with cheese. Roll up tortilla by folding in 1-inch ends first, and then each side. Serve with chopped lettuce and tomatoes.

Homemade burritos can be frozen, and then heated in the microwave for 2 to 3 minutes on HIGH.

Swift Substitutions

How often have we been in the middle of a recipe and run out of a very important ingredient! Below are some helpful substitutions for some items:

ITEM	QUANTITY	SUBSTITUTION
• Allspice	• 1 teaspoon	• 1/2 teaspoon cinnamon plus 1/8 teaspoon ground cloves
• Baking Powder	• 1 teaspoon	1/4 teaspoon baking soda plus 5/8 teaspoon cream of tartar
• Buttermilk	• 1 cup	• 1 cup yogurt
• Chocolate squares, unsweetened	• 1 ounce	• 3 tablespoons cocoa plus 1 tablespoon butter
• Cornstarch	• 1 tablespoon	• 2 tablespoons all-purpose flour
• Cream, heavy	• 1 cup	• 3/4 cup milk plus 1/3 cup melted butter
• Cream, whipping	• 1 cup	• 2/3 cup chilled evaporated milk or 1 cup nonfat dry milk powder whipped with 1 cup ice water
• Flour, self-rising	• 1 cup	• 1 cup all-purpose flour plus 11/4 teaspoons baking powder plus 1/4 teaspoon salt
• Honey	• 1 cup	• 11/4 cups sugar plus 1/4 cup water
• Lemon Juice	• 1 teaspoon	• 1/2 teaspoon vinegar
• Liquor	• 1/2 cup	• 1/4 cup fruit juice, unsweetened
• Milk	• 1 cup	• 1/2 cup evaporated milk plus 1/2 cup water or 1 cup water plus 1/3 cup nonfat dry milk powder
• Molasses	• 1 cup	• 1 cup honey
• Sour cream	• 1 cup	• 7/8 cup buttermilk or yogurt plus 3 tablespoons melted butter
• Sugar, granulated	• 1 cup	• 1 cup firmly packed brown sugar or 2 cups corn syrup
• Wine	• 1/2 cup	• 1/2 cup white grape juice
• Yogurt	• 1 cup	• 1 cup buttermilk

Make Your Own All-Purpose Mix

Instead of buying all-purpose mixes, make your own for a lot less.

All-Purpose Mix

8 cups flour
1/2 cup baking powder
4 teaspoon Salt
1 1/2 cup shortening

Combine dry ingredients, then cut in shortening until consistency of lumpy cornmeal. Store in airtight container in the refrigerator. This mix will keep for about six to eight months.

Biscuits

2 cups mix
3/4 - 1 cup milk

Bake at 425°F for 10 - 12 minutes. Makes biscuits for 6.

Muffins

2 ½ cups mix
2 tablespoons sugar
1 egg
3/4 - 1 cup milk

Mix ingredients well. Grease muffin tins, and fill each muffin cup 2/3 full. Bake at 400°F for 20 minutes.

Pancakes

2 cups mix
1 egg
¾ - 1 cup milk

Combine all ingredients. Pour on greased griddle heated on medium high heat.

Make Your Own Tomato Ketchup

10 tomatoes
1/4 cup salt
1/4 cup allspice
1/4 cup cloves
1 tablespoon sugar
4 cups white vinegar

Bring water to a boil in a large pan. Par boil tomatoes until skin peels off easily. Remove skin and return tomatoes to boiling water. Let simmer until tomatoes are soft. Place tomatoes in food processor and crush. Pour mixture into wire sieve. Rub mixture through with wooden spoon. Cook tomato mixture on medium high heat. Add remaining ingredients, bring to a boil and simmer for 1 hour.

To Meat or Not to Meat

My husband grew up as a vegetarian, and I was the one who introduced him to meat. I thought he was missing something by never having eaten meat. I felt it was my duty to get this guy on the right track. Ha! After a few years of observing his family cook vegetarian, live vegetarian, and be content without meat, he converted me to a vegetarian. Although I tried this for a few years, I never felt physically fit, and therefore returned to eating meat.

More years have passed, and I have experimented with different diets to find the right balanced diet for me. When I ate lots of vegetables and grains and no meat, I would sometimes feel weak. By no means was this because I wasn't getting enough protein. I was very careful about combining the grains and vegetables to complete the protein requirement. However, I am a jogger, and the energy required to exercise so vigorously never seemed to be provided by a strict vegetarian diet. On the other hand, I never felt as physically cleansed as when I was on a vegetarian diet. Too much meat seemed to clog my insides.

Today, my husband and I are experimenting with a diet that seems to be providing the best nutritional and physical well-being for which we have been searching. A very strict diet, it is based on the macrobiotic diet. We have greatly limited our intake of sugar, milk and milk products, fats and processed foods. However, it is impossible for us to completely ban these things from our diet, because we enjoy going out to eat or visiting friends and family. We eat meat one to three times a week, usually chicken or fish. Mostly, we eat lots of vegetables, beans and grains. We eat fruits three or four times a week, and these usually replace dessert.

We have spent a lot of time searching for a way of eating which meets our physical and nutritional requirements. In no way do we suggest everyone eat this way. Everyone must search for their own balanced diet. My concerns when considering vegetarianism were

Reasons We Should Cut Down on Meat

- Studies have shown we eat too much protein in the form of meat and suffer from the effects of excess animal fat in our diets.
- Beef comes from farmed animals that eat thousands of pounds of grain each year. Reducing our intake saves land and resources.
- Meat is one of the most expensive grocery items we buy. Reducing our intake could reduce our grocery bills significantly.
- Veal is from calves taken from their mothers a few days after birth. They are fed a diet of liquid milk substitute for 14 weeks.
- Many animals raised for meat are kept strictly confined. Pigs are chained, and chickens are confined to small spaces in which they never use their legs. Some of these practices are changing because of the efforts of people fighting against animal cruelty. Talk to your local grocery store or write the companies from which you buy most often.

not only nutritional, but philosophical as well. I had become uneasy with the way animals were being raised and treated to feed us. I was concerned about the drugs they were being given which I was ingesting too. For a long time, I was unable to reasonably justify eating meat when vegetables and legumes and grains seemed to provide all the nutrients and protein required for a healthy life. Actually, I still cannot justify this, at least in my own mind. I am simply aware I physically am not able to function at my best without some meat in my diet.

Is it right to kill animals for our benefit when vegetables, legumes and grains seem to provide all we need—especially if we choose to include milk products, such as cheese, in our diets? Cheese and milk complete the protein requirements.

Are we carnivorous or herbivorous beings? There have been studies demonstrating that vegetarianism increases passive behavior and eating lots of meat increases aggressive behavior in many individuals. Without a doubt, humans are complicated beings, and it would seem to reason that our diet would be as complicated. The key is to find a balance. For each of us, the balance may be different. Some of us may find that a vegetarian diet is the best diet, and others may find that they must have meat in their diet. Nutritional balance, with or without meat, seems to be the key to a healthy life, a healthy planet, and a healthy wallet.

Homemade Graham Crackers

- 1 cup flour
- 1 teaspoon baking powder
- 1/4 teaspoon salt
- 1/8 teaspoon cinnamon
- 1/4 cup shortening
- 2 tablespoons honey
- 1/4 cup water
- 11/4 cups whole wheat flour
- 1/2 teaspoon baking soda
- 1/3 cup brown sugar
- 3 tablespoons butter or margarine, sliced thinly
- 1 teaspoon vanilla extract
- 2 teaspoons molasses
- Dash of mace

Combine flours, baking powder, baking soda, salt, sugar and cinnamon using a whisk. Drop in butter or margarine and shortening and mix together with fingers until the mixture is coarse and crumbly. Set aside.

In a separate bowl mix vanilla extract, honey, molasses, water and mace. Pour half of this mixture over dry ingredients and mix, then pour the remaining half and mix thoroughly. Roll the dough into a ball, cover with plastic wrap and chill in the refrigerator for two hours.

Slice the dough in half and let it sit for 10 minutes. Preheat oven to 350°F. On a floured surface, roll the dough to 1/4-inch thickness. Slice away ragged edges. Cut into four-inch squares and prick the top of the dough with a fork. Place squares on an ungreased baking sheet and lightly sprinkle with mace. Bake for 10 - 15 minutes or until edges begin to brown. Meanwhile, roll and cut remaining dough. Let graham crackers cool.

Carpet Stains, Not

Carpet stains are easy to get and hard to get out. Carpet stain removers may contain perchloroethylene or napthalene. Perchloroethylene can pollute the air and irritate eyes and skin. Napthalene is toxic and can pollute the air. Therefore, try using more natural methods of ousting those stains. Use some of the products and methods below to remove stains with ease and without chemicals.

All stains will be easier to remove if they are caught as soon as they are made. Blot the area with a dry cloth or towel until it is just damp. Do not rub, and take your time!

A vinegar and water solution can be used on most stains. Mix equal parts vinegar with equal parts water and sponge the area by working from the outside in. Wring the sponge out thoroughly in another container after each application. After the stain has been removed, perform the same technique with only water to rinse the area well.

Removing Specific Stains

- To remove a coffee stain, apply club soda with a sponge and sprinkle with salt. Let sit for 30 minutes, then rinse with water and a sponge.
- To remove a grease spot, pour cornmeal over the spot and let sit overnight. Wipe up the area the next day.
- To remove chewing gum, place ice cubes over the gum until it hardens. Pull gum up. Rinse the area with water.
- To remove mud, sprinkle the area with salt and wait until mud is dry. Vacuum.
- To remove spilled soft drinks, sponge with cold water and rubbing alcohol.
- To remove blood, saturate area with cold water. Let sit for 30 minutes and rub gently.
- To remove wax from carpets, pick or scrape off as much as possible. Place cheesecloth or other thin cloth over area and iron with warm, not hot, iron. Continue ironing, moving the cloth to a cleaner area on the cloth each time until the wax is entirely removed.

Cheese Breeze

Many dishes call for cottage or cream cheese, such as lasagna, cheese cake or casseroles. If you do not have any handy or want to try a more inexpensive alternative, try these easy cheese-making recipes.

Cottage Cheese

Heat a quart of whole milk on low heat. When warm, add 1 tablespoon of lemon juice. Stir on low heat. When milk starts to curdle, remove from heat. Pour into cheesecloth or muslin and drain for a few hours.

Low-fat Cream Cheese

Pour one cup of plain yogurt in cheesecloth or muslin. Hang over sink and let drain overnight.

NOTE: This works best with fresh or homemade yogurt.

Earthsaver

Don't throw away those gallon milk jugs! Cut the bottoms off and use them to protect your tender vegetables or flowers from winds and cold. They can also be used to store small loose items from children's toys.

Choosing Environmentally-Correct Products

Check if products are made from recycled material.
If a product is made from recycled material, it should indicate this on the outside of the package.

Is the product wrapped in excess packaging?
If the product is double- or triple-wrapped, the manufacturer is using too much packaging. Such wasteful packaging of products contributes to the waste of wood for paper and wastes money.

Can the product be recycled?
If a product cannot be used, re-used or contains material which can not be recycled, it is a product which is not useful in solving environmental problems.

Does the price of the product outweigh its benefits?
A wave of environmentally-correct products has hit us in a big way, however are they all worth their promotional gimmicks?

Is the product made from rare raw materials or non-renewable raw materials?
If a product is made from materials which we will not be able to replace or have little of, it is not environmentally-correct to use it.

Does the product use too much energy to produce?

Some Environmentally Incorrect Products

Air fresheners pollute the air and deplete the ozone. Use potpourri or baking soda as natural alternatives.

Bleached paper coffee filters contain TCDD, a carcinogen, which according to the EPA is hazardous to human health at any level of exposure. Alternatives are cloth or metal coffee filters.

The market thirst for **Ivory** prompts the unnecessary destruction of wild elephants. The African elephant population has declined 60% since 1970. (An alternative to ivory is *tagua* which comes from the South American palm tree.)

Tropical woods, such as **ebony, mahogany, rosewood and teak** are harvested through the destruction of rainforests.

Animal flea and tick control products contain toxic ingredients, such as pyrethrins and DEET. These chemicals are not healthy for your pet or the environment. Natural controls can be made from garlic, pennyroyal or citronella.

Natural commercial products to control fleas and ticks on animals are available under the brand names listed below:

Safer - (800) 423-7544

No Common Scents - (513) 767-4261

Green Ban - (319) 227-7996

PetGuard - (800) 874-3221

Milk cartons are not recyclable.

OUTSIDE

The Call of the Wild in Your Backyard

If You Build It, They Will Come

If you want to attract wildlife to your yard or garden, you must create a place where they will want to come. Three things which attract wildlife are food, water and shelter. If you have one or more of these, wildlife will come.

Plant trees and shrubs in your yard to attract animals. Fill planter saucers or large seashells with water for all your visitors. Plant a wildflower area to attract wildlife to native plants.

Birds

Birds are relatively easy to attract. Set out some birdseed, and before you know it, they will be flocking to your yard. Provide water and some bushes, and they will nest there, too. Birds visiting your yard will help rid your garden of pesky bugs. The birds will visit your garden often to feast on the bugs.

Birds will also be attracted to your garden if you allow your flowers and other plants to go to seed. Plant some sunflowers at the edge of your yard every year. Other flowers which produce seeds attractive to birds are: Bachelor's Buttons, Coreopsis, Snapdragons and Sweet William.

If you want to see some hummingbirds in your yard, plant nectar producing flowers, such as Gladiolas, Trumpet Vine, Daylilies, Beebalm and Cardinal Flower.

Butterflies

Butterflies add beauty and delicacy to our garden. Butterflies need water, flowers and non-windy conditions. Flowers which attract butterflies are: Butterfly Bush, Daisies, Hollyhock, Dogwood, Purple Coneflower and Queen Anne's Lace.

3 Bird Feeders You Can Make for Under $3.00 Each

1. Materials: 66" of thick string, gallon milk jug, 4" X 6" piece of wood no thinner than 1", four tack nails and 2 nails.
Cost: $1.50 - $3.00.

Cut bottom off of gallon milk jug, so that it looks like a tray no higher than 1/2 of an inch. Place tray in center of wood with corners facing centers of each of the four sides.

Nail down with tack nails on each of four corners of milk carton bottom. Find center of each 4" side and place one nail on each side leaving 1/4" inch of nail showing.

Measure 46" of string and cut. Fold string in half, measure 10" down from fold and make knot. On each end of two free ends make 1" loops. Connect loops to nails on wood. Thread leftover string through 10" loop and around feeder, knot. Feeder should be supported by string on all four sides. This feeder is easy for large birds to reach.

If you like Butterflies, become a member of the North American Butterfly Association. For more information, write them at 909 Birch Street, Baraboo, WI 53913.

Chipmunks

Chipmunks will raid your bird feeder if it is accessible to them. With many shrubs planted and large rocks placed throughout the flower garden, chipmunks have plenty of hiding places on their journey to find food.

Squirrels

If you have some large trees in your yard, you may attract some squirrels to nest in them. At any rate, if you set out birdseed, you most likely will see them raiding your bird feeders.

If squirrels are invading your bird feeders, a new product, Squirrel Away, is available to help. Squirrel Away is made from a plant in the hot pepper family and will repel squirrels, but not birds. Check at your local garden center.

Rabbits

Rabbits usually feed at night on clover and vegetable gardens. If you have a high grassy area, you may harbor a mother with her young in the spring.

2. Materials: One Chinese take-out food container and string.
Cost: $.50 - $1.00.

Wash and dry take-out container thoroughly. Cut 2" X 2" square 1/2" from bottom on wide sides of container—for feeder opening. Hang by wire handle or string. This feeder is good for small birds.

3. Materials: One coat hanger and one corn cob.
Cost: $.50 - $1.00

Insert end of wire hanger into corn cob and hang by hook.

Do not place bird feeders on or near windows. Many birds are killed on windows when approaching window feeders.

Picnic Nit-picking

You can have a less expensive and more environmentally-friendly picnic by doing just a few things differently.

- Use dishes instead of paper plates. Use knives, forks and cups instead of disposables. If you must, use plastic dishes, knives and forks, but wash them and reuse them. Use cloth napkins instead of paper.
- Have containers set out for glass recycling.
- Have people bring food dishes.
- Set out a bin for collecting aluminum soda cans for recycling.
- Start your barbecue with a lighted wad of paper dropped in the coals instead of using lighter fluid.
- Use a reusable keg for beer instead of a disposable.
- Burn citronella candles to deter mosquitoes instead of spraying chemicals. Or place citrus-scented geranium plants or hang citrus peels around the area. If there are too many mosquitoes to handle, try using a natural bug deterring lotion instead of products which contain DEET. Dab your skin behind the knees, on the ankles, elbows and neck with citrus peels.

Charcoal used for outdoor grilling pollutes our air. **Nature's Fire Log**, made from banana leaves, coconut and lemon grass, leaves ashes which can be thrown in your compost pile. For more information, contact Nature's Distributors, P. O. Box 566, Grass Valley, CA 95945, (800) 407-5770.

Buzz Away contains peppermint, cedarwood, citronella, eucalyptus and lemon grass. For more information, contact Quantum, Inc., 754 Washington Street, Eugene, OR 97401, (503) 345-5556.

Do-It-Yourself Brick Patio

If you have leftover bricks or have torn down an old barbecue pit or chimney, reuse the bricks to create a walkway.

Use old oven mitts for heavy duty outdoor or gardening jobs instead of buying heavy duty gloves.

Materials & Tools

Mason's Sand
Play Sand
Bricks
Gravel
String
Lumber (1 x 8's) (Use cedar instead of treated lumber which contains toxic chemicals.)
Stakes
Weed Cloth
Screed
Tamp
Shovel
Broad-blade Brick Chisel
Mason's Trowel
Broom
Carpenter's Level
Hammer or Rubber Mallet

Finding the Materials

Use the telephone yellow pages to call various supply yards for quotes. Bricks and mason's sand will most likely need to be delivered unless you have a truck to haul it. Tools and some of the supplies can be found at hardware or home improvement stores.

How Much

Figure out how many bricks you will need by measuring the area where you are planning to build the patio and by keeping in mind bricks or pavers are typically 4 inches wide by 8 inches long. Decide whether you want a gravel base of 2 or 4 inches and count on a sand base of about 2 inches.

Starting the Patio

STEP 1

With stakes and string mark off the area where the patio will be built. If you have decided to place 2 inches of gravel with 2 inches of sand and the bricks are 1½ inches, you will need to dig out 5½ inches. Be sure to slope the area slightly away from the house or any buildings for drainage. After the area is completely dug out, tamp down the entire area firmly.

STEP 2

Lay out the weed cloth over the tamped area to help prevent weeds from coming up through the bricks. Place the 1 x 8 boards around the perimeter of the area and nail them together at the corners. Spread the gravel out evenly over the entire area to create a 2-inch base. Tamp down.

Re-use that old and dingy shower curtain. After cleaning, use it as a drop cloth for painting or as a floor protector in your shed. Or make a small tent for your children to play in.

STEP 3

Spread the mason's sand over one quarter or one-half of the area to a height of 2 inches. The smaller the working area, the easier it is to work. Use the screed to level the sand. Tamp down gently.

STEP 4

Before placing the bricks, choose a pattern. Keep in mind that most diagonal patterns will require more bricks to be cut than other patterns. One of the most popular patterns is basket weave. Basket weave is a pattern with two bricks placed together in one direction next to two bricks placed together in another direction and so on. Experiment with patterns and create your own pattern.

Lay bricks on the sand right next to each other. Tamp down on bricks gently. Use the carpenter's level to ensure the bricks are even and level.

Most likely you will need to cut bricks at some point in the project. Measure the area where the brick will be placed and mark the brick with the same measurement. Using the chisel and hammer or mallet, score the entire circumference of the brick. Place one end of the brick on another brick with the other end hanging over the edge. With the hammer or mallet gently tap that end of the brick to snap the brick off at the scored area.

After you have worked this area, spread the sand on the remainder of the area or a smaller area and work toward completion. You may now use the finished patio area as part of the area where you will stand and sit to complete the remainder of the patio.

STEP 5

Once all the bricks are in place spread the play sand over the entire area. Sweep the sand into the joints. With a hose, water the surface of the patio to pack the sand down between the joints. Let it dry, and then repeat the process.

TIP: Mix a little salt and pepper with the play sand when sweeping it into the joints. The salt will help prevent weeds from growing. The pepper will deter ants.

THE GARDEN

Planning Your Garden

In order to have a garden which is functional and beautiful, you need to plan it out on paper. Whether you have lots of land or a small yard you can have a vegetable garden with your favorite vegetables every year, if you plan well.

You need some grid paper or regular paper and a pencil. Convert the measurements of your yard or land from feet to inches and draw it on your paper. If you have lots of land, you may want to only concentrate on the part of it you are planning to garden.

Decide where you want to place the garden and how big an area you want to use for the garden. Consider other uses you have in mind for your yard or land. If you have children, you may want to have the garden away from the house, so the children may play in the yard close to the house. Or you may want the garden very close to the house for easy access. Will you be building a swimming pool in the future? Do you want to have an area for barbecues? These are all things to consider before planning where you want the garden to go and how big you want it to be.

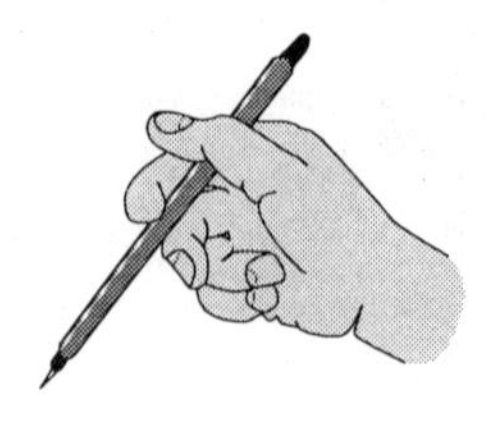

Draw the outline of your garden on your paper where you have drawn your yard or land. Decide what vegetables you wish to grow. If you will be growing cool crops and warm crops, you can use the space in your garden more wisely. Once the peas are on the vines, you can plant cucumbers in the same spot. By the time pea season is over, the cucumbers will be about ready to flower. Decide how much of each vegetable you want to grow. Write the vegetable names on your paper in your garden space. If you are companion planting, arrange your vegetables accordingly.

To make it easier, draw circles or squares for each planting. Consult gardening guides for individual vegetable spacing recommendations. This will be a trial and error or a draw and erase session until you have planned and arranged all your vegetables in your garden. Draw several views of the same garden in order to plan your spring, summer and fall gardens. Do not forget to include space for your herbs, nasturtiums and marigolds to repel those pesky pests. More about that later.

Use your master drawing every year when planning your garden to rotate the vegetables.

Xeriscaping is the use of plants in garden design which do not require lots of water. For more information on Xeriscape landscaping, contact your local extension service, the EPA at (202)260-2080, or check your library for some books available on the subject.

Clean up easy after gardening by hanging a soap bar in a clipped leg of a nylon stocking right by the outside faucet or hose. No need to remove the soap from the stocking, the soap lathers through.

Receive a free soil conservation packet from The Soil and Water Conservation Society by calling 1-800 THE SOIL.

Don't burn garden waste. Compost it. If you can't compost it, check with friends and relatives and neighbors to see if they would want to add it to their compost.

Preparing Your Garden

All gardens need preparation before planting. Whether you have a vegetable garden or a flower garden, you need to prepare the soil for spring planting. If you are not sure whether your soil is healthy, send a sample of it to your county extension service. They will tell you whether your soil is acidic or lacking in certain nutrients. Depending upon what you will be planting in your garden plot, this information will be very helpful in improving the conditions for your plants. Most organic material, such as compost, peat moss or cow manure will add nutrients to your soil. Lime will decrease the acidity.

After improving the soil or adjusting the acidity, prepare the soil for planting by clearing out the weeds and debris and turning over the soil with a shovel or spade. The goal is to loosen and aerate the soil for good drainage and root growth. If your garden area is very large or you are creating a new plot, it may be best to plow the ground using a tiller which will loosen and aerate the soil quickly.

If the weather is warm enough for planting, begin sowing seeds or planting seedlings in your garden, otherwise sow some seeds indoors for later planting.

Seeds can be easily started indoors. Place them on a damp tea towel. Roll up the towel, place it in a plastic bag and store it in a warm, dark place. In two to three days, the seeds will sprout and be ready to plant. If the weather is still too cold for planting, plant them indoors in a container covered with a plastic bag. Leave a few inches at the top of the plastic to create a little greenhouse. Place the container in your sunniest window. Once the seedlings are up, feed them with a little organic fertilizer to give them the strength to keep growing. When the soil is warm, plant them in the garden. If you are still in the planning stages and have not bought your seeds or seedlings yet, try to buy disease-resistant varieties. This will save you time and trouble later when you are fighting pests and diseases.

To save money when preparing your garden, use only compost you have created as fertilizer. Buy seeds instead of seedlings, and buy them on sale. If you need soil or manure, seek out farms in your area that are selling at low rates and in bulk. Top soil can sometimes be found at little or no cost around construction sites.

Composting Made Easy

Composting is an easy and inexpensive way of feeding your garden, your lawn and your house plants. You can save money on fertilizers and plant foods as well as save the earth.

Begin by choosing an area for your compost pile. Next, build a bin. You can build them from chicken wire or wood or blocks. Or you could use a barrel or just designate an area for a pile on the ground.

Making compost is easy. Simply throw in your garden waste, leaves, grass clippings and kitchen waste, such as fruit and vegetable peelings and cuttings, coffee grounds and tea bags. Do not put meat products, cooked foods or fat into the compost because these did not come from the ground.

You could pile your compost haphazardly, but the best compost will be created with 1/3 green waste plus 2/3 brown waste, adding water when needed. Green waste is garden waste, grass and kitchen waste. Brown waste is leaves, twigs and branches and straw.

Turn your compost pile often which helps decomposition through aeration. The compost will be ready when it is black and crumbly.

Mix compost with existing soils in your garden to enhance the nutrients. Spread it over the lawn as an organic fertilizer.

Discouraging Unwelcome Garden Visitors

Pests in your yard or garden are never welcome. The frustration of losing some of your most beautiful flowers or favorite vegetables can drive you to spray or sprinkle the deadly stuff, but don't! There are tried and true alternatives to using toxic chemicals. Even if you think you must kill those pesky beetles, you will probably also kill those beneficial ladybugs. And you do not want to do that.

WHAT TO DO ABOUT THE BIG ONES

Deer

Deer are repelled by human hair. Clean out your brushes and scatter the hair in the garden. Or leave piles of it every few feet. You must renew the hair supply in the garden every few months to keep the repellent *fresh.*

Sprinkle blood meal on plants usually eaten by the deer. The deer will stay away. After a couple of rains, sprinkle again. Besides being a good deterrent, the blood meal adds nutrients to the soil. Check for it at your local nursery.

Rabbits

Sprinkle cayenne pepper around plants you want rabbits to avoid. After a rain, sprinkle again. Tabasco sauce works well, too.

Try interplanting onions among vegetables to deter rabbits as well as other pests.

Gophers

If you see gopher holes, sprinkle black pepper inside the hole and cover the hole with dirt.

Companions Drive Away Pests

Instead of using chemicals to rid your garden of pests, try planting herbs, flowers and other vegetables in your garden to confuse or deter insects and improve the health of your plants. For instance, planting marigolds with your tomatoes deters nematodes and the tomato worm. Mint and chives improve tomato health and flavor. Here are a few more:

- Plant rosemary with your beans to deter bean beetles. Corn and eggplant interplanted with beans aid each other in growth and deterring pests as well as preventing diseases.
- Plant chives with peas to deter aphids. Mint improves health and flavor. Radishes and carrots aid peas in deterring pests and preventing diseases.
- Oregano deters pests when planted with cucumber. Tansy deters beetles and ants. Corn, beans and tomato improve overall health.

HOMEMADE CONCOCTIONS

Tomato

Tomatoes are very effective in warding off pests because of their strong smelling leaves. Use the leaves to create a mixture to spray on other vegetables to ward off insect pests.

Mince two cups of tomato leaves and soak in four cups of warm water for 24 hours. Strain and add four cups of water. Store in spray bottles.

Bug Juice

A very effective, yet disgusting, pest deterrent is a juice made from bugs. Evidently the insects are repelled by the dead bugs. Mix one part bugs with two parts water in a blender. Spray on vegetables and flowers.

Marigold

Besides planting marigolds all over the garden to deter pests, try preparing a mixture made with the flowers and leaves.

Gather 1/2 cup of flowers and leaves and add two cups water. Bring to a boil and let simmer for five minutes. Let cool and strain. Add one to two cups of water and store in spray bottles.

Herbs

Herbs, such as basil, mint, oregano and dill will deter pests if interplanted with vegetables. Try making a tea with any of these herbs and spraying it on vegetables.

Alcohol

Alcohol is a great pest deterrent for house plants and outdoor flowers. Dilute pure rubbing alcohol with water, one part alcohol to four parts water. Spray on infested plants and flowers. Sometimes mealybugs respond to a stronger solution of alcohol.

- Tansy and thyme deter the cabbage worm when planted with broccoli, cauliflower or cabbage. Dill improves growth and health.
- Horseradish deters most pests when planted with potatoes.
- Sage deters carrot fly when planted with carrots. Onions and lettuce improve general health and growth when planted with carrots.

NOTE: Marigold and Nasturtium provide general pest protection for the entire garden.

CAUTION: Be sure to research this area thoroughly. Some herbs may stunt the growth of particular plants. For instance, dill, when mature, stunts the growth of tomatoes. On the other hand, dill improves growth and health of plants in the cabbage family, such as broccoli, cabbage and cauliflower. Oregano, marigold and nasturtium provide general pest protection for most plants. For more information, check your local library for books on *companion planting*.

Nontoxic Poison Ivy Wars

Whether you have a large or a small patch of poison ivy in your yard, it can be a problem for anyone walking by who does not know it is poison ivy, especially children. We all know and expect poison ivy to exist in the woods, therefore we should leave it there and take precautions when near it. However, when there is a patch near the house or in an open area which is frequented by people or children, it is best to remove it from the area.

Chemical sprays exist to kill poison ivy plants, but non-chemical methods are less expensive and less damaging to the environment. Burning patches of poison ivy not only adds to the pollution problem, but can create problems since the poisonous oils may be carried by soot and infect anyone standing nearby. If winds are high, the soot could be carried further.

The location of the poison ivy determines the method of eradication. If the poison ivy is located in an open field or where few trees or obstacles are located, mow it close to the ground, then till the area thoroughly. If the area is kept mowed within one inch of the ground, the poison ivy will eventually die out. If the poison ivy is located near trees, fences or buildings, smother it with black plastic or any other material which will not allow light through.

USING THE GOOD INSECTS

To attract beneficial insects to your garden, never use pesticides. By using pesticides or any chemicals, you kill all insects —the bad ones as well as the good ones. Nature has created an excellent balancing system of predators and prey. Allow nature's system to work for you.

Ladybugs

Notorious for their beauty and their benefits to gardeners, ladybugs search out aphids, whiteflies and other insect pests.

If you have a serious infestation, purchase ladybugs from a garden supply store and set them free in your garden near the infestation. The best time to place them in the garden is early evening. Be very gentle with the ladybugs, releasing them on the ground at the base of your plants.

Praying Mantises

Hated by some for its fierce appearance, the praying mantis is a good friend to any gardener, eating aphids, beetles and other pests.

Gather the egg cases in early spring. Egg cases are light beige in color with an appearance of foam and usually about one to one and half-inches wide. They can be found adhered to small tree and bush twigs in forests or fields. Do not remove the egg cases from the twigs. Take the twigs with the attached egg cases and place them in your garden spaced 10 to 20 feet apart.

Spiders

Leave those spiders alone. They will catch most insects who try to raid your vegetables or flowers. In spring, the little ones hatch to go off and protect the remainder of your yard and garden.

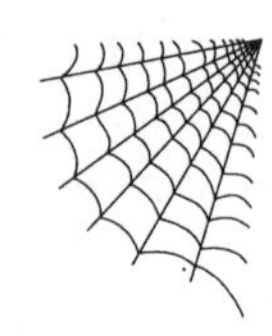

PREVENTION

Compost

Disease or an infestation of insects usually occurs because of a plant's lack of good health. Perhaps it has been overstressed with extreme heat, dryness or lack of water, —or it has not received all the required nutrients. Compost can provide the best nutritional source for plants as well as producing a better soil to hold water for longer periods of time.

Apply compost to the soil two weeks or one month before planting. Later, use compost as a mulch around plants.

Water

Water the garden on a regular basis to prevent plants from experiencing shock from very dry periods. Soaker hoses are the best tools for maintaining a constant flow of water to the roots of plants.

Set out barrels or buckets to capture and contain rain water for later use. Rain water contains nutrients which feed garden plants and flowers.

Companion Planting for Garden Health

Some planting combinations of vegetables and herbs can enhance the growth, health and flavor of vegetables. For instance, planting green beans with peppers can increase yields. Planting tomatoes with basil improves tomato growth as well as flavor.

Tomato companion vegetables are cucumbers, peppers, onions. Herbs which aid in pest control as well as health and flavor are basil, chives, borage and mint.

Potato companion vegetables are beans, eggplant, corn and peas.

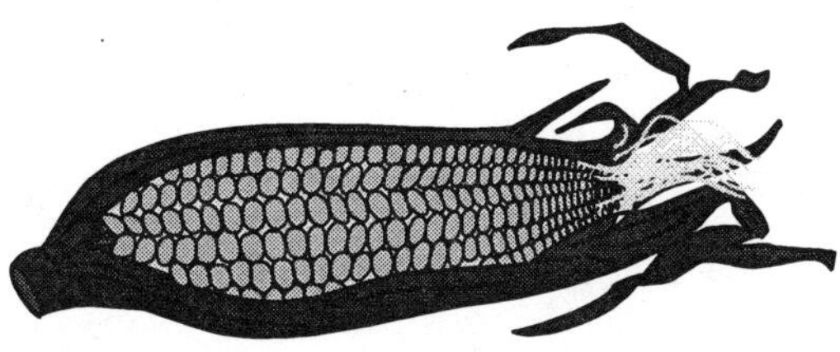

Bean companion vegetables are corn, cucumber, potato, carrot, radish. Summer savory improves growth and flavor as well as deters the bean beetle.

Lettuce companion vegetables are onion, radish, carrot.

Some interplantings of vegetables and herbs can stunt growth or increase the likelihood of pests. For instance, tomatoes and corn planted together will increase the likelihood of an attack by the corn earworm on both plants. The growth of beans can be retarded by an interplanting of garlic or onion. Do your research carefully.

Weeds

Some say weeds will attract pests into your garden if you do not weed religiously. Others say weeds in your garden will keep the pests from attacking your vegetables or flowers. One thing is for sure, weeds will take nutrients from the soil and growing room away from your vegetables and flowers. Therefore, it may be best to attempt to keep your garden free of weeds.

Mulch with grass clippings, pine needles or bark mulch to prevent weeds from sprouting.

Keep the ground covered for at least two weeks, then check to see if it has all died. Till the ground. Vines growing on trees or fences can be cut close to the ground or pulled out by hand. Be sure to wear gloves and cover arms and legs while working around poison ivy. Check the areas periodically for leftover seedlings, and pull them out.

Cut and pulled plants should be buried. All tools used should be washed thoroughly. All gloves, clothes and shoes should also be washed thoroughly to rid them of the infectious and poisonous oil.

Let spiders protect your garden from pests. Leave the webs alone and notice how few flies, gnats and other insects bother you or your plants.

Never allow weeds to come to seed. The seeds will forever be in your garden, sprouting year after year.

In the Garden or Yard

- To keep birds from nibbling on those berries, cover them with nylon netting or row cover material. Be sure to place the netting a few inches away from the plants so they cannot reach the fruit from the surface.

Use old pantyhose to store bulbs, such as daffodils or tulips. Hang in a cool, dry spot.

- Rabbits are cute and docile little animals, but they can wreak havoc in a garden. Fence the garden with chicken wire.

Cut strips of the pantyhose for tying tomato plants to stakes.

Get rid of crabgrass without chemicals. The key to this method is knowing when your crabgrass seeds begin to sprout. One to two weeks prior to this sprinkle cracked corn over the lawn. Evidently, the gluten in the cracked corn prevents the crabgrass seeds from sprouting. Cracked corn can be obtained at feed or pet stores.

- Tabasco sauce is effective in keeping deer and mice away.

- Many people have a strong aversion to snakes, but they are very useful animals in the garden and yard. If they are not poisonous, they cannot harm you, but they can help control insect and slug problems. If you are frightened of them because you cannot recognize the difference between a poisonous or a nonpoisonous snake, visit your local library to consult books which have big and colorful pictures of the poisonous snakes. Unless you live in Florida, you only need be concerned about three of the four poisonous snakes which exist in the United States. They are the copperhead, the water moccasin or cottonmouth and the rattlesnake. The coral snake is the snake which exists only in Florida. Besides the four poisonous snakes, there are many other species of snakes which are not poisonous. If you see one in the garden or yard, just leave it alone. Most of the time you will not even see it. Think before you kill. You may be killing a useful ally in the war against pests.

- To control white flies or flies in the house or yard, hang a yellow piece of paper coated with honey. They are attracted to the yellow paper and stick to the honey. Citrus oil repels flies also.

- Citrus and banana peels work well against insects in the garden and yard. In a food processor, slice up the peels. Place them in a cut piece of nylon stocking and tie a knot. Fill a spray bottle with water and place the stocking in the bottle. Let soak for a few days, then spray on plants.

- My favorite is garlic. Use the above method and spray on plants. Hot pepper flakes also work well with this method.

More on the Bug Battle

The Notorious Voracious Eater

A voracious eater, the Japanese Beetle causes havoc above and below the ground. As a white grub it feeds on roots of yard grasses. As an adult, it feeds on leaves of vegetable and ornamental plants. To rid the yard of grubs, apply milky spore disease to the yard generously. A disease which kills grubs, milky spore disease can be found in nurseries and garden centers.

Adults can be trapped in Japanese Beetle traps. Be sure to place the trap far from the plants on which they feed, otherwise they are attracted instead of deterred, from the yard. Another solution is to attract birds to the yard with feeders or sunflower plants. Japanese Beetles provide a feast for the birds.

Azadirachtin which is extracted from the seeds of the neem tree repels insect pests without harming most beneficial insects and is biodegradable. Ask at your local garden store for BioNeem or Concern Neem which contain azadirachtin.

Slugged

Slugs are voracious eaters primarily feeding at night. Traps can be created with salt or beer. Place a flat cloth or board around affected plants. Sprinkle the cloth or board with salt. The slugs will die when they come in contact with the salt. Be careful not to spill any salt in your garden. Salt can kill plants. To attract slugs away from your plants, place a shallow dish or pie pan of stale beer near the plants. Slugs are attracted to beer, but then drown in it.

Use old tin cans as flower pots. Paint or decorate them as you wish.

Charge! The Troops are Coming

Ants are usually not a problem except during picnics or barbecues. However, if you have a large problem with aphids, the ants could be transporting the aphids to other areas of your yard or garden. Ants are attracted to the sweet secretion of aphids, therefore will tend to make their home near these feeding areas.

Black pepper or lemon juice will keep ants away from eating areas. Sprinkle the pepper around the outside of the table or blanket. Pour the lemon juice in small plastic containers and place them around the area to be protected. Mint planted near problem yard and garden areas should deter ants, too.

White Like Cotton

Mealybugs can infest yard or garden plants as well as indoor house plants. White and with the appearance of cotton, they are usually found on the underside of leaves. Effective controls are Safer's soap or a diluted alcohol spray.

Generally Speaking

Most bug problems in the yard and garden can be solved with the garlic spray mentioned earlier or hand-picking.

Safer's soap is another general organic insecticide which is not harmful to the environment, humans or animals. Spray it on vegetable and yard plants to deter insect pests.

Dill Vinegar

11/2 cups white wine vinegar
1 tablespoon dill seeds
1 sprig dill

Place seeds and dill sprig in bottle. Pour vinegar over the seeds and sprig. Let sit covered in dark place for two to three weeks. Strain and store in clean covered bottle.

Herb Harvesting

If you have an herb garden or a few herbs in your flower or vegetable garden, the best and easiest way of having them on hand during the winter months is to harvest as much as possible. The best time for harvesting most herbs is in the spring right before flowering, however herbs will still add aroma and flavor if harvested in the fall. Below is some helpful information on some common herbs:

Basil is an annual. Therefore you must pull it up before the first frost comes or plant it in a planter to take indoors. Basil does very well in a sunny window.
Chives, a perennial, will be slightly affected by frost. The standing leaves will bend over, however the leaves are still good for harvesting. Use scissors to clip off the tops for the best flavor.
Dill is an annual and will have to be harvested throughout the warm season. Pinch off the delicate leaves or pull up the entire plant and cut off the leaves.
Lavender may need some protection in the winter. Pinch off tips or plant in a container for indoors.
Lemon Thyme can be considered a tender perennial, but if well sheltered during a cold winter, may survive. Clip off the tips of each stem.
Marjoram is an annual in cold climates. Bring it indoors in a pot and place by a sunny window. Pinch off the tops of each stem.
Parsley is a biennial and can be harvested even under snow during its lifetime. Pinch off the heads.
Peppermint is a pretty hardy perennial. Cut stems and pull off leaves from stem.
Sage is a hardy perennial. Cut tips and pull off leaves from stem.
Thyme is a hardy perennial. Clip off the tips of each stem.

There are several methods of preserving herbs after harvesting. Drying is the traditional method of preserving herbs but can be messy and tricky and require lots of space. Freezing is another method which is convenient and retains lots of herb flavor. Preserving herbs in salt is yet another method of keeping herbs handy for later use. Always wash herbs before preserving.

Drying

In order to dry herbs, you need a drying rack. However, if you have a warm, dry room where air is well-circulated, you may hang them from the ceiling on hooks or nails. If you choose to dry them on a rack, spread them out separately. Place them in a warm room where air is well-circulated. Check them every day. When the leaves are dry, store them in jars with dark-colored glass to diffuse the light which deteriorates herb flavor.

When drying herbs from the ceiling, hang in bunches. And repeat as above for storing.

Freezing

Wash herbs and let them dry on a dry towel. When herbs are dry, pack in containers and place in the freezer. Another way of preserving herbs by freezing, is to chop herbs finely and place in a bowl of water. Pour the water and herbs in ice trays. When the ice is frozen, pour the ice cubes in a large container and store in the freezer. Use the herbs as needed.

Preserving in Salt

Lay herb leaves in the bottom of a large jar. After each layer, cover with coarse salt. Repeat until the jar is full. Pour olive oil to cover the herb leaves and salt. Cover and seal the jar tightly and store in the refrigerator. The herbs will keep for several weeks.

Herb Vinaigrette

1/2 cup red wine vinegar
3/4 cup olive oil
1/2 teaspoon crushed mustard seeds
1 clove chopped garlic
1/2 teaspoon water
1/2 teaspoon chopped basil leaves
1 teaspoon chopped chives
1/2 teaspoon crushed dill
1 sprig marjoram
pinch of black pepper and salt

Add all ingredients except olive oil. Mix well. With whisk, slowly beat in olive oil.

What to do with the Harvest

Always let tomato plants remain in the garden until the first frost when they wilt. After they have wilted, remove the remaining green tomatoes and bring them inside to ripen. Place them in a cool dark place on newspaper. Some of the tomatoes will be lost due to partial freezing from the frost, but most of them will ripen normally and be ready to eat.

Freezing

- Freeze all those extra vegetables.
- Make sauces from tomatoes and freeze. Make dishes from beans and squash and freeze.
- Chop onion and garlic and freeze for cooking later.

Drying

- Dry onions and garlic in a dark, dry room with good air circulation. Barns and sheds work well for this purpose.
- Dry flowers from your garden for arrangements, gift baskets and decoration.

Storage

- If you have a basement or cellar, store carrots, potatoes, tomatoes and beans.
- Use a wooden container of sand to store vegetables for long periods of time. Bury them in the sand.
- Outside, dig a deep hole (below the frost line) to store vegetables. The ground must be well-drained and lined with straw or leaves. Cover vegetables with sand or sandy soil and straw.
- Store vegetables in a cold frame lined with straw or leaves.

Gifts

- Make baskets of vegetables, fruits or flowers as gifts.
- Make baskets or bouquets of herbs and spices as gifts.

Decoration

- Make centerpieces with vegetables. Arrange them around a candle or in a bowl with ribbon.
- Tie up bunches of herbs and slide them behind a picture frame or put them in a vase.

Herbal Earth

One of the best ways to appreciate the earth is to create a flower, vegetable or herb garden. Herbs, for example, can be used straight from the garden for cooking or for medicinal teas or for making dried flower wreaths. In addition, herbs add texture and color to any garden or landscape.

To begin an herb garden, the first step is to plan where you wish to place it and how large a space you wish to designate. Keep in mind most herbs do not do well in rich soil.

The second step after deciding what design you wish to create and where you wish to place your herb garden, choose the herbs you wish to plant. Do you wish to grow cooking herbs, medicinal herbs or both? Make a list of the herbs you wish to grow in your garden. Also, draw a sketch of your planned herb garden. Write in your herb choices, considering the height and light requirements of the herbs. Keep in mind some herbs are perennials and some are annuals. This may affect your placement of specific herbs in the garden.

Herbs grow best in a soil which is not too dry or not too wet. The soil should be a mixture of sand, clay and humus with good drainage. The ideal soil pH for herbs is within the range of 6.5 to 7.0.

Start your herbs from seed or purchase them from a nursery. Some herb seeds are very hard and may sprout more easily if soaked in water overnight before planting.

If you wish to grow an herb garden consisting of primarily herbs for cooking, consider planting basil, chives, dill, garlic, mint, oregano, parsley, sage and thyme. If you wish to grow an herb garden consisting of primarily herbs for medicinal purposes or teas, consider planting chamomile, echinacea, fennel, garlic, goldenseal, marigold, mullein, peppermint, rosemary and sage.

Remember herbs do best when neglected a bit. Plant them and leave them be.

If you plan to have a separate herb garden, there are several designs to choose from.

- The traditional herb garden comes from the Romans. Consisting of two three-foot paths crossing at their centers, this garden creates four square herb beds. The paths can be of stone, wood or gravel. The entire bed can be bordered with stones, brick or wood.

- Use containers. Containers are easy to use because you can move the herbs to the sun or shade depending upon what they require. Use pots, window boxes, strawberry jars, hanging baskets or an old wheelbarrow.

- Create an herb border. Plant against the house or a fence. Add a border to the vegetable garden.

- Plant a triangle herb garden. Border with brick, stone or wood.

- Another idea is to plant a circular herb garden with a path to the middle and circling around.

CHILDREN/PETS

Thrifty Ways Kids Can Entertain Themselves During the Summer

Whether you will be home with your children or working in the summer, you probably want them to entertain themselves for the majority of their time at home. Camp is an educational and productive time for children, but it does not usually last the entire summer. Going to a local pool is fun for you and your children, but you will probably want to be there with them to ensure their safety. If this is an everyday activity, you will not have much time to yourself. If you work outside the home, you will not be able to do this at all unless you can trust a neighbor or friend to watch your children at the pool. Plus, kids get bored rather easily which means they need lots of ideas for activities to keep them busy. Below are some ideas which may help save you time, money and headaches:

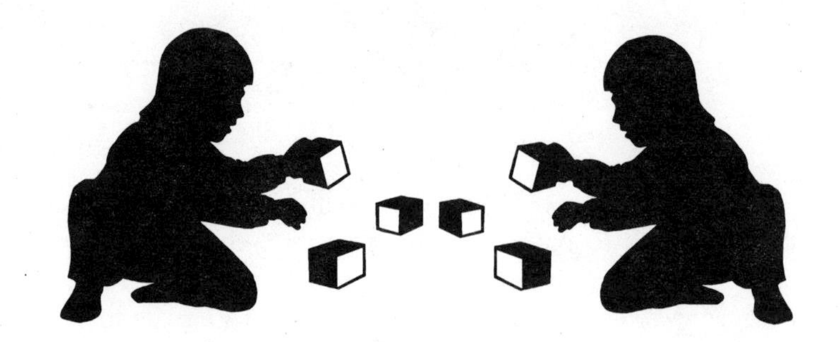

Creating

1) Set aside a time for your children to draw. Bring out scrap paper, construction paper, magic markers, pens, colored pencils and coloring books with crayons. If your children have a hard time deciding what to draw, assign projects where they spend several hours completing them.

   For older children, bring out papers, glue, felt, magazines, scissors and burlap. Ask them to create collages or posters for their rooms.

2) Bring out the macaroni, beans and dried flowers to create pictures. Assign projects which require several hours. Or ask your children to work on birthday or holiday gifts.

3) Make homemade clay out of one cup flour, one cup salt and water to make dough hard but pliable. Ask your children to make figures of themselves and each other.

Homemade Baby Wipes

1 tablespoon baby oil
One roll of soft absorbent paper towels
1 tablespoon baby shampoo
2 1/2 cups water

Cut paper towel roll in half. Remove the cardboard roll inside. Place one of the two halves in a large plastic container. (You could use an old baby wipes container.) Pour above mixture over the towels and keep tightly covered. Start the roll by pulling one towel up from the inside center.

Make your own bubble mixture by mixing 1 cup water, 1 tablespoon Joy dishwashing liquid and a drop of glycerine.

Games

4) Bring out old boxes and line them up as a train. Each child can occupy only one box. The child in the first box decides on a destination for the train. Without revealing the destination, he or she describes characteristics of that place by saying, "I see palm trees and beaches. I see women in grass skirts." And so on. The answer being Hawaii. The first person to guess the destination takes over the first box and the other child moves to the open box. After the children have played awhile, they will become more creative in describing the destinations, so that the process will last longer. Before or after the game, have the children decorate the boxes which will be their train cars.

5) Cut a hole in the center of an old sheet or blanket. Hang it up in the center of a room. The children may attempt to throw soft sponge balls through the hole at varying distances. Later, the game can change to each person placing his or her face in the hole and each child attempting to hit the target with the sponge balls.

6) One child chooses three items out of the house, such as a picture, a piece of furniture and a plant. The child writes them down on a piece of paper, then begins describing the items without mentioning what the items are. All the other children must walk around the house trying to discover what is being described. The person who returns with all the answers becomes the next person to choose the three items. If no one guesses the right answers, the game is played again.

Projects

Send the children out into the backyard, a nearby forest or field. Ask them to bring back three to five nature items to make an environmental poster. When they return with the items, allow them to create posters with messages or paper booklets.

That's Using Your Head

Children often pick up lice from other children at school or at play. Instead of using chemical remedies, try natural ones.

Use rosemary, eucalyptus or coconut oil. Rub into the scalp and leave for 2 to 3 minutes. Using a steel comb, remove the dead lice.

Be sure to wash all clothing and bedding to ensure complete eradication of the lice.

Make your own face paint for children. Mix 1 tablespoon of petroleum jelly, 1/4 teaspoon of glitter and enough food coloring for desired color.

Make Your Own Baby Powder

1/4 cup oatmeal
1/4 cup chamomile flowers, dried
1 tbsp. peppermint leaves, dried
1 tbsp. baking soda
4 tbsp. cornstarch

In a spice mill, grind oatmeal, chamomile flowers and peppermint leaves until a fine powder. It may be helpful to grind each ingredient separately. Sift and bottle the finest powder.

If you wanted another fragrance of powder, omit the chamomile and peppermint and add only a few drops of your favorite scent to the remaining mixture.

Another idea would be to take your favorite herbal tea and grind the contents of a few tea bags—the equivalent of the above measurements. Sift and add to the powder.

Use cotton sleeping bags instead of synthetic ones. Polluting chemicals are used to produce synthetic fibers.

Field Trips

8) Take turns with a neighbor or friend to gather all the kids together for field trips once a week or month to the library, local newspaper, farm or city.

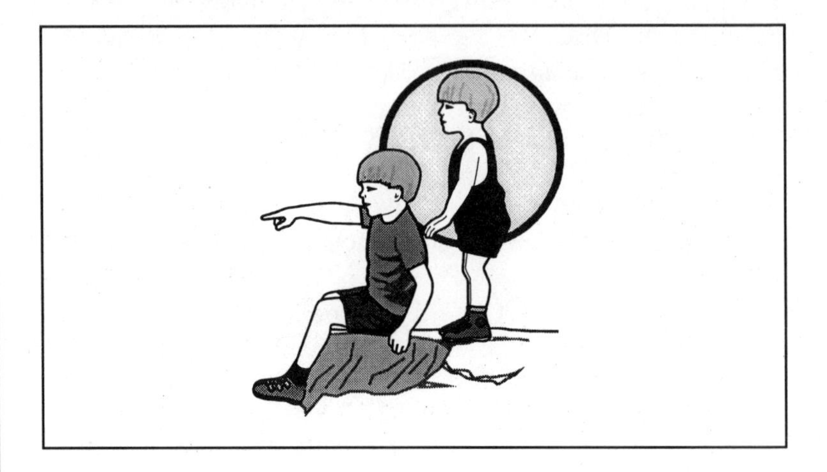

A Little Education

9) While your kids are home for the summer, why not teach them something? Tape some classical music on some cassette tapes. After giving them a short and simple course, have them play some of it on their own. One person places the cassette into the player and the others try to guess the composer.

10) Bring out an art book or borrow one from the library. Spend a small amount of time teaching the children about painters. Have one child hold the book up to the children while the others try to guess the painter.

These are just a few ideas to keep your children occupied during the summer at no or little cost. Use your imagination and create some activities of your own. To children, life is a discovery, therefore nearly anything can become a game or be of interest to them.

Earthsaving for Kids

Children, as a group, seem to be more concerned about the fate of the earth than adults. Perhaps because they want a better world in which to grow up. Or perhaps they have the luxury of focusing on one issue, one problem, whereas adults must face many issues every day. Possibly, they see things more clearly in their young, yet enlightened, minds. Whatever the reason, their thirst for new ways of saving the earth is endless.

Many children find outlets for their environmental concerns through school projects. However, if you find your children are interested in more ways of saving the earth, get them involved in your own projects. Ask them to help you sort the recycling, all the while teaching them the difference between plastics and glass. They might even teach you something.

When you make a decision to reuse an item instead of throw it away, tell your children why you are planning to do this. Through your example and your communication with them, they will learn the what, how and why of recycling and reusing. They will carry this with them into adulthood, and consequently pass it on to the next generation. Your small effort in sharing and communicating with your children can make a big difference in their development as stewards of the earth.

If you desire to teach your children more, begin by taking them out on nature walks or to parks to peak their appreciation of earth's nature. Show them the trees, plants and animals. Teach them how the forests sustain themselves through the forest floor of plant and animal debris.

Assign your children fun projects. Have them create collages on a particular environmental concern, such as pollution or saving energy. Hang these on your walls to display your children's efforts and their earth concerns. Ask them what they can do to improve conditions or solve particular problems. However small the solutions may be, have them bring those solutions into action.

Get your children involved in Earth Day activities. Attend community activities or create your own activities at home, such as planting trees or cleaning up a nearby forest or stream.

However you decide to teach your children about the earth and its beauty, its complexity and our taxing of it—keep in mind you are saving the earth simply by sharing your love and concern for it with them.

Snowy Treats

SNOW CONES

Make real snow cones. Collect snow in a large bowl. Using an ice cream scoop, scoop balls in a cup or bowl. Pour 1/4 cup or more of grenadine, soft drinks or anything of your choice over the top. This works best with slushy snow.

SNOW ICE CREAM

Collect snow in a large bowl (about 6 cups). Stir in 1 teaspoon of vanilla, a dash of nutmeg, 1/4 cup of sugar and 1/2 cup of milk. Put in freezer for 30 minutes.

Variations can be created by using sugar and chocolate milk, sugar and fruit, such as strawberries or blueberries or sugar and eggnog.

NOTE: Use only freshly fallen snow and always brush away the top layer of snow. Be sure to check if any soil or discoloration is visible.

Make Your Own Baby Food

Buying baby food can be expensive. Most of the products are simple vegetables or fruits. These can be made easily at home for a fraction of the cost. Since some baby food products contain preservatives, making it at home can be healthier, too. When feeding your baby vegetables, cook them until very tender. Mash them thoroughly or use the blender or food processor to make a fine mixture.

When feeding your baby fruits, wait until the fruit is very ripe and soft. Mash thoroughly or use the blender or food processor.

Oatmeal and cream of wheat are excellent cereals and cost much less than the food in baby food jars. Just make sure everything is very soft and digestible for the baby.

Meats are easy to puree in your food processor. Add a little water to make it easier. Poultry is easier than beef or pork, but you may want to try them. Fish is very soft when cooked. Once pureed, it is a very fine texture.

You may think this is all a lot of extra work, but it is not. Since you fix meals for yourself and your family, use some or all of those dishes you made for your baby.

Snowballs and Such

Snow Crunchies
Boil maple syrup until candy thermometer registers 230°F. Pour on clean snow. The syrup hardens and creates a crunchy treat!

Snow-sicles
Mix fresh clean snow with fruit juice. Freeze with popsicle sticks.

Kitty Litter Box Hints

To rid your house of kitty litter odor, follow some of the suggestions below:

- Use one half to one cup of baking soda on the bottom of the kitty litter box to absorb odors.
- Kitty litter will last longer if you use a generic (fragrance free) brand of kitty litter mixed with some homemade potpourri.

- Kitty litter will last longer if it is cleaned out every day.
- If you use a hooded kitty litter box, be sure to check the inside walls for urine stains. Cleaning the hood may solve that *mystery odor* problem.
- New kitty litter boxes with charcoal filters are very effective in controlling odors. Be sure to change the filter often.
- If you have more than one or two cats, try adding another kitty litter box.

Homemade Dog Biscuits

2 cups flour
2 tbsp. oil, melted butter or fat
1 tsp. Bone meal
1/4 cup unsulfured molasses
1/4 cup sunflower seeds, shelled
2 eggs combined with 1/4 cup milk
1/2 cup soy flour
1 tsp. sea salt
1/4 cup cornmeal

Mix dry ingredients and seeds together. Add oil, molasses and all but 1 tbsp. of egg and milk mixture. Add more milk if needed to make a firm dough. Knead a few minutes, then let dough sit for 30 minutes or more. Roll out to 1/2-inch thickness, cut into shapes and brush with egg and milk mixture.

Bake on cookie sheets at 350°F for 30 minutes, or until lightly toasted. Turn off heat and leave biscuits in oven to cool for an hour or more.

Make Your Own Pet Flea Repellents

Prepare a rosemary flea rinse. Use 1 teaspoon of rosemary per cup of water. Boil water and let steep and cool. Wash your pet thoroughly with castile soap. Rinse thoroughly. Submerge your pet's body up to the neck in water for 10 minutes to drown any existing fleas. Apply cooled rosemary rinse with a sponge to the head to rid of fleas.

Another natural and inexpensive flea rinse can be made from lemons, limes or oranges. Chop the fruit with the skin. Add to one pint of boiling water. Steep for at least 10 minutes and let cool. Apply over entire body with a sponge.

BEAUTY

Make Your Own Natural Shampoo

Using nonmetal containers, boil 10 ounces of water. Add herbs, such as hibiscus, rosemary or lavender. Let simmer for 5 minutes. Strain and add enough Castile soap for desired consistency. Add 2 ounces of olive oil or rose oil.

Make Your Own Hot Oil Treatment

Use almond oil or olive oil. Just pour one to two tablespoons in a vitamin or prescription bottle and place in a bowl of hot water for a few minutes.

Lemons, Strawberries and Hair

Harsh chemicals are used to color our hair in the salon whether we highlight, tint or color. Below are a few natural alternatives. First try these on a small section of hair to see what results you have on *your* hair.

To lighten hair...

Squeeze lemon juice from a real lemon onto hair and let sit for 15 to 30 minutes. For more lightning, sit in the sun for the 15 to 30 minutes. (Also, the longer you let the mixture stay on your hair, the lighter it will be.) For blond highlights, rinse hair with 1/4 cup lemon juice and 3/4 cup water.

NOTE: This will not bleach your hair as peroxide does. It will lighten it only to a certain point.

To redden hair...

Puree ripe strawberries or raspberries. Drain. Spread mixture on hair and leave for 15 to 30 minutes. You will have to experiment with a small section of your hair to find out how long to leave the mixture on to get the desired result.

You can also use henna found in your drug store, health food store or Asian Indian store. Mix a little with water to make a paste. Spread on hair and leave for 30 minutes to an hour depending on the desired result.

To darken hair...

Rinse hair with coffee or tea.

Earthsaver

Take hair clippings into the garden. The hair slowly releases nitrogen to the soil to feed your vegetables and flowers. Or throw the clippings into the compost pile.

Homegrown Herbal Beauty

Some say natural beauty is the most beautiful. Herbs have been used for thousands of years to accent the beauty of women and men. Herbs have a timelessness about them, mostly because of the incomparable reputation they possess for being effective healing plants. If, for instance, the skin is in need of repair, herbs can help internally and externally. Beauty is the reason the herb is originally sought, however good health is the ultimate goal.

Using things readily available from the backyard is convenient and inexpensive. If you do not have an herb garden, most of these herbs can be found at a nursery or on an herb farm. You may even have some of these in your kitchen. Fresh is best to use, however dried will suffice.

SKIN

Facial Cleansers

Yarrow
3 teaspoons yarrow leaves and flowers
1 cup boiling water

Pour the boiling water over the yarrow and let steep until cool. Strain and use as a mild cleanser for oily skin.

Lady's Mantle
2 tablespoons Lady's Mantle leaves
1 cup boiling water

Pour the boiling water over the leaves and let steep until cool. Strain and use as a mild cleanser for normal skin.

Peppermint
4 tablespoons almond oil
3 teaspoons peppermint leaves

Heat oil, add leaves and simmer for 4 to 5 minutes. Let cool. Use this oil to cleanse the skin deeply.

Stimulating Bath

1 cup dried rosemary leaves or pine needles
1 tbsp. dried lemon balm
3/4 tbsp. dried mint leaves
1 tbsp. orange peel, finely minced
1 tbsp. lemon peel, finely minced
1/2 cup rose water

Mix ingredients together in a jar. Let sit for two to three weeks and strain. Add a little to bath water for a stimulating and refreshing bath.

Cut *empty* plastic lotion bottles in half with a sharp knife. Use a spatula to scrape out the 1/4 to 1/3 cup of lotion you will find.

Facial

1 tablespoon rosemary leaves
1 tablespoon peppermint leaves
1 tablespoon anise seed
4 cups water

Boil the water and sprinkle the herbs over the top. Simmer for 1 minute. Remove the pot from the heat and place on a table. Lean your face over the pot. Place a towel around your head and the pot to trap the steam. Let the steam surround your face for 10 to 15 minutes.

Feet Moisturizer

Marigold
5 teaspoons marigold flowers
1 cup almond oil

Heat oil, add flowers and simmer for 4 to 5 minutes. Let cool. Use at the end of the day to massage tired or dry feet.

After-shave Lotion

3 tablespoons sage leaves
1 tablespoon peppermint leaves
1 cup alcohol

Mix the above ingredients in a jar. Close the jar and let mixture steep for 2 weeks. Strain and use full strength or diluted with a little water.

HAIR

Use herbal infusions to rinse the hair after shampooing to add strength and shine. Use chamomile for lighter hair, sage for darker hair.

BATHS

Refreshing Bath
2 tablespoons rosemary
1 teaspoon sage
1 tablespoon peppermint

Add the herbs to your bath as the water is running. Do not use very warm water for this bath. Lukewarm is best. Be sure to rub the herbs over your skin to receive the full refreshing effect.

Relaxing Bath
2 tablespoons rose flowers
1 tablespoon catnip leaves
1 tablespoon chamomile flowers

Add the herbs to the bath as the water is running. Use very warm water. Rest and soak with your eyes closed, breathing deeply and slowly for a few minutes.

To prevent runs, wash pantyhose in cold water and let dry. Then soak pantyhose in a mixture of 1 cup salt and a half gallon of water for two to three hours. Rinse in cold water and let dry.

OTHER BEAUTY TIPS

Facial Mask for Dry Skin
1 tablespoon milk
1 tablespoon dry skim milk
1/2 teaspoon honey
1 egg yolk

Mix the above and beat until blended well. Apply thickly all over face and throat. Leave on for 10 to 15 minutes. Rinse off with water.

Facial Mask for Oily Skin
1 tablespoon dry skim milk
1/2 teaspoon honey
1 egg white

Mix the above and beat until blended well. Apply thickly all over face and throat. Leave on for 10 to 15 minutes. Rinse off with water.

Hair Highlights
2 tablespoons apple cider vinegar
4 cups water

Mix and pour over just-washed hair. Leave on for 5 minutes and dry as usual. There is no need to rinse with water.

Flexible Fashion

These days the fads of fashion change so rapidly, we hardly have time to keep up with them. The styles we wore last year are out. What are we supposed to do with those "outs?" Not many of us can afford to change our wardrobe yearly or seasonally, therefore we must try to make what is really *out—in* again.

Accessorize

Add belts and scarves to your outfits. Use scarves as belts. With some outfits wear more than one belt.

If you have a long string of fake pearls, use them as a belt, clasping the ends with a pin.

On a blazer or jacket, fasten one end of a gold necklace with a pin at the top button and the other end at the top buttonhole on the other side with another pin.

Don' t Follow Fads

If you buy classic clothes, you can save lots of money because they are always in fashion. Fads die quickly. If you must have fads, sew them yourself or buy them at discount stores.

Trade-ons

Trade clothes with friends to vary your wardrobe. Your friend may have colors you need or pieces of clothing which you are dying to wear.

Alternatives

Wear your husband's blazer or belt or shirt. Be creative. Take time out to try things on to see how they look.

Grungy Sometimes

When working out in the garden or painting the house, never wear good clothes. Wear torn and stained clothing.

New Changes

Change your clothes by cutting off sleeves or sewing on new buttons or raising a hem. Some clothes just need a small change to make them "in."

Organic baseball caps made from organically grown cotton or natural wool are available from Eco-Heads, 1341 West Fullerton Ave., Suite 184, Chicago, IL 60614, (312) 665-2004 or from Make a Difference, 2284 Hills Point Road, Charlotte, VT 05445, (802) 425-3214.

The **Eco-Mat**, a Manhattan-based *wet-cleaning* laundry service, hand washes or steams delicate fabrics, such as silks and wools. They do not use perchloroethylene, the dry cleaning solvent which is blamed for much of our pollution. **Eco-Mat** is becoming a national chain. Check in your area or contact them at **Eco-Mat**, 180 West 80th Street, New York, NY 10024, (212) 779-1777. Another green laundry service is **The Greener Cleaner** of Chicago, (312) 784-8429.

Earthsaver

Avoid disposable contact lenses. Besides filling up landfills along with the accompanying packaging, they cost more in the long run than long-lasting contact lenses.

Chapter 2

The Kids' Room

Nature never did betray
The heart that loved her.

- William Wordsworth, *Lines Composed a Few Miles above Tintern Abbey*

RECYCLE SOCKS: Make Sock Puppets

Materials

Old Sock
3-inch String
Some Stuffing Material
Black Felt
Red Felt
Brown or Yellow Yarn (for hair)
Scissors and Glue

Instructions

Turn sock inside out. With stuffing, stuff toe of sock about 3 to 4 inches. Tie sock at end of stuffing with string. Turn sock right side out.

Make oval eyes and triangle nose on black felt. Cut out.

Make oval tongue from red felt.

Glue these onto face of sock at the top. Glue only one edge of tongue, so part is sticking out or hanging down.

Cut strands of yarn for hair, and glue onto the top of the sock.

The top of the hand reaches inside to touch the top of the sock. The thumb reaches toward the heel.

Save the Earth Collage

Materials

Old Magazines
Used Aluminum Foil
A Plastic Bottle
Newspaper
Junk Mail
Scissors
Glue
A large piece of cardboard

Instructions

Look through old magazines for pictures of the earth or recycling or letters to spell a word or phrase you want on the collage. Cut them out. Set aside.

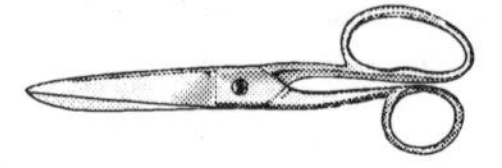
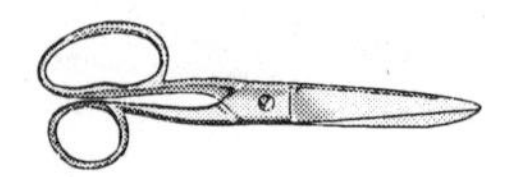

Use the aluminum foil, newspaper, junk mail and plastic bottle to draw shapes on. Draw the earth or snowflakes or just cut strips of each. Cut out and set aside.

Arrange all your shapes on the cardboard as you want them until the cardboard is covered. Then glue each piece onto the cardboard.

To hang your collage, tape the ends of a long string to the back of the collage.

Ideas:

- Cover the cardboard with newspaper or aluminum foil, then glue the shapes on top.
- Make each shape to represent one thing, such as all circles to represent the earth or all strips to represent the products which are recyclable.
- Make a picture or a scene shapes and colors.

Measuring Waste

Here's how to learn how much waste we throw away in a week, a month or a year. Perhaps if we all realized how much garbage is thrown away, we could take steps to reduce consumption.

- Gather a group of friends and commit to this project. Each friend must weigh the family's trash on trash day before it is collected. Log the total weight for the week per family.
- At the end of a month, add the weekly weights to arrive at the monthly total for each family.
- If you wish to measure waste for a longer period of time, repeat this process for six months to a year.
- At the end of your project, discuss among you which family had the most garbage and why. Was this family a larger family? Did this family purchase lots of packaged items? Was this family recycling and reusing?
- If you want to take this project a step further, start sorting the trash every week. Create separate piles for product packaging, such as bread wrappers or cosmetic boxes; possible recyclables, such as paper, glass, cardboard, plastic or cans; compostable items, such as fruit peels, tea bags, coffee grounds or vegetable stems.
- Examine each family's level of waste by what did not have to be thrown away, such as recyclables or compostable items. Could the family reduce the purchase of packaged items? Can some of the items be reused, such as aluminum foil or non-recyclable plastic bottles?
- After all your notes and figures have been logged, you may want to write a report, offering suggestions to each family on how they can reduce waste. Educate them on recyclables and on the local recycling program.

Plant Trees

Materials

Small shovel
Tree seedlings
Watering pail

Instructions

Have your parents provide you with seedlings from your trees or from a nursery. Some places give them away during Earth Week. You can choose to plant them on your property or, with permission, someone else's yard, a park or public land. Ask your parents to help.

Choose an open spot which receives sun. Dig a hole two to three times bigger than the roots of your seedling. Place the tree in the hole, and have someone hold it while you place the dirt around it. Be very gentle. Pack the dirt when you are finished, then water your seedling thoroughly.

Earthsaver

Avoid using mosquito repellents which contain DEET. Studies have shown it can be absorbed through the skin. Try organic mosquito repellents which contain oils (usually citronella oil) that ward off insects naturally.

Throwaway Magic

Adopt a Wild Horse or Burro. The federal government gathers excess healthy wild horses and burros and offers them up for adoption. You will need adequate facilities for housing your adopted horse or burro. For more information, contact the Bureau of Land Management, 7450 Boston Boulevard, Springfield, VA 22153, (703) 440-1699.

Learn how to make toys and creations with things which are usually thrown away.

Milk Carton Animals

Open the top of a milk carton and wash and dry thoroughly. Fold the top of the milk carton to be flat. With a pair of scissors, cut a hole out of the bottom center about the size of a penny.

Cut some construction paper to cover the entire milk carton. Glue on smoothly.

Take 5 pipe cleaners and twist them together. Insert them in the hole at the bottom of the milk carton and glue in place. This makes the tail of the cat.

On a large piece of cardboard, draw the 4 legs of the cat. Cut them out and cover them with construction paper. Glue them in place on the milk carton. For the face, draw eyes with crayons. Cut out ears, a mouth and a nose from construction paper and glue on.

NOTE: Use different colors of construction paper to create spots or stripes on the cat.

Cardboard Tube Kaleidoscope

With a wrapping paper cardboard tube, make a kaleidoscope. Trace one end of the tube onto waxed paper. Double the size of the tracing and cut out two of the same-sized circles from the waxed paper.

Use a hole-punch to make many small colored pieces in various colors of construction paper. Place the hole-punched pieces on one piece of the waxed paper. Bunch them all together in the center of the circle. Place a circle of glue all around the edges of the wax paper circle. Immediately place the other wax paper circle on top to glue them together over the hole-punched pieces. Let this dry.

Now, place the waxed paper over one end of the cardboard tube. Center it and glue the ends down on the outside of the tube.

Cover the tube with aluminum foil, but do not cover either end of the tube. Look through the open end of the tube and twirl. You can see many colors.

NOTE: Decorate the kaleidoscope with different shapes glued on the outside of the tube.

Oatmeal Box Drum

Wipe out an empty oatmeal box. Take the lid off and cover the bottom with red construction paper. With a small strip of aluminum foil, wrap around the center of the box. Cover the top with white paper, and glue on the top of the box.

Use old chopsticks or wooden spoons as drumsticks.

Community Recycling Center

If your community does not have curbside recycling, create a community recycling center.

- Ask your neighbors if they would be interested in having a community recycling center and if they would be willing to help with the small cost of building one. Tell them it would be an area where all community members could drop off their recyclables. Once a week or every two weeks all the recyclables would be taken to the nearest recycling center.

- Decide where the recycling center could be located. A good spot would be behind or beside a neighbor's home in a centralized location where neighbors could drop off their recyclables at any time. However, you could decide to use the center only on specific days. Consider your schedule and talk to neighbors before making your final decision.

- Check with local government or your homeowner's association to see if any permits are required.

Use your imagination to create your recycling center. Here are a few ideas:

- Use old rubber or plastic tubs set in a row.
- Make a frame out of wood and hang burlap bags inside.
- Have neighbors donate old garbage containers.
- Use bushel baskets or whiskey barrels.
- Hang wooden or cardboard signs over each bag or container specifying whether that container is for glass, plastic, cardboard or newspaper/paper products.

Organize the recycling center just as the recycling center where you will be delivering the recyclables. This will make things easier when dropping off the recyclables. Be sure your signs are in big and bold letters.

Include your community in all aspects of creating the recycling center. Volunteers can alternate delivering the recyclables to the recycling center. Get all the kids in your neighborhood involved.

Help out the senior citizens in your community by offering to go by their home once or twice a week to pick up their recyclables.

Environmental Youth Groups

KIDS F.A.C.E. (Kids For A Clean Environment)
P. O. Box 158254
Nashville, TN 37215
(800) 952-3223

Children's Earth Fund
40 West 20th Street
New York, NY 10011
(212) 727-4505

Earth Force
1501 Wilson Boulevard
12th Floor
Arlington, VA 22209
(703) 243-7400

The Natural Guard
142 Howard Avenue
New Haven, CT 06519
(203) 787-0229

Tree Musketeers
136 Main Street
El Segundo, CA 90245
(310) 322-0263

Ten Things Kids Can Do for the Earth

Earlier generations of children did not need to worry about the earth's fate. However, the children of the last half century have been increasingly faced with the imminent danger of a gradually deteriorating planet. The carefree life of a child has been somewhat hampered by the fate of an uncertain future. Nevertheless, there are things, no matter how small, children can do to save the earth and feel as if they have control over making their future a green one.

1. Start a *Green Club* in the community. The club could meet once a week or once a month to discuss and create environmental projects, such as neighborhood clean-up, recycling and organic gardening.

2. Plant more trees in your yard. Trees planted near the house may save energy by shading the house in warm weather and protecting the house from cold winds in cold weather.

3. Campaign at your school for refillable ink pens to be used by teachers, students and staff. Millions of disposable pens are thrown away each year to pile up in landfills.

4. Use your bicycle more often rather than driving or asking your parents to take you somewhere. Always consider safety first. If the ride will not be safe, then ride the bus.

Energy Audit

- Make a list of all the electrical appliances in your house. Go into every room in the house and see what is plugged into the wall outlets. Do not forget to count all the things in drawers, cabinets and closets which are not used every day.

- Once you have completed the list, go through it and decide which items you could do without. Circle them. Could you choose not to use these items for a day, a week, a year? Just think how much energy that would save!

- Ask your grandparents or great grandparents which items on the list were available when they were children. Ask them what they used instead.

- Go to the library and read what people were using instead of electricity 100 years ago, 200 years ago. Do you have any ideas of how to do without some of the electrical items you and your family use?

5. Propose to your school that a section of the campus be used to create an organic garden. The garden could be a vegetable, herb or flower garden. Classes, clubs or groups of students would be assigned tasks to prepare the garden, plant and care for the garden. Projects could be assigned to document the garden's progress or document the success and failure of miscellaneous natural pest deterrents.

Use lead-free fishing weights. Lead can be hazardous to waterfowl and other wildlife especially when the weights are lost in water. Alternatives in tin rubber or tungsten polymers are available.

6. Compost. Keep a bin in the kitchen for your apple cores and banana peels. Empty it daily in a bin or pile in your backyard, and then use it as fertilizer for the grass or the garden once the waste has decomposed.

7. If you live within a few miles of school, try walking home from school with some friends once in a while. Make an afternoon of it by stopping somewhere to eat dinner or study. Always check with your parents and only do this if it is safe.

8. Save throwaways such as plastic caps, cardboard paper towel rolls and product packaging. Use your imagination to see what useful items you can make from these items. Try making some toys.

9. If you use a computer at home, try to buy recycled diskettes. Encourage your school to do the same.

10. Have a party on Earth Day! Invite all your friends and relatives to celebrate recycling, saving energy and using solar energy.

Earthly Fun

~~The SAVing Source~~	earth	non-toxic	saving
baking soda	earthsaver	organic	share
carpool	energy	potpourri	solar
compost	environment	recycle	tree
conserving	green	renew	vinegar
do it yourself	natural	reusing	weatherize

r l c f v b q y j k u t l l h z r a T

o d o i t y o u r s e l f j d c e s h

n n m s x y f l p h j j j n a a n e e

h b p x r t w w e a t h e r i z e v S

b j o o e y e l v r e e a d s x w r A

u h s d u j k l m e r t z c d o a a V

r o t x s a v i n g u l f f r l l m i

d o i f i c b a k v c a r p o o l p n

n e l c n v a c c x x q j s p g i t g

e n e r g y k o o n n a t u r a l c S

e v i c m v i n e g a r e e s i i y o

f i n i i t n s h a h e l p k n a b u

o r b x k c g e x x r i c d a j t u r

c o h o o n s r v t u s l g e n w z c

i n x t s v o v l n d u r e c y c l e

o m s n a k d i g y r o s b b u g e t

r e n o q u a n p o t p o u r r i k k

n n l n j k f g q i o g b t f d k x y

j t h e a r t h s a v e r e a r t h m

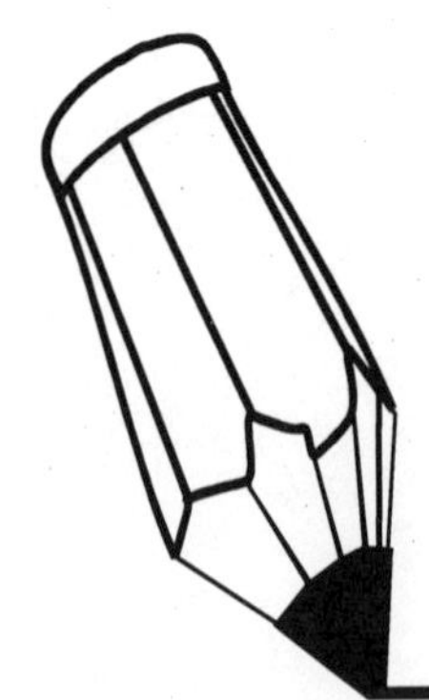

Chapter 3

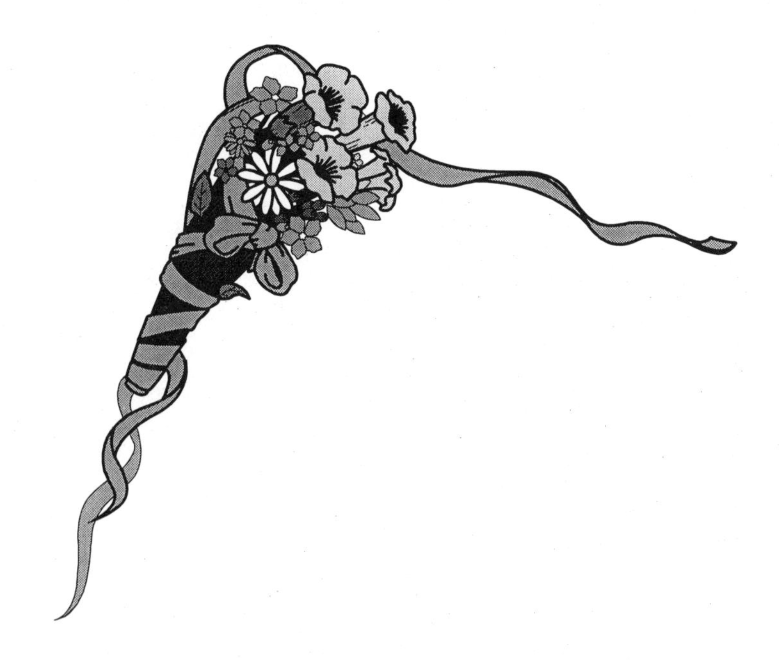

THE NATURAL WAY

Here's good advice for practice: go into partnership with nature; she does more than half the work and asks none of the fee.

- Martin H. Fischer, *Fischerisms*

Natural Deodorizers

Rose Potpourri

1/2 cup pink rosebuds and petals
1/2 cup red fragrant rosebuds and petals
1/2 cup rosemary
1/4 cup broken cinnamon
1 tablespoon whole cloves
1/4 cup lemon verbena
1/4 cup bay leaves
1 tablespoon orris root
6 drops rose oil

Getting rid of odors whether it be in the kitchen or the bathroom or the living room is a necessary chore if we want our homes to smell nice and clean. Besides buying sprays and solid deodorizers, there are some natural and inexpensive things we can use to rid our homes of those bothersome odors.

BAKING SODA is an excellent deodorizer because it absorbs odors without a distinct odor of its own.

- Sprinkle some in the bottom of the garbage container in the kitchen, bathroom and outside garbage cans.
- With the water running, pour some down all drains in the house as well as the garbage disposal.
- Open small boxes and leave in the refrigerator and freezer.
- Clean the refrigerator and freezer with a little baking soda mixed with warm water.
- For an odor-free carpet sprinkle some on the carpet or rug and vacuum.
- Pour some in the toilet bowl and leave for an hour or so, then flush.

- Clean coolers with a little baking soda and water.

CHARCOAL is another deodorizer which absorbs odor without a distinct odor of its own.

- Hang a mesh bag of charcoal in the basement or garage.

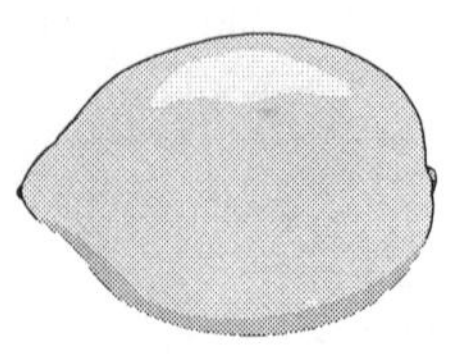
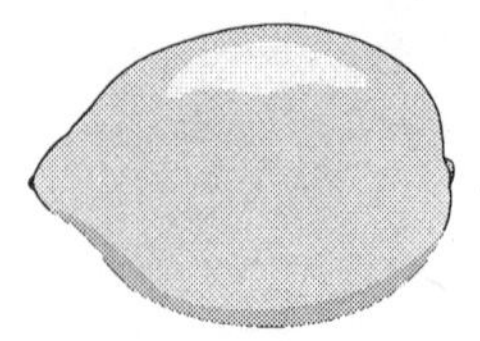

CITRUS PEELS, such as lemon, orange, lime and grapefruit are great deodorizers because they strip the odor away while leaving a fresh clean smell.

- Use them in the garbage disposal.
- Grate some to deodorize the garbage can.

WHITE VINEGAR is a deodorizer which strips the odor away, but does not leave a vinegary smell.

- Sponge kitchen counters and stove with a solution of white vinegar and water.
- Pour down all drains in the house.
- Sponge cat litter boxes and pet carriers with a solution of white vinegar and water.
- Pour some in a small bowl and heat in the microwave until boiling. This will not only deodorize, but clean the microwave by leaving a mist around the edges to wipe off.
- Sponge inside of garbage cans with white vinegar and water.
- Use some in the dishwasher rinse cycle to deodorize the dishwasher and rinse off dishes.
- Sponge coolers with a solution of white vinegar and water.

We all enjoy walking into our home and noticing a nice clean smell or the subtle fragrance of flowers or herbs. Below are some simple ways to add fragrance to your home naturally and inexpensively:

CEDAR is a fragrant wood and the odor lasts for a long while.

- Leave cedar chips or shavings in bowls around the house.
- Place cedar blocks in clothes drawers or make sachets from shavings or chips and hang in closets.
- Buy or build your own furniture from cedar and let the fragrance fill the room.

SANDALWOOD is a fragrant wood, and the odor lasts a long time.

- Make sachets from shavings or powder and place in drawers or hang in closets.

SCENTED SOAPS are very fragrant. You can use any soap you wish. Soaps made with natural ingredients are available in health food stores.

- Place bowls of soap shavings around the house.
- Place bars of soap in clothes drawers.
- Make sachets with soap shavings and hang in closets.

PERFUMES AND COLOGNES are very fragrant, and we all have some in the house. A little will go a long way. You may even try the perfume or cologne that was given to you as a gift but unfortunately did not mix well with your natural oils. Maybe it would smell nicer using the next tip. It would be better to find a use for it rather than throwing it out.

Herb Potpourri

1 cup pink roses
1/4 cup chamomile
1/4 cup lemon verbena
1/4 cup rosemary
1/4 cup marjoram
1/4 cup spearmint or other mint
1 tablespoon orris root
2 - 3 drops each of rose and bay oils

Mill some coffee beans with cinnamon for a natural and wonderful kitchen deodorizer.

Deodorize exercise shoes by placing kitty litter in nylon stocking feet which have been cut from a pair of stockings. Knot the top and place in shoes.

Deodorize the strongest odors by adding vanilla in a bit of water and place in bowls around the house or simmer on top of stove.

Rid garments of cigarette smoke by tossing them in the dryer with a washcloth soaked in herbal tea and baking soda.

Libraries rid books of musty odors by placing books in resealable freezer bags and storing in the freezer for a week. Try this with other small musty items instead of throwing them away.

- Spray or dab a little of your favorite perfume or cologne on all the light bulbs in light fixtures in your house. When the light is turned on, the heat of the bulb will slowly release the fragrance. This tip is especially useful if you are expecting company or having a party.

POTPOURRI is a natural and inexpensive deodorizer for your home. Even more natural and inexpensive if you make it yourself.

To make potpourri requires flowers or herbs or spices. Pick them from your garden or from the nearby woods. You can use roses, lavender, honeysuckle, chamomile, marjoram, peppermint, rosemary, cinnamon, cloves, nutmeg and citrus fruit peels. Combine your favorites.

Once you have chosen your ingredients you need to dry them. You can dry them on the bottom shelf of your oven on a very low setting or use the microwave. To dry flowers, herbs and spices in the microwave, place them between two tea towels and start the microwave on HIGH. Check them at one minute intervals.

Preserving and strengthening the fragrance of your potpourri is a must. Orris root, available in powder or chips, is the best preservative.

To enhance the fragrance of your potpourri, you need oil. Spice or herb mixtures usually do not require oil, although flower mixtures do. Choose from floral and citrus scents and match them to your mixture.

Various amounts of orris root and oils can be used. Experiment with what amount works for you. The standard is 1 to 2 tablespoons of orris root to one pint of dried flowers plus 3 to 6 drops of oil. Mix thoroughly and you have potpourri.

Potpourri ingredients are available from your garden or in most herb or specialty shops.

Save on Cleaners

Using common items to replace toxic cleaners can not only save the environment but save money, too. Usually we buy window cleaners, scouring powders, disinfectants, toilet bowl cleaners, tub and tile cleaners, bleach, oven cleaners, drain cleaners and the list goes on.

Nearly all cleaners and disinfectants have a non-toxic counterpart. Most have more than one. And it just so happens that these counterparts are very inexpensive and have many uses.

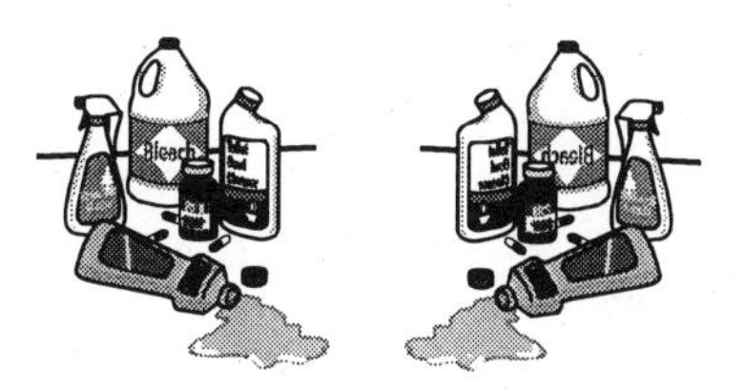

Replace scouring powder with baking soda. Baking soda will effectively scrub your sinks, bathtubs and toilet bowls. Baking soda contains no bleach or phosphates to hurt the environment. When used with vinegar, it produces a foaming reaction which is very useful in the toilet bowl to scrub off dirt. Pour one cup of vinegar into the toilet bowl, then toss a handful of baking soda. Leave for one minute, then scrub.

Baking soda also cleans fiberglass showers and tubs. Use with a little water and it performs just as scouring powder.

Instead of using fabric softeners, use 1/4 cup of baking soda in the wash cycle. Vinegar is another alternative to fabric softeners. Use 1/4 cup in the wash cycle.

Vinegar has many uses. As a cleaner, use equal parts of vinegar and water in a spray bottle for washing windows. For tougher jobs,

Use a soft-drink bottle carton as a cleaning caddy. Store your cleaners, brushes and cloths in the individual compartments. Carry it with you as you clean the house.

Remove grease stains from the walls by applying cornstarch. Leave for a few minutes and wipe off. The cornstarch absorbs the oil.

Use baking soda to get rid of tea stains in cups. Baking soda or salt can be used instead of abrasives.

Avoid using chemicals to polish your silver. Line the bottom of a pan with clean aluminum foil. Fill with 3 to 4 inches of water plus 1 teaspoon each of salt and baking soda. When water begins to boil, put in the silver for 2 to 3 minutes. Cool, rinse and dry the silver.

try cleansing off the chemical build-up of other window cleaners with alcohol first. Always use *white* vinegar for cleaning and deodorizing.

Substitute phosphate laundry detergents with washing soda and borax. To rid clothes of stains, use hydrogen peroxide for tough stains, such as blood. For common stains, such as chocolate or coffee, rub with washing soda or borax, soak and rinse.

Cleaning the oven is one of the most undesirable cleaning jobs in the house. Rubber gloves must usually be donned, as well as a clothespin, to resist inhaling the lye in commercial cleaners. They do a good job, but at what cost?

Instead of using commercial oven cleaners, try using baking soda with a little water, and scrub with steel wool. To loosen baked-on foods, place a pie pan of water in the oven and heat the oven on high heat for approximately 30 minutes. The best method of cleaning the oven is to prevent spills from happening in the first place. Place a baking pan or dish on the lowest rack to catch spills.

Replacing commercial cleaners with less toxic and less expensive ones takes time. When you have run out of your commercial cleaners, try alternatives. Soon you will not have one commercial cleaner in your home and your savings will show it.

NOTE: Some environmental product stores and health food stores sell nontoxic cleaning products.

Natural Cleaning Tips

- To clean gold jewelry, sprinkle baking soda on a wet sponge. Rub jewelry gently, then rinse and rub with a soft sponge in cold water.
- Clean the garbage disposal with lemon or lime rinds by throwing them in the disposal and turning it on. Run water to rinse.
- Mix one cup white wine vinegar and one cup milk in a bowl. Place silver items in mixture and let soak overnight. Rinse in hot water and dry.
- To naturally bleach out stains on white sheets or tablecloths, wash or rinse with warm water and spread out on the lawn on a bright sunny day. The sun will naturally bleach the white fabric.
- To disinfect areas, make a large pot of sage tea. Let cool until warm. Wash areas with cloth soaked and rinsed in tea.

Polish furniture with olive oil. For varnished woods, mix with a little vinegar.

Make your own ironing starch. Dissolve 1 tablespoon of cornstarch to 1 pint of water.

Cleaning Metals

Copper
Spread a tarnished pan or other copper product with a paste of 2 tablespoons of lemon juice and 1 1/2 tablespoons of salt. Let sit for one hour. Check by scraping off a bit of paste. If not completely clean or shiny, let sit for 30 minutes to an hour more. (Vinegar can be substituted for lemon juice.)

Stainless Steel
Dab wet cloth or sponge in a little baking soda. Rub until clean. Rinse well in warm water and dry with a cloth.

Silver
Soak in lemon juice checking every 15 minutes. Rinse and dry well.

Earthsaver

Clean drains with natural ingredients instead of using commercial drain cleaners which are caustic. Unfortunately these caustic cleaners end up in sewers and in our waters. Instead, pour 1/4 cup of baking soda down the drain, then pour one cup of boiling hot vinegar down the drain. This will loosen the dirt and clean out the pipes.

You can also use a plunger or plumber's snake to clean your drain.

Use borax for many household cleaning tasks. Borax is made from boron, a mineral from the earth, and is a disinfectant. Use it to clean bathrooms, kitchens and laundry.

Clean Indoor Air with House Plants

Indoor pollution is hard to avoid today since most of us have homes with carpet, paint and plywood. These items contain chemicals, such as formaldehyde, benzene and trichloroethylene. Studies have shown the development of significant health problems in humans due to prolonged exposure to these chemicals. Memory loss, headaches and cancer are just some of the illnesses linked to chemical exposure.

Luckily, nature has provided a simple purification process through the common house plant. Since plants take in carbon dioxide, they also take in the chemicals in the air around them. For instance, the spider plant takes in formaldehyde.

For each average-sized room, two or three plants will clean the air of these chemicals. In each room try having different plants for different chemicals. For example, in the living room place a spider plant for formaldehyde, a bamboo palm for benzene and an English ivy plant for trichloroethylene (TCE). If you have the room, place more plants for cleaning the air of formaldehyde, a commonly used chemical found in plywood, particleboard, some insulation and permanent press clothing.

All plants clean the air in some sense, however the plants below have been found to be the most effective in cleaning the air of particular chemicals found in our homes.

Spider Plant - Formaldehyde
Bamboo Palm - Benzene, Formaldehyde
Aloe Vera - Formaldehyde
Azalea - Formaldehyde
Corn Plant - Benzene
Weeping Fig - Formaldehyde
Gerber Daisy - Benzene, Formaldehyde
Philodendron - Formaldehyde
English Ivy - TCE
Peace Lily - Benzene, TCE
Dieffenbachia - Formaldehyde
Dragon Tree - TCE, Benzene
Pothos - TCE
Chrysanthemum - Formaldehyde
Boston Fern - Formaldehyde
Snake Plant - Benzene, Formaldehyde

If you are moving into a brand new house, these plants can be very effective in cleaning the air of the chemicals due to new construction.

Cheap and Natural Cold Remedies

Instead of using medications to relieve the symptoms of colds, use something natural and very inexpensive.

The most natural and most inexpensive cold remedy is to protect yourself from getting one in the first place.

1. Take good care of yourself.
2. Reduce stress and eat healthy foods.
3. Bundle up when going out in the cold weather.
4. Never share a glass or anything else from someone who has a cold.
5. When in public places, such as work, wash your hands often to prevent the spread of germs from others.

For a stuffy nose:
1. Eat hot foods, such as Mexican or Indian dishes made with cayenne pepper or jalapeno pepper. The *hot* from the pepper helps to drain and clear your nasal passages.
2. Suck on a clove of garlic to clear nasal passages.
3. Soak a washcloth in very warm water. Wring out and place over the face for a minute. Repeat twice.

To soothe a sore throat:
1. Gargle with warm water and salt.
2. Slippery Elm Bark lozenges found in your local health food store ease the sore throat discomfort naturally.
3. Drink or gargle with chamomile tea.
4. Mix 4 or 5 whole peppercorns in a tablespoon of honey. Take small bites and chew.

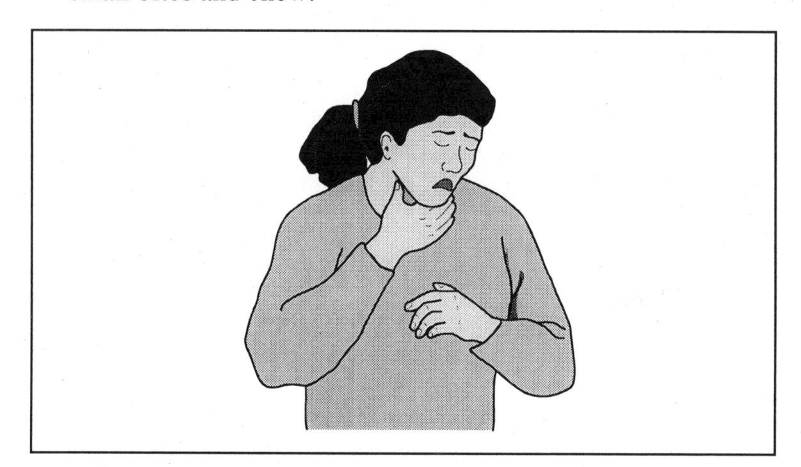

To ease that overall achy feeling:
1. Make basil tea by bringing a cup of water to a boil and steeping 3 to 4 basil leaves. Sprinkle with a dash of freshly ground black pepper and drink.
2. Eat foods high in vitamin C, such as oranges and potatoes.
3. Drink lots of fluids, such as water and juices.

More Natural Remedies

Allergies

To clean out the pollen which irritates the nasal passages, pour a little salt in your palm. Mix with a tablespoon or two of water and breath in and up the nose.

To relieve irritated and itching eyes, brew some eyebright tea. Let cool. Rinse eyes with the tea.

Insect Bites

Aloe vera gel rubbed on the bites helps heal the skin and lessen the itching.

Sunburn

Brew some chamomile tea. Let cool. Using a soft cloth soaked in the tea, pat skin all over burned area. (You could add some aloe vera gel* to the tea, also.)

Apple cider vinegar can be used as above to relieve the discomfort of sunburn.

Discomfort from the Heat

Drink lots of fluids. Stay away from *heavy* meals.

*For more information on the benefits of aloe vera, contact Aloes International, 2421 Curry Ford Road, Orlando, FL 32806-2503.

Naturally Healthy Cats

Recently, I received a scare when my 13 year old cat began bleeding from his eye and his nose. As I rushed him to the veterinarian, all I could think was I was not ready to let go of him, not yet.

After x-rays, tests and $400, there was no conclusive answer to the question, "What is wrong with my cat?" Although there were tissue samples sent off to the lab for tests, the results would not be available until for a week or two. In the meantime, I was given antibiotics and a cortisone drug for my cat.

Because there was the possibility that an abscess was causing the swelling on the right side of his face and the bleeding from his eye and nose, the vet put my cat under anesthesia to examine his mouth. His age, his illness and the fact that anesthesia was administered by injection, as well as with gas, contributed to the long amount of time my cat took to recover from his ordeal. He was a pitiful sight. And as a result, I was beside myself.

Last year, I contacted a homeopathic veterinarian to help with another cat with health problems. Last month, I gave her another call. Because holistic medicine does not advocate the use of drugs, I waited to hear from the homeopathic vet before I gave my cat the drugs. Instead, she suggested a homeopathic remedy and warned me of the possible negative consequences of giving the drugs to my cat. I was very frightened. Although I have been a disciple of natural health for many years, I was afraid my cat would die if I did not give him the medicine.

A month has passed and my cat is still alive. I did not give him the drugs. I gave him the homeopathic remedies as well as some herbal, nutritional and vitamin therapies. He is not completely well, but he is improving. The drugs may have cured him in a few days, but the effects of the drugs may have lasted a lifetime by weakening his body to be susceptible to more illness. Holistic medicine may take a little longer, but the effects are easier on the body and last. These are the beliefs of natural medicine.

I do not profess to be an expert, however I will impart as much information as I can based on my experiences. Holistic medicine is based on the belief that our bodies and the bodies of animals can heal themselves. Sometimes they may need just a push or to be given natural supplements which will strengthen the immune system. Allopathic medicine or traditional medicine sometimes uses strong drugs to produce a quick reaction from the body. But holistic practitioners believe this sometimes shocks the body and may produce long-lasting weaknesses in our natural healing system because of the immune suppression most drugs cause.

Homeopathy is based on the belief that like cures like. Simplified, this means that by introducing a small amount of a substance which produces similar symptoms as the illness, the immune system will be stimulated to fight the illness. As a result, the patient is cured and has more resistance to that illness.

The New Natural Cat is a book which takes a holistic view of health care and maintenance for cats. The book covers homeopathy for cats, nutrition for better overall health, and some natural home remedies for minor illnesses. I have used it as a reference with great success. I used the goldenseal tea, a natural antibiotic, to help my cat fight his illness last month. I have been giving my cats vitamin supplements for years. And I have completely changed my cats' diet using raw food, including raw meat and vegetables. The aim is to fill all cat's nutritional requirements for optimal health.

The use of holistic medicine may also save you money. I spent $400 at my first visit to the veterinarian. I spent $100 for five phone consultations with the homeopathic veterinarian. The homeopathic remedies cost approximately $10 in all.

And so, how does this affect the earth? Holistic medicine benefits us all by using nontoxic and safe methods of treating health problems. Obviously, there is a need for traditional medicine in cases of extreme emergency. However, the tendency of holistic medicine to treat the entire individual for the long term is, in my opinion, more beneficial to our physical, mental and spiritual well-being.

NOTE: The cat referred to in this article has since died, but I felt the article would still be of interest to readers of this book. Although we would like our pets to live forever—sadly, there comes a day when they must leave. No manner of medicine can make them live forever.

Natural Remedies for Cats

- For hairballs, fast the cat once a month.
- For flea and tick prevention, feed a little garlic in food.
- To improve a cat's overall health, give a little of the herb Echinacea every day for three days.
- For a shiny healthy coat of hair, give your cat a little brewer's yeast as a diet supplement.
- For feline acne, open a small capsule of vitamin A & D and squeeze into the food. Do not do this too often because vitamin A & D could build up to a toxic level.
- When your cat is ill, add a little Vitamin C to the food. Stress depletes vitamin C in the body.
- Whenever your cat is placed under a large amount of stress, give a few drops of the Bach Flower Remedy, Rescue Remedy.*

To find a homeopathic veterinarian in your area contact the American Holistic Veterinary Medical Association, 2214 Old Emmorton Road, Bel Air, Maryland 21015, (410) 569-0795

*Always consult with your veterinarian.

Chapter 4

RE-USABLE

Accuse not Nature, she hath done her part;
Do thou but thine.

- John Milton, *Paradise Lost*

Loose with Reuse

Recycle old eyeglasses by donating them to needy people around the world. Send used glasses to New Eyes for the Needy, 549 Millburn Avenue, Short Hills, NJ 07078. If you include your name and address, you will receive a notice of receipt of your tax-deductible contribution.

Or recycle glasses by donating them to Vision/Habitat, 542 Southerfield Road, Americus, GA 31709. The glasses will be sold to needy people around the country for a couple of dollars.

Everyday we throw away things because we feel their use has expired. However, some things can be used in other ways. Try saving the earth and saving money by using those throwaways again in another way.

GLOVES

Old gloves can be worn and used to dust and polish furniture. If you have some good gloves which have holes in the fingers, darn them as you would socks.

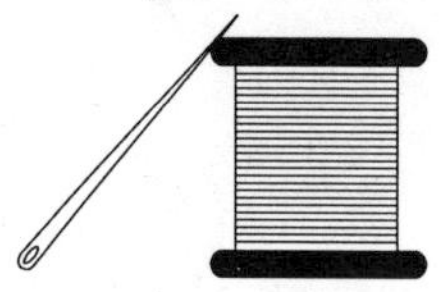

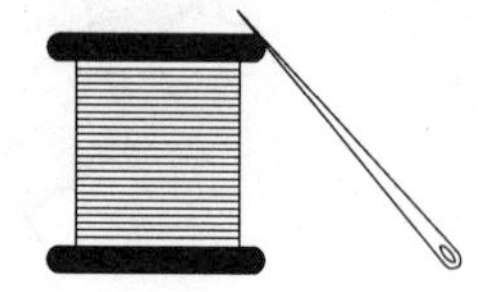

BED SHEETS

Make your own duvet cover out of sheets. Sew three sides together, the two sides and the top. Sew from each end of the bottom until there is a 20- to 30-inch opening in the center. Sew Velcro™ inside the opening. Slip the duvet inside and secure the duvet cover.

CARDBOARD TUBES

Cut part of the tube to create a trouser hanger. Place the cut tube across the lower bar of the hanger to prevent trousers from creasing.

Save long cardboard tubes for sending papers, posters or artwork in the mail.

MILK CARTONS

Use old milk cartons to start a grilling fire. Fill the milk carton with charcoal and light. In many instances, you will not need to use lighter fluid.

POTPOURRI

Heat potpourri two or three times instead of once. Then let it dry and use it as a gift decoration. Glue it on the box in the shape of a flower. Or fill the mailing package with potpourri to scent the box.

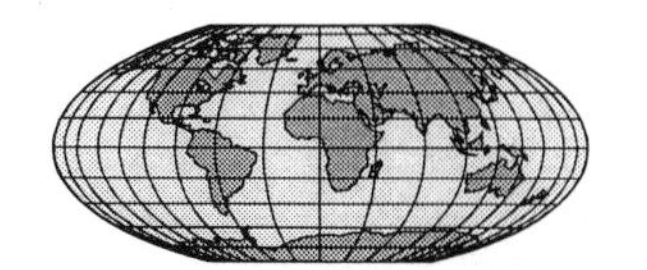

TOOTHBRUSHES

Use old toothbrushes to scrub tile or dirty floor corners.

OLD PILLOWS

Tie fabric around a pillow and use it as a decorative pillow for couches or chairs.

OLD WALL CALENDARS

Save the pictures for making your own envelopes. Using an old envelope which has been unglued, lay it flat on the back of the picture. Trace it, cut it out, fold and glue it together. Use white labels for the address and fun stickers to close the envelope.

PLASTIC LIDS

Use plastic lids as planter saucers.

OLD CEREAL BOXES

Cover with fabric or wallpaper to make magazine storage boxes.

EGG CARTONS

Use egg cartons at Easter for storing decorated eggs. Decorate the egg carton with paint or ribbon.

WIRE HANGERS

If you cannot donate your leftover hangers, make mobiles out of them. Take two and stretch out the wires. Crisscross them and hang any objects you like with string.

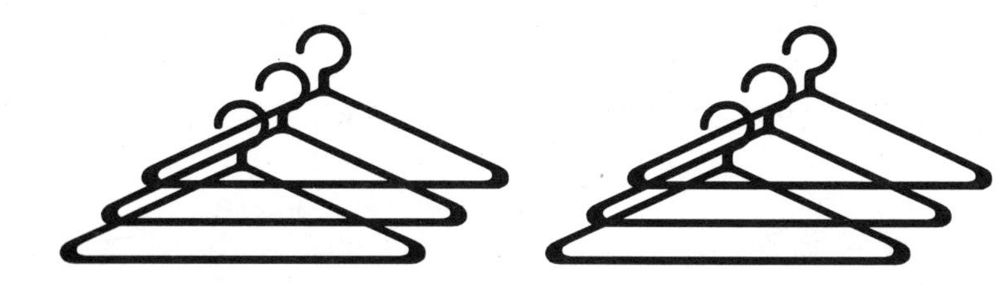

FLOUR BAGS

Clean the inside of paper flour bags gently with a damp sponge. Use as decorative gift bags.

GLASS JARS

Save glass jars for storing small items or toys. Use them to store snacks, such as nuts or pretzels.

OLD LINENS

Those yellowed linens you thought old and ready to be trashed can be saved. Boil them in water and bleach in a large pot on the stove. Simmer for 10 to 15 minutes, then rinse in lukewarm water. Squeeze all the water out. Place in plastic bags and refrigerate for an hour. Remove from refrigerator and bags, and iron immediately.

BURLAP RICE BAGS

Some brands of rice bought in bulk come in burlap bags. Use these bags as cloth shopping bags. Use them to store birdseed or flower bulbs.

PLASTIC TAPE ROLLS

If you use tape for tape dispensers, you usually have a plastic ring leftover when the tape has all been used. Paint this and use as a napkin ring.

OLD GREETING CARDS

Cut off the front of the card from the back. Paste this in the center of a gift box instead of a bow.

LOTION BOTTLES

Use old lotion bottles as liquid soap dispensers.

PLASTIC DETERGENT BINS

Store birdseed in washed plastic detergent containers.

PLASTIC FILM CONTAINERS

These are perfect for storing paper clips or thumb tacks. Use as a stamp dispenser. Slit hole in side with sharp knife, place roll of stamps in container, and pull out of slit.

Scratch Pads

We all need scratch pads for grocery lists, notes to ourselves and phone messages. Fancy notepads can be bought at greeting card stores or department stores, but it is very easy and inexpensive to make your own.

If you haven't written the Direct Marketing Association* to stop your junk mail or you are still getting some junk mail, save all envelopes and sheets of paper with one blank side. Save other sheets of paper, such as note paper and letters which have one blank side. Store these in tins or baskets loosely or make a pad by stapling, clipping or gluing them together. You will never have to buy a pad again, and you are recycling.

*If you wish to have up to 75% of your junk mail stopped, write to: Mail Preference Service, Direct Marketing Association, 11 West 42nd Street, P. O. Box 3861, New York, NY 10163-3861.

A booklet, *Stop Junk Mail Forever* by Marc Eisenson and Nancy Castleman and Marcy Ross is available for $3.00 from Good Advice Press, Box 78, Elizaville, NY 12523, (914) 758-1400.

Those *Darn* Socks!

Socks need not be thrown away just because of one hole. Sometimes one hole can ruin an otherwise perfect sock. Here's how to save money and recycle all those *holey* socks:

1. Darning by hand...

Materials

Matching darning cotton (sewing department of most stores)
A darning egg or a plastic Easter egg

Instructions

Stretch the sock over the darning egg to expose the hole. Pull the *unknotted* thread through the edge of the hole and secure with three tiny stitches on top of each other. Make small stitches completely around the hole. Sew horizontal stitches across the hole 1/16 inch apart. Repeat this vertically, but weave the thread over and under the horizontal threads. End with a small knot made with one single loop.

2. Darning by machine...

Materials

Matching darning cotton (sewing department of most stores)
Embroidery hoop
Sewing Machine

Instructions

Place area to be darned into embroidery hoop. Take presser foot off of machine. Use straight-stitch setting, drop or cover feed dog, and set stitch width on 0mm. Place hole under needle and freehand stitch a circle around it. Then closely stitch back and forth across the hole until it is completely covered. Move the piece around to stitch in the opposite direction.

Hol(e)y Socks!

Holey Socks! Do you have any? Most of us do. The question is what to do with them. Should you throw them away, darn them, damn them or leave them in the dryer hoping they'll disappear like those *other* socks?

If we are to be earth conscious, we should find ways to reuse those socks rather than discard them to the land of landfills. Here are a few ideas:

- Use old socks as dusting cloths. Pull one over your hand and dust.
- Slip socks over the ladder to keep it from making marks on the walls or the outside of your house.
- Use old socks to cover shoes or other items when packing a suitcase or when packing summer or winter items away for the season.
- Keep old socks in the car for changing the tire or other dirty jobs.
- Cut the cuffs off of socks to create sweat bands or ponytail holders.

Earthsaver

Save plastic nursery flats and plastic planters from the nursery. They are great to use for starting plants from seed or giving plants to friends or relatives.

New Ideas for Old Clothes

Before you send those clothes out to the Salvation Army, try to update them or repair them. Stains and holes can be repaired or covered. Out-of-date clothes can be updated. Shoes can be repaired and embellished.

Stains Be Gone

Sometimes we have a perfectly fine blouse, but it has one stain which will not disappear in the wash. We are sure we could never wear it again.

Stains can be concealed by adding some embroidery either just over the stain or all over the blouse for a uniform design. Embroidery transfers are available at fabric shops. Some sewing machine models will create embroidered designs on clothes.

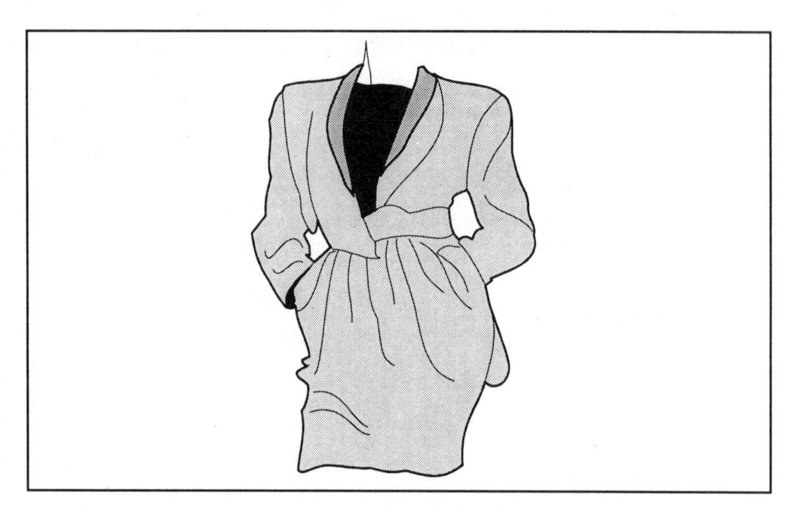

Use extra buttons to create a design which will cover your stain and add a new look to your blouse. Sequins can be sewn over the stain to add a beautiful flower design. First, draw the design on the blouse lightly with a pencil.

Dying the blouse another color may conceal the stain and give you a whole new look. When using dyes, follow the directions carefully.

If the stain is on a sleeve, cut off the sleeve and create a short-sleeved blouse.

Old Shoes Into New Shoes

Heels can be repaired and replaced at any shoe repair shop. After repairs, dye the shoes another color with shoe dye. Follow the directions carefully. Gold shoes can give you a new elegant look.

Shoes can be embellished with a strong glue and small craft rhinestones. Be sure to plan out your design very carefully before applying the rhinestones because there is no going back after you have begun.

Never Too Late to Update

Use accessories to update old clothes. Add scarves, belts and pins.

Take out those large shoulder pads and wear without.

Shorten tops by cutting fabric to the waste. Lengthen tops by adding fabric to reach the thighs.

Bring out your old bellbottoms. They are back.

Below are some more ideas:

- Make pillows.
- Use old clothes for cleaning rags
- Make cloth puppets.
- Make an apron.
- Sew the ribbed end of tube socks to the sleeves of a child's jacket when the child is outgrowing the jacket.
- Learn how to quilt.
- Use old slips as linings for wool skirts.
- If a sweater has become too tight, turn it into a cardigan by trimming and sewing the front.
- Cut off the top of a dress and make it a blouse. Use the bottom as a skirt.
- Spice up old clothes by embellishing them buttons, sequins, ribbons and beads.

Sweater Issues

With normal wear and tear, sweaters develop holes and tears in them. Darn these holes just as you would socks. Add a suede patch if the hole is on the elbow. If the hole is on the body of the sweater, embroider a design over the hole or embellish with sequins and fabric paint.

Drastic Changes

If a shirt or blouse has too many stains or holes, use a pattern to cut out and sew a vest. Add an assortment of patches to the vest for a casual look over jeans.

White canvas shoes which have stained very badly can be dyed or embellished with rhinestones. Add decorative laces.

Use the remaining fabric from cut-off jeans for creating jean patches. Use jean patches on blazer elbows, other jeans and on other casual slacks. Embroider designs on the patches.

If the sun has faded an item of clothing, dye it the same color. If the colors are too varied, plan a new design with fabric paint or sequins or buttons.

Cheap and Easy Gift Pillows

For the New Bride

Start with a plain square pillow. You can find them at yard sales or craft stores for very little money. Use a fabric of your choice. You may want to use colors which match the bride's dress or the colors of the wedding. If your fabric has frayed edges, sew a hem of 6" or more. You don't want to see the hem when you tie the bow. This means you will have to cut the fabric 18 inches on each side of the pillow. Center your pillow on a piece of fabric and cut the fabric 12 inches larger on each side of the centered pillow. Bring all sides together in the center of the pillow to make a *bow*. Tie around the bow with braid or ribbon. Leave the pillow as is or decorate around the edges with lace trim using a glue gun. Use potpourri inside the pillow. Sprinkle some under and on top of the pillow before you tie up the fabric. Add some dried flowers inside the bow for a bouquet.

For the New Home

Start with any bed pillow. Use fabric which matches a room in the person's home or use white or natural. Roll the pillow into a round oblong shape. Tie the middle and each end. Do not tie too tight. Use one leg of nylon stockings to pull over the pillow to keep it in the shape. Tie the end of the nylon stocking and cut off the excess. Measure your fabric to cover the pillow with 6 to 8 inches left on each end. Sew the seam to cover the pillow or use a glue gun to secure the seam. Tie the ends into a bow with braid or ribbon. Add potpourri or extra trim.

It's *New* from Rubbish

With a little imagination, some of the things we normally throw away can be transformed into things we use. Thus, preventing some items from ending up in the landfill. Below are some ideas for creating usable items from your trash:

***Plastic Bottles w/Handles* = A Pooper Scooper**
Cut around the handle of the plastic bottle enough to create a scoop.

***Jar Lids* = Cookie Cutters**

***Milk Carton* = A New Desk Pencil Holder**
Cut off top with spout and cover with decorative magazine pages.

***Scrap Paper* = Paper for Notes, Lists, etc.**

***Old Nylon Stockings* = A Washer Blade Cover for Delicate Items**
Before washing delicate items in the washer, cover the washer blade with the legs of nylon stockings to soften the blade motion during the cycle.

***Round Plastic Lids* = A Hamburger Patty Shaper**

***Old Umbrella* = Clothes Drying Rack**
Remove the torn or old fabric from the umbrella frame and hang from the handle on the outside clothesline. Hang small items from the frame, such as socks and children's clothes.

***Egg Cartons* = Storage for Screws and Nails in Toolbox or Tool Shed**

***Cardboard Egg Cartons* = Fire Starters**

***Old Toothbrush Handles* = Plant Stakes**

***Facial Cream Tubs* = Bobby Pin Holder**
Store the empty tubs in drawers with loose items, such as bobby pins.

***Carpet Remnants* = A Mat at the Door of the Shed**

***Berry Baskets* = Refrigerator Storage for Small Items, such as yeast and sauce packets.**

***Styrofoam Meat Trays* = Shoe Cushion Inserts**

***Old Door* = A New Table or Desk Top**

***Old Towels* = Liners Protecting Car Trunk When Carrying Mulch or Other Garden Items**

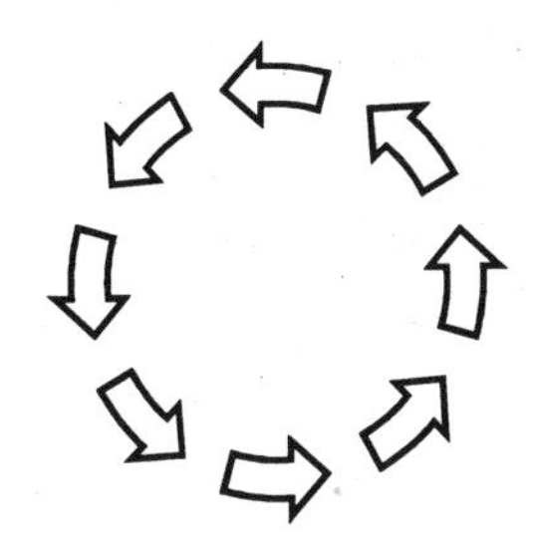

***Old Broom Handle* = Closet or Curtain Rod**

***Old Magazines* = Packing Material**

***Old Baking Pans* = Seed Starting Flats**

***Deflated Mylar Balloons* = Kids' Party Placemats**

***Old Sheets* = A Car Seat Protector during Feline Trips to the Vet when the Hair Flies**

***Old Blue Jeans* = Beach Bag**
Cut the legs off of a pair of jeans and sew leg openings closed. Use the fabric from the cut off legs to create a shoulder strap and attach to the bag.

***Old Clothes* = New Rags**

***Bread Wrapper Tabs* = End of Roll of Tape Marker**
Use tabs on a roll of tape to mark the end of the tape.

EARTHSAVING WAYS TO INCREASE YOUR SAVINGS BY $1000 OR MORE THIS YEAR

- When using canned goods, such as tomatoes or peas, drain off the juice and freeze it for later use in soups or stews. ($10 - $50)
- Save attractive wine bottles and use them as flower vases. ($10 - $50)
- Buy a used car or buy a car at an auction instead of buying a new car. ($3,000 - $10,000)
- Re-use aluminum foil. First, wash in hot soapy water. ($10 - $25)
- Use elastic band at waist of pantyhose as a giant rubber band. ($5 - $10)
- Use plastic bags from the grocery store as trash bags instead of buying new trash bags. ($10 - $25)
- Re-use tea bags. ($5 - $15)
- Save water from boiling eggs or soaking legumes for watering plants. ($10 - $25)
- Use old pillowcases as storage bags for toys, craft items or yarn. They can also be used as travel bags for kids. Pack clothes inside and tie the opening with thick string. ($10 - $25)
- Save stale bread for making your own bread crumbs. ($5 - $15)
- Use old shower caps as food dish covers. They are washable, and you don't need to use aluminum foil or plastic wrap. ($10 - $25)
- Save cotton from vitamin bottles for later use. ($5 - $10)
- Pantyhose can be used as nightwear. Simply cut off the feet and you have something similar to long underwear, but lighter. ($10 - $50)
- Use plastic bags as packing material for packages. ($5 - $10)
- Snip old and run pantyhose into small pieces for craft stuffing. ($10 - $25)
- Have shoes re-soled or repaired instead of buying new. ($20 - $300)
- Roll up plastic bags to stuff in boots. These can replace shoe trees. ($10 - $50)
- Do not throw away torn rubber gloves. Cut across glove to create heavy duty rubber bands. ($5 - $20)
- Cut or tear old clothes to make cleaning rags. ($10 - $20)*

*Figures are estimated for a family of four. Your savings may be more or less.

Rechargeables

Batteries are something we use often enough not to even think about the fact they may contain toxic chemicals. Chemicals, such as mercuric oxide, silver oxide, zinc and carbon are most commonly found in batteries. When these batteries are discarded to endlessly sit in landfills, they leach these toxic chemicals into the air, soil and water. Just think of the toxic effects if every family threw out five to 20 batteries a year.

Rechargeable batteries, on the other hand, do not have to be discarded for a very long time. They can be recharged hundreds of times. All you need to use these batteries is a battery recharger which you use to recharge the batteries over and over again. Most battery rechargers plug into any electrical outlet in your home. However, there are battery rechargers available which can be set outside to recharge using solar energy.

One thing to remember about rechargeable batteries is to completely drain them of power before recharging them. This is also true of rechargeable vacuums, flashlights and cordless phones. Leave these items out of their rechargeable pockets until they no longer have power. Then recharge them fully.

Disposable and even rechargeable batteries contain toxic materials which can pollute our environment. The only battery which is safe for landfills is the 'Zinc-air' battery offered by ***Seventh Generation.*** If you still have disposable batteries, wait for a day when the landfill is accepting hazardous waste. Battery recycling programs are available in some areas. Check with your local government.

Earthsaver

Make your watch battery last longer! When you are not wearing your watch pull the stem out fully. Before you put your watch back on, set the time and push the stem back in.

Rechargeable Products

Rechargeable Lawn Mower is cordless, gasless and bagless. This mulching mower can be recharged by plugging it into an electrical outlet or using a solar charger.

Solar Battery Charger will charge AA, AAA, C and D batteries.

Both available through ***Real Goods***, 966 Mazzoni Street, Ukiah, CA 95482-3471. (800) 762-7325.

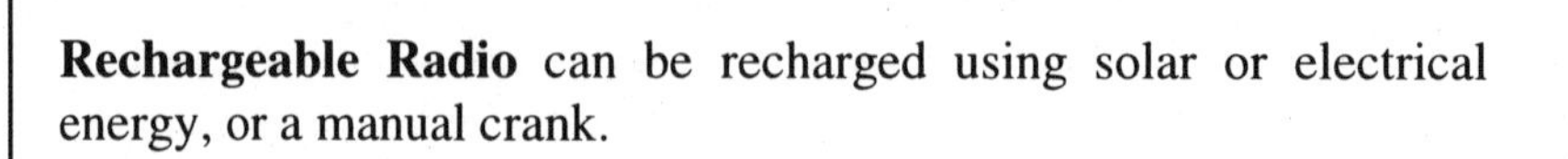

Rechargeable Radio can be recharged using solar or electrical energy, or a manual crank.

Mercury-free and Cadmium-free Disposable Batteries are safe for landfills.

Both available through ***Seventh Generation,*** Colchester, VT 05446-1672. (800) 456-1177.

Rechargeable Batteries last long and can be recharged as much as 500 times. Check local drug and electronic stores.

Chapter 5

RESOURCE-FULL

Come forth into the light of things,
Let Nature be your Teacher.

- William Wordsworth, *The Tables Turned*

Staying Warm Without Turning Up the Heat

Heating costs are the major contributors to your electrical bill each month. Below are some ideas for reducing those heating bills and saving energy:

- When you have finished baking, leave the door open to allow the heat to enter the room.
- Run a humidifier to keep the air moist in the house. Moist air creates an impression of more warmth due to high humidity.
- Close doors of unused rooms and place a towel or draft guard at the bottom of the door.

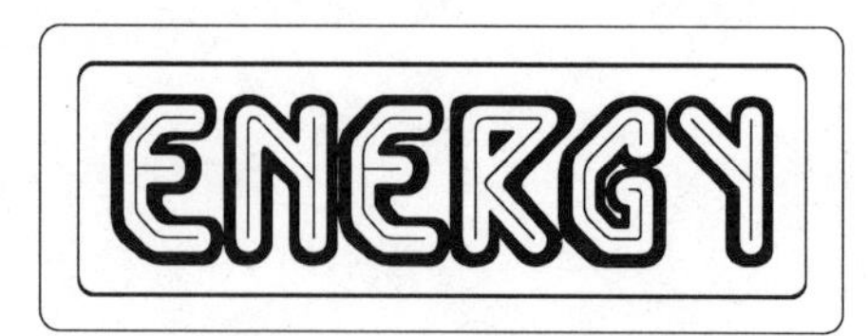

- Close heating vents which are not in use. There are vent coverings on the market to make a tighter seal.
- Wear more clothing. Buy several sets of long underwear and wear them under sweats. Wear two pairs of socks and a pair of slippers. With all this clothing you can bear to turn the thermostat down a few degrees and save on the monthly bill.

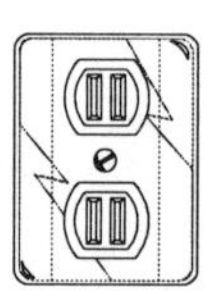
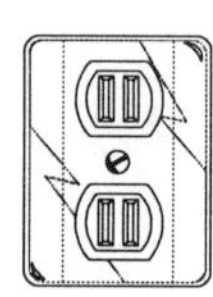
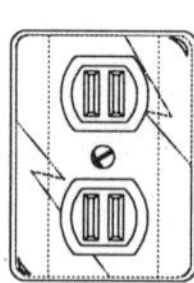

- Cover all electrical outlets if not in use. Several products are available. Check your local hardware store.
- Caulk around the outside openings of all windows and doors to prevent heat from escaping. Place weather-stripping around all doors and windows.
- Storm doors and windows can add a lot to preventing heat from escaping. You can also use clear plastic over windows. Kits are usually available at home centers.
- Use or make window quilts to cover windows.
- Use a woodstove instead of a fireplace. A woodstove is more efficient.
- Have periodic checks on your heating system to ensure it is running efficiently.
- At night use lots of blankets to keep warm and turn down the thermostat.

Make an Autumn Wreath for Less than $1.00

Materials

Pampas Grass (soaked in water for 30 minutes)
Autumn Leaves (dried and pressed)
Ribbon (yellow, orange, brown)
Acorns
Glue Gun

Take the pampas grass out of water and pat dry. Lay the strands out so as to be even from top to bottom. Shape into a circle keeping in mind the desired size for the wreath. Tie with string or tie with cut pieces of the grass. Shape into circle and let dry for 24 hours.

Starting at the bottom, wrap ribbon around wreath 4 to 5 times to reach start of ribbon. Repeat this with 1 or more other ribbon colors. Tie ribbon into bow at bottom of wreath. Glue leaves around and under ribbon bows. Glue acorns in clusters of three on leaves.

- Stay in the warmest rooms of the house.
- Keep thermostat temperature low. Try keeping it between 60°F and 68°F. Add another layer of clothing, such as long underwear you will hardly feel the difference in temperature. Another way to keep yourself warm while you have lowered the thermostat is to keep a space heater going in the room where you are spending time. While sitting, cover yourself with blankets.
- If you are in the room with the fireplace, turn off the heating system and enjoy the heat of the fire.
- Exercise every day which will raise your metabolism and help you feel warmer throughout the day.
- Open curtains while the sun is shining. Keep them closed when it is not. This allows heat to enter your home. Close the curtains after the sun has set or is no longer shining. This seals the heat in the house.

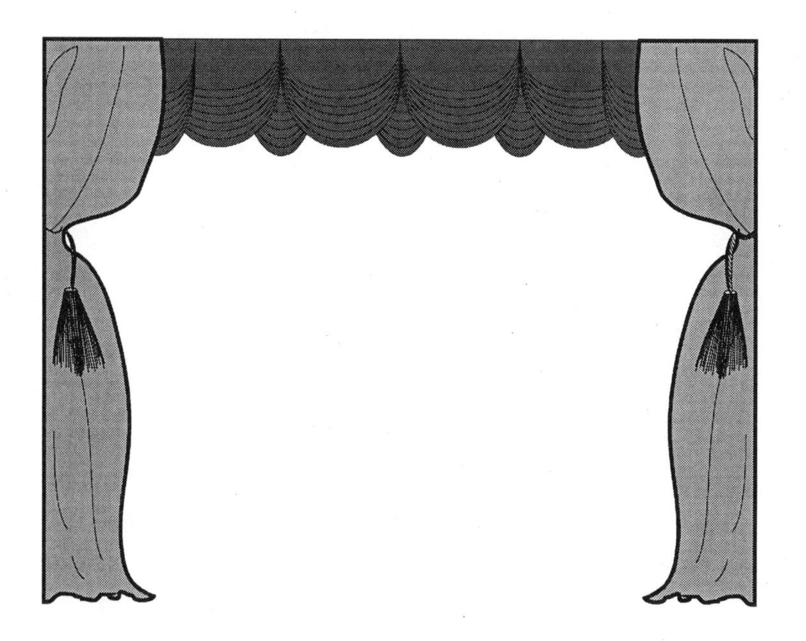

- Invest in ceiling fans. They push the warm air down from the ceiling and circulate it through the house.
- Turn the thermostat down while you are away.

Gas Saving

- Use public transportation.
- Carpool.
- Travel by train instead of air.
- Stay home for vacation this year.
- Drive at the speed limit. Driving 70 mph compared to 55 mph increases gas consumption by 25%.

If you are sitting in traffic or waiting for someone, turn off your car engine. Cars require more fuel to idle for 60 seconds than to restart.

Earthsaver

Buy compact fluorescent or halogen light bulbs. Compact fluorescent bulbs produce less heat, use less energy, and last up to ten times longer than standard bulbs. Halogen bulbs are very bright and last up to three times longer than standard bulbs.

Make A Window Quilt

Materials

Measuring Tape
Magnetic Strip
Fabric or Quilted Fabric
Batting

Instructions

The first step is to measure the windows. Measure top to bottom and side to side. If you want the quilt to fit over the window inside the frame, measure inside the frame. If you want the quilt to fit around the window on the outside of the frame, measure 1 1/2 to 2 inches outside of the frame all around the window except the bottom.

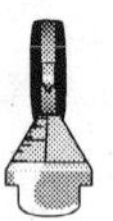
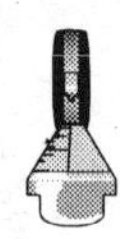
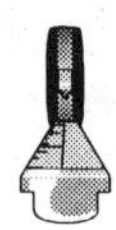

I originally made my quilt with magnetic strip to seal the window, but I have cats who insist on seeing outside and have therefore, repeatedly broken the seal.

If you think you will not have such a problem, measure the windows to figure how many feet of magnetic strip you will need. Double this measurement because you will have magnetic strip on the window and on the quilt. If you have metal windows, you may be able to use enough magnetic strip just to rim your quilt. The quilt with the magnetic stripping will seal onto the metal.

Of course, the quilt can be made without the magnetic stripping, but the quilt is the most effective when it seals the window. On the other hand, the quilt will still be better alone than if you only had a curtain.

Make Your Own Liquid Soap

What can you do with all those leftover soap pieces? Make liquid soap.

Measure the soap and pour it in a blender. Measure half the amount of water as soap chips and pour in the blender. Turn on the blender for a minute or two until the soap and water have mixed. Check the consistency of the soap. Is it too thick? Add more water.

The next step is to buy the fabric. You can buy quilted fabric or fabric plus batting. Be sure to buy double the amount of fabric in order to have a front and back to the window quilt. Always buy a little more fabric for hems and seams.

If you use magnetic stripping, you may not need a curtain rod. The quilt seals in place with the magnetic stripping. If you have a large window or are not using the magnetic stripping, you will need a curtain rod. Be sure to increase your measurements for the top of the window if the rod is outside the window frame because you will need more fabric.

Now, cut the fabric to fit the windows. You may sew the magnetic stripping on the inside or apply it to the outside of your fabric. If you choose to put it on the outside, make sure you purchase magnetic stripping which has a sticky side for adherence. With quilted fabric, sewing the magnetic stripping inside may reduce the effectiveness of the magnet because of the thickness of the fabric.

Sew your seams to fit the window. If you sew the magnetic stripping inside the fabric, your measurements must be exact in order for the magnetic stripping to match to the window metal or magnetic stripping. If you are using a rod, you must allow for enough fabric to loop over the rod. You may make this separately and sew it onto the quilted part of the window quilt.

If you are not using quilted fabric, be sure to place batting between the two pieces of fabric before sewing the seams. Then quilt the piece to flatten it.

Place the magnetic stripping all around the window. Press the rest of the magnetic stripping to the back of the window quilt. Place the quilt on the window on the magnetic stripping. If you are using a rod, hang the quilt, then press it against the magnetic stripping.

If you do this on every window in your house, you will save lots of energy and see significant savings on your heating bill.

The Water Watch

Energy Savers

Do not let the dishwasher run through the dry cycle. Open the door and let them air dry after about 30 minutes.

Contact your local utility company for incentive energy programs in which you can participate.

Turn lights off when not in use.

Change light bulbs to compact fluorescent or the new energysaver bulbs.

Use automatic timers for outside lights. You will never waste energy again by forgetting to turn your lights off.

Upgrade insulation in attic and walls.

Plant bushes and small trees around the house to insulate your home from the cold and shade it from the heat.

Save energy and make your bed warmer by placing a blanket under the fitted sheet.

Water sustains us in many ways. First, we need water for basic survival. Second, we need water to maintain growth in our gardens. And third, we need water for bathing and cleaning. Since we require so much water for so many different uses, we must use it conservatively in order to ensure we have a constant supply.

Below are some ideas for saving your water usage:

- Save water shaving in the morning by filling the sink with enough water to rinse your razor instead of running the water for rinsing.

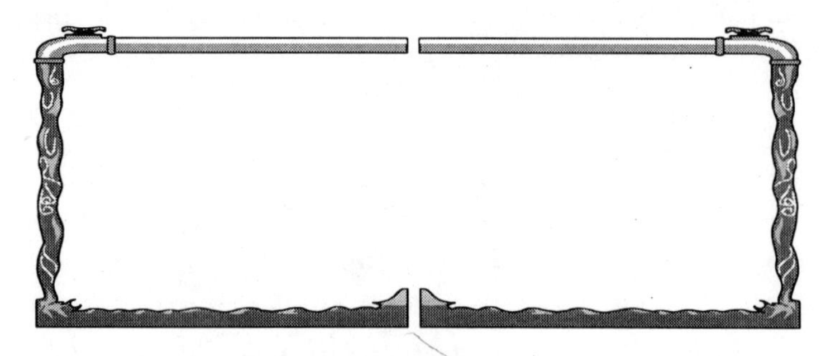

- Invest in a low-flush toilet. Standard toilets use between five to seven gallons of water for each flush. Low-flush toilets use only one to three gallons of water for each flush.
- Wash full loads of dishes in the dishwasher.
- When showering, run the cool water in a bucket when waiting for warm water. Use the cool water for watering house plants.
- Avoid using the hose to clean sidewalks, porches or driveways. Instead, fill a bucket and use it to rinse these areas.
- Run the shower only long enough to have water for lathering and to rinse.
- When soaking dried beans, such as black beans, save the water from the soaking. This water provides a good food source to house plants.
- Wash full loads in the washing machine.
- Avoid running the water at all times.
- When cleaning, use a bucket of water instead of rinsing out in the sink.
- Install water dams in toilet tanks to reduce water usage by about 30%. A soda bottle filled with water may also be placed in the toilet tank to reduce water usage.
- Install faucet aerators on all bathroom and kitchen faucets. Most faucets run at two to 12 gallons of water per minute, however faucets installed with aerators run at one to nine gallons of water per minute.
- Install low-flow shower heads in all showers. Low-flow shower heads reduce the flow of water up to 50% to 70%.

- Capture rain water in buckets or barrels to use for garden plants.
- Use mulch around garden plants and flowers to reduce evaporation.
- Avoid watering lawn and garden on a regular basis. Stay aware of the weather forecast. If rain is predicted, take advantage of the rain on your lawn and garden.

- Water the lawn and garden in the early morning to reduce evaporation..
- Invest in a soaker hose or a drip irrigation system for your flower or vegetable garden.
- When having a sump pump installed, try to have the water drained toward the garden to conserve water.
- If you are building your house, install a gray water drainage system which allows the gray water from your house to be used for outside watering.
- Be sure faucets are not dripping.
- Plant lots of trees and shrubs to create shade and reduce evaporation.
- Use horticulture polymers which absorb water several times their own weight, and then release the water slowly as the soil dries.
- Use plants in your garden which don't require a lot of water.

Trees which do not require a lot of water are: pine, crape myrtle, locust and Japanese pagoda.

Shrubs which do not require a lot of water are: sandhill sage, juniper and Oregon grape.

Perennials which do not require a lot of water are: lamb's ear, thyme and ice plant.

Bulbs which do not require a lot of water are: iris, daffodil and windflower.

Grasses which do not require a lot of water are: silverado, bonanza, mustang and trailblazer.

Buy a water heater timer.

Use a pressure cooker which cooks food more quickly, therefore saving energy and money.

Reduce the amount of times you open the refrigerator or freezer. Decide what you want before you open it.

Use floor fans and window fans.

Saving Energy

Use solar-powered calculators. They require no batteries nor electricity.

A complete list of appliance energy ratings is available from the American Council for an Energy-Efficient Economy, 1001 Connecticut Ave., NW, Suite 801, Washington, D. C. 20036, (202) 429-8873.

Saving energy not only conserves energy but saves you money on your utility bill every month. If you can cut down your usage by even $1.00 a day, that would be a savings of $30.00 a month, $360.00 a year.

Saving Energy in the Kitchen

- Always use cold water to fill pots or run the garbage disposal. This will save energy to heat water.
- Boil water in a covered pan. The water will boil faster.
- Keep the stove clean. Burners and reflectors operate better when clean.

- Turn burners off several minutes before food is completely cooked. The same applies for baking in the oven.
- Turn up the refrigerator/freezer temperatures. Good temperatures for the refrigerator are between 38°F and 40°F; 5° F for the freezer.

Saving Energy in the Bathroom

- Take showers instead of baths. Limit your showering time by turning on the water only long enough to get wet, then turn off the water while you lather. Turn the water back on long enough to rinse. You can save gallons of water each day, as well as save money, because you are using less hot water.

Saving Energy in the Laundry Room

- Wash clothes in warm or cold water, rinse in cold. Use hot water only for items needing disinfecting or when items are very soiled.
- Soak very soiled items to eliminate another wash.

Earthsavers

During good weather, dry clothes out on the line or on a drying rack brought from the inside. Not only does this save energy, but the clothes smell naturally fresh.

Do not buy ivory products. Elephants are killed by poachers purely for their tusks. There are approximately 600,000 elephants left in Africa. In 1979, there were 1.5 million.

Chapter 6

Waste Not, Save Much

To gild refined gold, to paint the lily,
To throw a perfume on the violet,
To smooth the ice, or add another hue
Unto the rainbow, or with taper-light
To seek the beauteous eye of heaven to garnish,
Is wasteful and ridiculous excess.

- William Shakespeare, *King John*

Sew sachets with scrap fabric and fill with potpourri—for closets and drawers.

Create a Budget

One of the first steps to saving money is to create a monthly budget. Not only does a budget allow you to save money, but it allows you to observe your spending habits.

Below are steps to creating a budget:

1. Write down the take home pay for each individual after taxes.

2. Add to this any interest, dividends or other income received consistently each month. This is your total income.

3. Decide what your fixed expenses are including—mortgage, car payment, insurance and loan payment. Add these and subtract them from your total income. This is your flexible money.

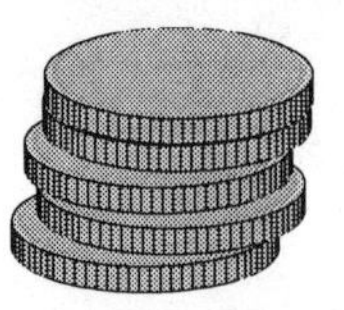

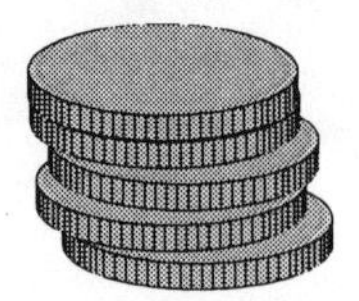

4. Decide what your semi-fixed expenses are by looking at each minimum payment of your credit cards. Decide whether you would like to pay the minimum payment or a little more. (Be sure to take into account how much interest is being charged every month.)

   Electric, water and telephone payments are semi-fixed expenses also. By looking at your average payment over a year's time, decide how much should be allotted each month for these items. (Examine whether you could cut usage down on some of these and budget accordingly.)

   Subtract these items for your flexible money.

5. Decide what expenditures you make consistently, such as food, clothing, automobile maintenance, medical, household (non-food), entertainment, transportation and home maintenance.

6. By looking at your average expenditure, decide how much should be allotted each month for these items. (Can you cut the food bill a little? How about entertainment? Or clothing?) Subtract these items from your flexible money.

7. Decide whether to put the remaining money into savings or take a small amount from it for miscellaneous expenditures or emergencies, such as gifts, charities or small accidents. If there is any money left, put it in a savings account.

How did you do? Were you left with a big chunk for savings which you have blown in the last years, or were you left with nothing? You may need to go back and forth over some of the steps until you come up with a budget that fits your income and your needs and wants. Using the budget for a few months is the real test to see where you may want to cut or add to create a final budget.

In order to maintain the budget effectively, write all your expenditures and budgeted figures down. Each month when you make a payment on a particular item, check it off. If the payment is more or less than the expenditure, write the difference beside it with a plus or minus sign. At the end of the month, you will see where your money goes. For instance, if you budgeted $90 each month for your electric bill but see in the last few months you have consistently paid under $80, redo the budget, so the extra money can go into savings. If you budgeted $150 each month for food costs but see in the last few months you have consistently exceeded

that amount by $20 or $30, examine carefully where that $20 or $30 is going. Couldn't you cut that small of an amount? If you budgeted $80 each month for food costs but are consistently over by $50, you may need to increase that allowance.

With the flexible expenditures, there is always some way to cut these costs by $5 to $50 or more each month leaving you with more for savings. Even if you cut three or four of these flexible items by just $5 each month, that would leave you with $150 to $240 by the end of the year.

One last point. This is a guide for you to use. Each family may have different expenditures. Feel free to experiment and add or subtract items to accommodate your household.

A Sample Budget

Monthly Budget ______May______

Expenses	Budget Amount	Amt. Used	Result
Mortgage	$600.00	$600.00	—
Electric	70.00	63.00	-7.00
Telephone	60.00	51.00	-9.00
Transportation	25.00	21.00	-4.00
Insurance	36.00	36.00	—
Credit Card	50.00	50.00	—
Water	25.00	20.00	-5.00
Food	150.00	163.00	+13.00
Home Maint.	35.00	55.00	+20.00
Auto Maint.	20.00	.00	-20.00
Entertainment	35.00	42.00	+7.00
Pocket Money	45.00	45.00	—
Miscellaneous	100.00	92.00	-8.00
Savings	225.00	225.00	—
Total	**$1,476.00**	**$1,463.00**	**+40.00 -53.00***

*Although this family stayed within their overall budget, they do need to look at their spending on some individual items. As you can see, it is not enough to stay within the total budget.

Weekly Worksheet

In order to save more money, we all need to take a closer look at our spending. Once we are aware of where the money goes, it is easier to see in what areas we can cut back. Keep this worksheet as a log for 3 to 4 weeks, then evaluate each area. Decide in what areas costs could be cut, make the changes, and keep the log for 3 or 4 more weeks. Evaluate again to see where the savings have increased.

Expense	Mon	Tues	Wed	Thurs	Fri	Sat	Sun
	$	$	$	$	$	$	$
Mortgage/Rent							
Electric/Gas							
Telephone							
Water							
Transportation*							
Auto Maintenance							
Home Maintenance							
Auto Insurance							
Home Insurance							
Other Insurance							
Groceries							
Clothing							
Laundry							
Dry Cleaning							
Cosmetics, etc.							
Barber/Beauty Salon							
Health Club							
Entertainment**							
Gifts							
Cable Television							
Medical***							
School Fees							
School Lunches							
Baby-sitting							
Allowances							
Toys							
Other							
Total	$	$	$	$	$	$	$

Weekly Total $_____

* Include gas, public transportation, parking and tolls.
**Include eating out, trips, sporting events and movies.
***Include doctor and dental fees and prescriptions not covered by insurance.

Cutting Health Care Costs

Prevention

- Many insurance companies support preventive medicine, such as regular check-ups by paying most or all of the cost.
- Be more aware of your body. Notice slight changes and observe whether the change is more painful, disappears or re-occurs. Tell your doctor.
- Keep a Health Diary. Write down pains and discomforts and when they appear. This will greatly assist your doctor and may help you to catch something before too much damage is done.
- Eat healthy! There are numerous articles and books which have researched the health benefits of eating healthy.
- Maintain a positive attitude! Research shows anger, worry and resentment are killers!

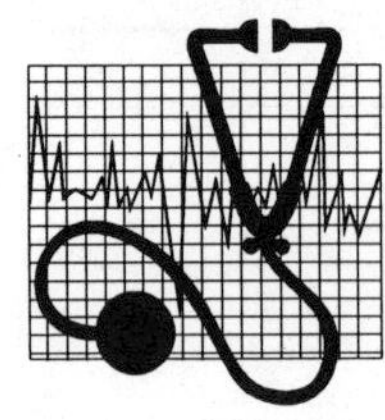

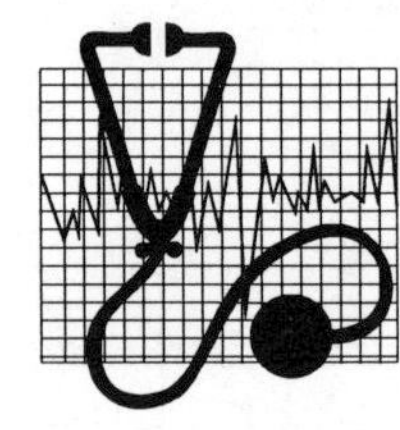

Tidbits

- Pay your doctor ahead of time in cash. Many doctors offer cash discounts.
- Check with medical associations before seeing a new doctor. Be sure your doctor is certified, licensed and has no complaints filed against her or him.
- Some states offer free health care to children. Eligibility requirements of families are based on annual income. Check with your State Department of Health.
- Read about your aches and pains. Your research could educate you on better prevention and new treatments.
- Call university hospitals to inquire about current studies in which you may participate for your particular ailment.
- Reduce your exposure to toxic chemicals. Research has shown exposure to some chemicals can cause mild to very noticeable symptoms.
- Fill your home with house plants to clean your indoor air.
- Investigate alternative methods of treatment.
- Try holistic medicine which treats the entire individual, not only the symptoms.
- Research has shown exercise increases immunity to disease and illness.
- Express feelings of hurt, anger and fearfulness. Research has shown individuals who do not express emotions are more susceptible to disease.

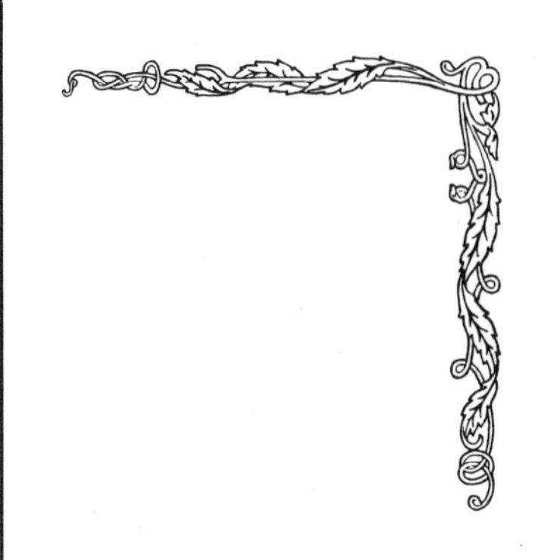

- Forget the telephone or television in your hospital room. These are usually unnecessary costs.
- Never ask for a private room.
- Choose outpatient surgery wherever possible. The difference between minor surgery in a hospital or as an outpatient can be thousands of dollars.
- Always check your hospital bills. Mistakes are often made. If you find a mistake, contact your employer or insurance company.
- Before you become ill, compare the hospital costs among several hospitals. For-profit hospitals and university hospitals usually have higher costs.
- Senior citizens are eligible to join health cooperatives which can save 20 - 25 % on medical care and 10 - 15% on prescription drugs. If there is no health cooperative in your area, start one. For information about senior health cooperatives, contact the United Seniors Health Cooperative, 1334 G Street NW, Suite 500, Washington, D.C. 20005.

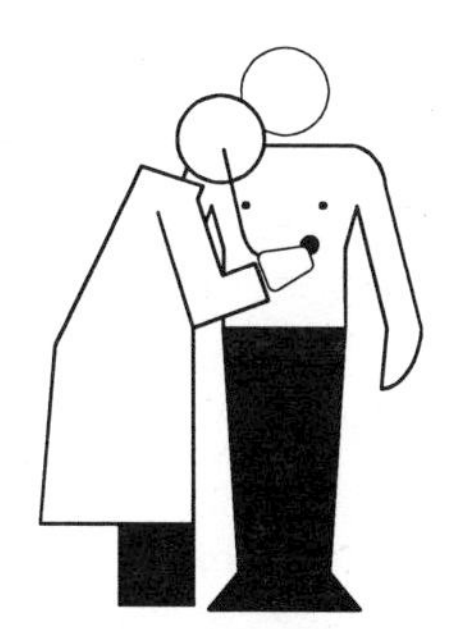

- If you take prescription drugs regularly, get them through the AARP (American Association of Retired Persons). If you are a member, you can receive discounts on prescription drugs and medical supplies. For more information, contact AARP, 1909 K Street NW, Washington, DC 20049.
- Use generic prescription drugs wherever possible.
- Ask your doctor for drug samples as your prescription.
- If you are reasonably healthy, increase your deductible which will reduce your insurance payment.
- Eligibility for Medicaid varies from state to state. For more information, contact the Medicare Hotline, Health Care Financing Administration, 330 Independence Ave., SW, Washington, DC 20201at (800) 638-6833.
- If you are a member of AAA, you may be able to receive added insurance for only $5 a year.
- Contact your local health department for free medical treatment. If the treatment is not free, a small fee is usually charged.
- Choosing a nursing home can be difficult. Write the Consumer Information Center for a pamphlet on choosing a nursing home at P. O. Box 100, Pueblo, CO 81002.

Earthsaving and Moneysaving Weddings

Weddings these days can cost thousands of dollars leaving anyone who has to pay for one scrambling for ways to save wherever possible. Actually, saving money on weddings and receptions is very easy because there are so many components to them. Moreover, saving money can mean saving the earth, too. For instance, throwing finch seed instead of rice at the couple after the

wedding is less expensive and better for the birds. Rice, when swallowed by a bird, may expand inside the bird's stomach and cause health complications, even death. Depending upon your area, rice may cost $1.99 per pound whereas finch seed may cost $1.29 per pound. In recent years, rose petals have become a popular alternative to rice.

First, decide what kind of wedding you want to have formal, thematic or very simple. Next, create a budget for every single expenditure. Write everything down from the invitation costs to the decorations; from all the wedding apparel to the food for the reception. This may take some time and research. Be sure to comparison shop.

Below are a few ideas to cut costs:

Invitations

- Paper product companies provide a variety of paper choices for making your own invitations. Many have attractively designed postcard-type papers which could be used as invitations with matching envelopes or stationery. Write by hand the invitations or if you have a computer, print them yourself. Paper companies include:

  Idea Art
  (800) 433-2278

  PaperDirect
  (800) A PAPERS

- Check with several printers to get the best price.
- Do not order very heavy invitations because your postage will increase.

Save the Earth Theme

- Wear only natural fabrics, such as cotton or silk.
- Wear green and use green accents in decorating.
- Arrive on a bicycle.
- Hold wedding and reception outdoors or on a commercial organic farm.
- Decorate with living plants and flowers.
- Use china and silverware instead of paper plates and plastic forks and knives.
- Use cloth napkins instead of paper ones.
- As a small gift for all the guests, have tree seedlings available.
- For the honeymoon, accompany scientists on a study tour of a rainforest.

- Choose simple invitations in white.
- If having the reception at the same place as the ceremony, do not include a separate reception card. Have the printer add *Reception Following* on the bottom of the invitation.
- Instead of formal invitations, have a calligrapher design and write them on stationery you purchase from the store. Or have an art or graphics student from your local college design them on recycled paper or stationery you purchase from a recycled paper outlet.
- Design and write your own invitations, and take them to a campus desktop publisher. After receiving the camera ready copy, take it to your printer for printing. Choose your paper and matching envelopes.

Where to Hold the Wedding and/or the Reception

- Hold the ceremony in your or a relative's or a friend's backyard. Have the reception inside.
- Clubs, parks, beaches, historical sites, public gardens and community centers can be used at little or no cost. Be sure to obtain permission.
- Have the ceremony in a judge's chambers with a few relatives and friends in attendance. Have the reception at someone's home afterwards.

Decorations, Flowers, etc.

- Use your local craft store to buy silk and dried flowers, ribbons and bows to make decorations.
- If you use a florist, try to pick flowers in season or ask for what is on sale in pots.
- Decorate with flowers, greens, candles and baskets.
- Ask relatives and friends if you can borrow potted plants and flowers. Wrap pots with fabric and ribbon or just a bow.
- If in the spring, prune flowering trees and bushes for use in the wedding ceremony or reception. Place the cuttings in large vases or decorated buckets.
- If in the fall, use fall-colored leaves for table decorations.

- Give away or keep all decorations after the ceremony or reception. Most of the items can be used for other things in the future.
- Rose petals for the flower girl can be obtained from a relative or friend's rose garden. Or use rose potpourri.

Adopt a Puffin and receive a color photograph of your bird, newsletter and information about puffins. Project Puffin, The National Audubon Society, 159 Sapsucker Woods Road, Ithaca, New York 14850, (607) 257-7308.

- The bride's bouquet and other bouquets can be made of fresh cut garden flowers or wildflowers; dried or silk flowers; or herbs.
- A rose bouquet can be made by wrapping the rose stems in a thin wet cloth, then with aluminum foil. Wrap a ribbon all around the stems or use fabric.
- Instead of a bouquet, carry a small wreath.
- Make a lei of flowers instead of carrying a bouquet. Cut flowers short and thread the small stems through thread or thin string. Use living plants and flowers wherever possible, so all can be reused.

Photography

- Ask relatives and friends to recommend a photographer who does a good job at a reasonable cost.
- Always ask to see a portfolio of the photographer's work.
- Go to your local college and recruit advanced class photographers or college newspaper staff. Advertise in the paper or place fliers on all campus bulletin boards.
- Ask a relative or friend to be your official photographer. Set up your own photos, provide the film and develop them yourself.
- Do not buy frames or photo albums from the photographer. Buy them separately.
- Instead of having a photographer, have an artist or caricaturist draw from the ceremony and reception.

Wedding Apparel

- Check with both families for a wedding dress family heirloom.
- Check at consignment shops, thrift shops and classified ads for wedding apparel.
- Have dress made by a local and reasonable tailor or seamstress. Buy matching pumps and decorate them with lace, flowers or faux pearls.

- Use scraps of same fabric to make ring bearer's pillow and other decorations.
- Ask at your local trade school for a good fashion design major to make your dress.
- Buy or have a dress made which can be used for other occasions in the future.

- If you can, make your own dress.
- Make your own veil. Buy fabric which does not need hemming.
- Instead of having a veil, decorate hair with dried flowers and ribbon.
- Bridesmaids can use big bows or large silk or dried flowers in the hair.
- Rent, instead of buy, a tuxedo.
- Buy a formal suit which could be worn later for other occasions.

Food

- Have wedding cake made by a relative or friend. In many communities, there are people who run baking businesses out of their homes.
- Serve small appetizers and punch instead of a complete meal.
- Buy alcohol in bulk.
- Have family and friends help in preparing food for the reception.

Miscellaneous

- Check with music schools or colleges for students who would be willing to perform. Be sure to audition them first.
- Make cassettes of preferred music to be played during the ceremony or the reception.
- Set the date of the ceremony on a weekday, such as a Friday evening—instead of a weekend.
- Instead of renting a limousine, use a nice family car or a horse and carriage or sleigh or motorcycles.
- If you know someone who owns horses, use horses for arrival.
- Instead of having a rehearsal dinner or dinner reception, consider having a buffet or dessert reception.
- Call local Antique Car Clubs and ask for their prices on using their cars for the arrival.
- Make your own Guest Book.
- Select any month for the ceremony other than May, June, September or October.
- Ask relatives and friends to help with all preparations.
- Use the Bridal Registry.

What to do with all that Stuff

The overwhelming production of waste and accumulation in our landfills is becoming a serious problem. We have a responsibility to do something about it, and do it now. We must think about the future of our children by thinking of the future of this planet. If we do not, the human race will no longer exist. We exist on what the planet supplies—oxygen, plants and animal life. If we destroy the planet, we destroy ourselves. It may not happen in our lifetime. It may not even happen in our children's lifetime, but it could happen soon.

Understandably, we have much less time and energy to seek out alternatives when setting things out on trash day seems so quick and easy. However, if the knowledge were available to us as easy as knowing when trash days are, it would be easier. So, let's explore some alternatives to *trashing*.

REUSE

Maybe that old end table could be used in your shed as a storage shelf. Or maybe you could paint it and put it in another room in your house, such as your child's room. That old worn out chair could be re-upholstered and added to your living room. Sure would beat the cost of buying a new one! That old trunk could be re-painted or re-varnished and used as a fancy coffee table. Lamps can be painted, and lamp shades can be painted or re-decorated with bric-a-brac or lace trim. Old clothes can be used as rags (instead of paper towels), scraps for making quilts or scraps for making stuffed animals or toys for children. Use leftover bricks to rim your flower garden or to make stepping stones. Use leftover deck wood to make bird feeders or to rim your flower garden.

GIFTS

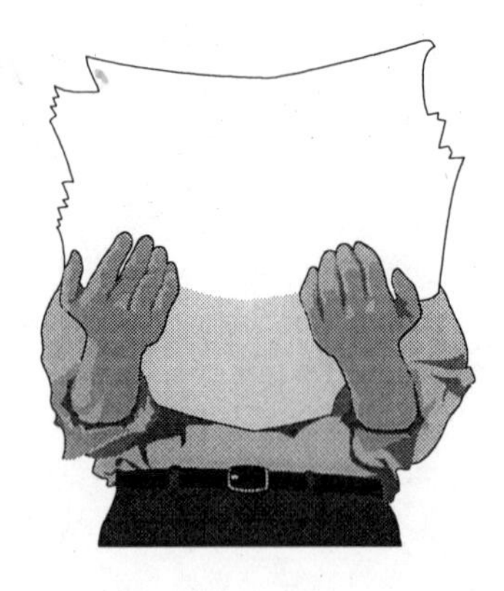

That old end table that doesn't go with your decor anymore could be given to a relative or friend as a gift. If it is in good condition, give it to a college student or ask your friends if they need it. If it needs a little work, decide if you would like to take the time to fix it up for that relative or friend. This goes for couches, chairs, appliances, electrical equipment, tools, planters, knickknacks, comforters, trunks, dressers, beds, desks, lamps and wall units. Books, encyclopedia sets, plants and some clothes could be given as they are.

YARD SALE/FLEA MARKET

If your spring cleaning has unearthed lots of items which are in good condition, but for which you can find no use, have a yard sale or join the many flea markets in your area. Join in with neighbors or friends when you have a yard sale. Price things fairly, and be prepared for some haggling. Flea markets are had by many schools, church groups and volunteer organizations. Check your newspaper for details.

DONATE

Donating unwanted items is an excellent way to reduce waste and to give back to the community. Some places will even estimate the cost of your donation and give you a receipt for tax deductions. Church groups, schools and volunteer organizations are places you may want to check. They have drives throughout the season.

Some organizations send out fliers or advertise in the newspaper when they are accepting donations or when they are picking up donated items. Three places you can take your items or call for pick up are Disabled American Veterans, The National Children's Center and Goodwill. Disabled American Veterans accept clothing, books, appliances, toys, household items and furniture in good condition. The National Children's Center accepts clothing and accessories, shoes, draperies, toys, small appliances, kitchenware and jewelry. Goodwill accepts clothing, household items, toys, books and wooden furniture in good condition. They do not accept appliances or upholstered furniture.

Disabled American Veterans - (800) 343-1407
National Children's Center - (800) 296-1122
Goodwill International - (301) 530-6500 or call your local branch

RECYCLING

If you have items which are not in very good condition and cannot be repaired, call your local landfill and ask them if they have sources for recycling these items. Call your local recycling center to find out if they recycle glass, plastic, aluminum and tin cans, phone books, corrugated cardboard and magazines and newspapers. Many service stations accept motor oil for recycling. Call your landfill or recycling center to see if they hold Hazardous Waste days throughout the year for car batteries, antifreeze and other items.

Scrooge's Budget: Getting Out of Debt

Scrooge may have been a penny-pincher and an unkindly old fellow, but he did know one thing—how to budget wisely. We may not want to take after his example of excluding charities and joy from his life, however we may want to learn how to pinch those pennies, especially if we are in debt.

Many of us have been in debt at one time or another whether it be for one month to pay off those holiday bills or for a few years to pay off those credit card bills. Some of us are still in debt unless we paid off that mortgage or that car. And all of us know getting out of debt is NOT easy.

First, we must find a way to pay off the debt. Are there expenditures we can cut or eliminate, at least for a while? Scrooge would have known what to cut.

Making the Commitment. Each time you make a payment on loaned money, such as a mortgage, car loan or credit cards, you are taking one step forward and more than a half of a step back.

For instance, if you pay a minimum payment of $50 a month on a loan or credit card balance of $1,500 with an annual interest rate of 22%, you are only paying approximately $23. The 22% interest on $1,450 is $319. Divided by 12 months equals $26.58. So, you pay $50.00 which leaves you with $1,450. Then they add the interest which leaves you with $1,476.58. Actually, you have only paid about $23.42.

If you make a regular monthly mortgage payment on a house costing $75,000 with a 10% annual interest rate for 30 years, at the end of 30 years you will have paid $300,000 for your house. You are paying four times the price of the house. You are not making much headway at this rate.

To get ahead of the interest game, make the commitment to sacrifice a few extras for a while. Once you have paid off your loans, credit cards, and begun adding a little more principal to that mortgage payment, you can start reaping the long term benefits of being out of debt and saving more money.

Scrooge's Budget

Monthly Expense	Scrooge's Budget	Normal Budget	Savings
Mortgage or Rent	$700.00	$700.00	$0.00
Utility (Gas or Electric) plus Water	$50.00	$100.00	$50.00
Telephone	$30.00	$75.00	$45.00
Transportation (Includes gas, public transportation fees, etc.)	$25.00	$40.00	$15.00
Automobile Insurance	$100.00	$100.00	$0.00
Other Insurance (Includes homeowner's, life, medical, etc.)	$136.00	$136.00	$0.00
Food (Includes groceries, toiletries, home cleaning, etc.)	$100.00	$300.00	$200.00
Home Maintenance (Includes repairs, condo fees, etc.)	$10.00	$35.00	$25.00
Automobile Maintenance (Includes oil changes, tune-ups, etc.)	$15.00	$20.00	$5.00
Entertainment (Includes movies, eating out and vacation)	$0.00	$50.00	$50.00
Miscellaneous (Includes gifts, charity contributions, other expenditures)	$0.00	$100.00	$100.00
Savings/Investments	$0.00	$200.00	$200.00
Total	**$1,166.00**	**$1,856.00**	**$690.00**

Freezer Squeeze

Using a freezer to store items, such as leftovers, garden surplus and bulk food purchases is a great way to save money. It can also save time if meals are prepared ahead of time and then frozen for later popping into the microwave.

1. Make more than you need when preparing soups and stews and freeze the rest.
2. Freeze tomatoes, green peppers, beans, peas, squash and other vegetables from the garden.
3. Freeze herbs, such as basil, dill, thyme, oregano, sage, parsley and others for using in foods as needed. The flavor and aroma are stronger than when herbs are dried.
4. Buy meat, poultry and fish in bulk and separate them into smaller sections. Freeze for meals.

Credit Cards. They have increased the ease of shopping as well as the ease of getting into and staying—in debt. In other words, we can't live with 'em and we can't live without 'em.

The first thing to do is **stop** using the cards. No need to add to the debt. If you cannot buy it with cash, do not buy it. Next, if you have a Visa or Mastercard with a good interest rate, transfer all your other cards to that card. Or you could call or write to the Bankcard Holders of America for a list of banks with low interest credit card rates and no annual fees. Some of these banks offer credit card interest rates as low as 8.%. So back to that $50 payment...

If you make your $50 payment on that credit card balance of $1,500 with an annual interest rate of **8%**, you will be paying approximately **$40.34**. The 8% interest on $1,450 is **$116.00**. Divided by 12 months equals **$9.66**. After you make your payment and they add the interest, your balance is **$1,459.66.** Not bad when you compare the 22% interest rate scenario.

The address for the list is Bankcard Holders of America, 524 Branch Drive, Salem, Virginia 24153 or call them at (540) 389-5445.

Mortgage. Few of us can pay off a mortgage, however we can increase the time we pay it off or decrease the interest we will have to pay.

- If the interest rates have dropped enough to make a significant difference between your original interest rate and the current interest rate, check with your bank about refinancing. A good rule is to refinance when the interest rate drops 2% or more below the original interest rate. You could save thousands of dollars.
- Adjustable rate mortgages are not for everyone, but they do offer some advantages. Paying 5% interest on $75,000 sure beats paying 10%. Check with your bank for more information.
- Consider a 15-year mortgage instead of a 30-year mortgage. You will pay far less in the long run because more of your payment goes to principal and less to interest.

If your mortgage is $75, 000 with a 10% annual interest rate and you agreed to a 15-year mortgage, at the end of 15 years you will have paid $187,500. That is far better than $300,000!

Try increasing your principal payment every month. One way to do this is to write a check for more than your monthly mortgage payment with a note asking the mortgage company to apply the additional amount to your principal. Or you can write two checks —one is the payment, the other is strictly a principal payment, specifically noted on the check.

Car Loans. I know an electrical engineer who saved up for years to pay cash for a red Corvette. And he did it, too.

Most of us don't have the time to be without reliable transportation while we save up for our dream car. On the other hand, we could opt for public transportation or sharing a ride with a co-worker. Using a bicycle or purchasing an inexpensive motorcycle or scooter for transportation could provide an adventurous transition to *owning* your car.

- When buying a car, try to put down as much as you can towards the purchase price. The less you need to finance, the less you will have to pay in interest.
- Buy a used car while saving for the new car. You may find a used car you can afford in cash.
- If you are a two-car family, reduce to one car to save for a new car.

Paying interest on a car loan is not the same as paying interest on a mortgage. At least the home or property appreciates. The car, unfortunately, depreciates. So, not only are you losing the money you pay in interest, but you are losing re-sale value every day. At least when you pay cash, you have saved paying the interest.

Paying Off. When you pay off credit cards and loans, you save money which would otherwise be used for interest payments. These savings can be invested or added to savings accounts.

The best way to pay off credit cards and loans is to pay off quickly in order to decrease the amount of interest paid. Scrooge's budget illustrates areas where cuts could be made. This will not be easy, however once you have paid your debts, you will be able to increase your budget to include more entertainment or increase your savings for vacations, education and retirement.

The perks have to go. Entertainment is either cut drastically or cut out all together. Use your creativity to invent inexpensive ways of having a good time. For family outings, visit parks and free museums. Have friends and family over for a potluck gathering.

Cut your toiletries and food bill by a few dollars. Eliminate fancy items, such as perfumes, special soaps and shampoos, gourmet cheeses, bakery items and packaged foods. You can last for a few months. You may even like saving so much you make it a permanent way of life.

Miscellaneous items can be cut by making shower, wedding and birthday gifts yourself. Offer services, such as catering or photographing for a wedding or hosting a birthday party or shower.

Cut utility bills by lowering the thermostat, if only at night. Wear more clothes. Make fewer long distance telephone calls and talk less on the phone. If repairs are needed for the house, try to put them off for a while.

5. Buy breads in bulk and freeze for later use.
6. Make broth and freeze for soup-making later.
7. Freeze meal and party leftovers.
8. Prepare and freeze sweet snacks, such as cookies and brownies for those unexpected visits.
9. When using canned goods, such as tomatoes or peas, drain the juices and freeze them for later use in soups and stews.
10. Before those bananas go bad, peel them and freeze them for later use in breads and cakes.

According to Scrooge, you can save $690 a month by cutting your budget. Use these savings to pay off those credit cards and loans and to increase your principal payment on your mortgage. Of course, your personal savings may be more or less. Sit down and draw up your budget. Analyze it and discover where you can cut just for a few months until those debts are paid off. Determine where you could permanently cut to add to your principal payment every month on the mortgage.

You sat down, you looked over the budget, and you just can't cut anything? Ah, Humbug!

Investment Newsletters

Investment Resource - (800) 950-8765
All Star Funds - (800) 299-4223
InvesTech - (800) 955-8500
The MoneyPaper - (800) 842-3993
Dick Davis Digest - (800) 654-1514

Earthsavers

If your telephone is broken and cannot be repaired, recycle it instead of throwing it away. Take or send it back to the manufacturer. They can use many of the parts in making new telephones.

When you are through reading your magazines, trade them with friends or relatives. You can also donate them to doctors' offices or schools.

Plastic six-pack rings have become a wildlife hazard for birds and other small wildlife. Use them to make a trellis for your garden by tying them together with string or rope. If you must throw them away, snip the rings open and take them to a recycling center.

Yard Sale Success

A yard sale is a great way to rid your house of unwanted items, make money and recycle by not throwing away.

First, organize what you want to sell at your yard sale. If you feel it is not enough to warrant the trouble of a yard sale, ask some neighbors or friends if they would like to join in your yard sale. If you like making crafts, you could make some for a little extra money.

Next, check with your community to see whether you need a permit. Run ads in community newspapers and newsletters giving the date, time, place and rain date. Create posters or fliers to distribute at local stores, community centers, bus stops and homes if legally permitted. Be sure to stop by the bank a day or two before the sale to get change. Thirty dollars worth of bills and loose change should be enough to start.

On the day of the sale, set out your items early, organizing them neatly. Use tables for smaller items. First impressions may make a sale. Price items with tags. Price items reasonably. Prepare yourself for bargaining, especially during the last few hours of the sale, so you can rid yourself of everything. If there are leftovers, give them to charity or take them to a consignment shop. Do not forget to remove all posters and fliers.

Here are a few tips to add a few more dollars to your yard sale earnings:

- Serve refreshments, such as brownies or cookies and soda or lemonade. You may just attract some more visitors to your sale.
- Arrange all your items in a neat and organized manner. For instance, hang clothes on tree limbs or rods. Lay books and albums out on the grass or table so people can see the titles. Dress up dolls with baby clothes if you are selling both.
- Make small repairs. You might get a few more dollars.
- Say hello to people when they stop by. Offer them something to eat or drink. Be friendly.
- Lay rugs out on the grass for display.
- Try to clean up all your sale items as much as possible. The better they look, the more chance they have of selling.
- Mark all items with a price. If you have good prices, people may respond by buying. If you don't mark items, people may not ask.

Yard Sale Magic

If you want a successful yard sale, spend a weekend visiting other yard sales to see what makes some successful and some not so successful. Notice pricing and what items are selling. Are the sellers interactive with their customers or do they allow the customers to look around for themselves? Which seems to work best? (Usually a little of both works well.)

- Ask neighbors and friends if they would like to join you in your yard sale.
- Plan to hold the yard sale on a Saturday or Sunday preferably not on a holiday weekend. Plan a rain date.
- Create fliers and colorful posters with large dark letters. Place in local stores, bus stops, busy intersections and community centers. Run ads in the local paper, listing some of the better items for sale to attract more people. Again, be sure to give the date, time, place and rain date.
- Use masking tape and scrap paper to place pricing on items.
- Price all items reasonably. If you price too high, you may not have a buyer. If you price too low, you may be shortchanging yourself.

- Have plenty of tables for arranging items neatly. Arrange all items so they are visible.
- Play soft music and try to have all electronic equipment plugged in or an outlet available for the customer to try the item.
- If you have items which are inside because they could not be brought outside, be sure to have big signs telling your customers more items are available inside.
- Begin reducing prices two to three hours before the end of the sale.
- Try not to accept checks unless you feel comfortable doing so.
- Have fun! If you seem to enjoy the day, customers will, too.

EARTHSAVING WAYS TO INCREASE YOUR SAVINGS BY $1000 OR MORE THIS YEAR

- Read books and magazines from the library instead of buying them. ($10 - $100)
- Use the front and back of stationery. ($10 - $25)
- Instead of buying new power tools, borrow and share them with neighbors and friends. ($50 - $200)
- Use plastic containers instead of food wrap when freezing. ($10 - $25)
- Use cloth diapers. ($100 - $300)
- Buy grocery and household items in bulk. ($50 - $500)
- Use old rags or sponges instead of paper towels. ($50 - $200)
- Use half as much laundry soap as you usually do. The clothes will probably still come clean. ($10 - $50)
- Use handkerchiefs instead of tissues. ($50 - $200)
- Buy whole poultry instead of parts. At home, cut into parts yourself. ($50 - $300)
- Use permanent coffee filters instead of paper ones. ($5 - $25)
- Trade children's clothes with friends and relatives. ($50 - $200)
- Be creative in repairing items instead of replacing them with new ones. Sometimes they simply need a good cleaning. ($50 - $500)
- Bring your lunch to work and use plastic containers for everything, no waste. ($50 - $1000)
- Dilute dishwashing liquid by ¼ or ½ with water. ($5 - $25)
- Use cloth instead of paper napkins. ($10 - $50)
- Carry eating utensils, such as a fork or spoon with you to reduce waste. ($5 - $20)
- Save outdated fabric and clothing. Use to make new clothing or gift items. ($50 - $200)
- Use old clothes as cleaning rags instead of buying disposable ones. ($5 - $25)*

*Figures are estimated for a family of four. Your savings may be more or less.

The New Budget

If you have been budgeting and saving money, but you want to save even more—consider the following ideas.

1. Add the following entries to your existing budget: property taxes, homeowner's insurance, home maintenance and repair, car maintenance and repair, pet care, newspapers, magazines, books, life insurance, church contributions and charities.

2. When calculating all earnings, subtract taxes. If you usually receive money back from the IRS, calculate the average amount into your year's earnings. If you usually pay the IRS, subtract more from your annual or monthly earnings.

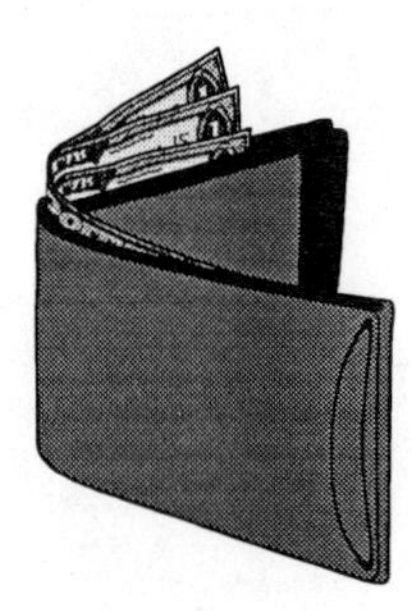

3. Cut back on snacks and reduce your grocery bill by about $10 to $50 per month. $50 X 12 months = $600!

4. Start a carpool in your area if one does not exist. Place a notice on the office bulletin board for people to join your carpool. If one does exist in your area, join it. You could reduce that transportation budget entry by $10 to $25 or more per week by carpooling. The more people involved in the carpool, the more you will save. $25 X 50 weeks = $1,250!

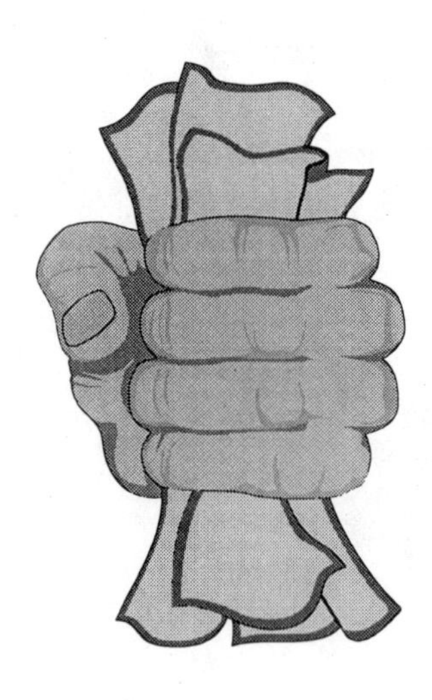

5. Find a neighbor who provides child care in her home. You could reduce your child care budget entry by $50 to $75 a month. $75 X 12 = $900!

6. Have your children earn their own money through performing chores around the house. You save time and money by having them help maintain the cleanliness of the house. They learn how to earn money through work.

7. Before making purchases, always ask yourself whether you really need that new jacket or chair or pair of shoes. Most purchases are impulse purchases. We see something we want and we buy it. Think before buying. Nine times out of ten, you will realize you did not really need it once you reach home.

Chapter 7

Holiday Saving

By viewing Nature, Nature's handmaid, art,
Makes mighty things from small beginnings grow.

- John Dryden, *Annus Mirabilis*

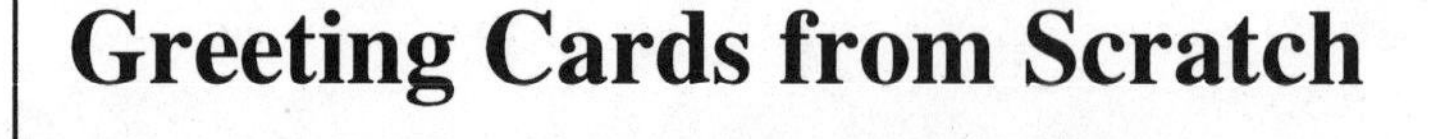

Greeting Cards from Scratch

Greeting cards are a necessity. Birthdays, weddings, illness, births and deaths are a fact of life. During times of celebration and sadness, we will always want to express ourselves to others with cards. However, instead of buying these greeting cards, we can find new ways to recycle or reuse items we already have to create even more personal cards, cards made by hand. Below are some ideas, however use your imagination and perhaps you can come up with some ideas of your own.

Happy Birthday!

1. Pantyhose in flat packages are wrapped around a white piece of cardboard. This cardboard is very useful in making greeting cards. Take one of these and fold in half. Unfold and edge the entire card with a marker in the color of your choice. Only edge the very thin part of the card which gives it its thickness. The marker will bleed a little away from the edge and give the card a nice border.

With a thin piece of colored ribbon or string, make the letters "H" and "B" for the first letters of Happy Birthday on the front of the card. Glue in place. Write the rest of these two words with your marker.

Using a pencil, draw a rectangle the size of a business card in the center of the right side, inside the card. With a sharp craft knife make four cuts at each edge of the rectangle as if you were cutting off all four corners of the rectangle. Make the cuts about 1/2 of an inch wide and erase the pencil markings. The cuts are for inserting money in the card. Fold the bill twice and insert it into the card. If you wish to write something, write in a circle around the inserted bill.

Congratulations!

2. Take an 8 ½" x 11" piece of construction paper and cut it into an 8½" x 8½" square. Fold this square at an angle to form a triangle. Flip through an old magazine looking for ads which have big bold letters. Cut out the letters to form the word "Congratulations." Cut the letters out or just cut them into a square. Place all the letters on the front of the card across the top in a straight line. Or place all the letters down to and up from, the bottom. Once you have chosen how you want the letters to be placed, glue them with a glue stick. Inside, glue a picture of a baby cut out from an old magazine. Write your message around it.

Envelopes are easy to make. Take an existing envelope, preferably the size you want to use for your cards. Pull the glued flaps apart and unfold it. Flip through an old magazine and choose a page for the envelope design. Lay the unfolded envelope on top of that page and trace it. Cut out the tracing and fold as the other envelope. Glue in place. Place a white label on the front of the envelope for the address. To seal the envelope use a sticker or glue.

NEW YEAR'S DAY

Earthly Resolutions

Every year we make commitments to ourselves on losing weight, being kinder or working harder. Below are 25 New Year's resolutions we can make for our commitment to saving the earth.

1. Hang cloth shopping bags near the door or place in the car so they are not forgotten

2. Recycle, reuse and renew.
3. Talk to your employer about instituting small recycling programs at work, such as separate trash cans for recyclables or specified parking for cyclists or planting a tree every year.
4. Volunteer to clean up parks or recreational areas.
5. Start an organic garden. Or eat organically grown foods.
6. Propagate plants instead of buying them.
7. Compost as much as possible.
8. Use alternatives to indoor and outdoor pesticides.
9. Buy and use recycled products as much as possible.
10. Buy a fuel efficient car.
11. Share driving chores with a relative, friend or neighbor. If your children go to the same school or activities, or you both shop at the same places, try to share these chores or the ride.
12. Recycle yogurt, sour cream, butter or margarine tubs. Use them for storing food and toys.
13. Turn down the heat. Turn up the thermostat for air conditioning.
14. Use solar energy products.
15. Think twice when you are about to throw something away. Can you use it for something else? Can it be recycled?
16. Always snip the holes of plastic six pack rings.
17. Use less chemicals. Seek out alternatives.
18. Take showers instead of baths.
19. Ride your bicycle more often.
20. Buy rechargeable batteries.
21. Use natural cleaners which can be homemade or bought.
22. Use handkerchiefs more often than tissues.
23. Sell or trade books instead of throwing them out.
24. Buy more natural fabrics instead of synthetics.
25. Get involved in at least one environmental group or local program.

VALENTINE'S DAY

Valentine Hearts

Using your favorite cake recipe, bake a cake in a 9 x 12-inch pan. Let cool.

Take a heart-shaped cookie cutter and cut out heart shapes from the cake. Set aside.

Make white frosting and color it pink with a few drops of red food coloring. Frost the hearts.

Sprinkle the hearts with chopped nuts, sprinkles or small chocolate chips. Write messages on top of the hearts with leftover white frosting or with some sprinkles.

EARTH DAY

Community Earth Day

What did you do for Earth Day this year? Last year? What did your community do? Below are some ideas for next year. Start planning now!

Earth Day Cooking Contest
Hold a cooking contest for the best dish which used the most natural ingredients and used the least amount of energy!

Earth Day Spelling Bee
Prepare a list of earthsaving words and hold a spelling bee for the children in the community. Have a small prize available for the winner.

Ask for Donations or Charge a Small Fee for Playing Games
The money will be used to fund next year's festivities.

Hold Classes or Workshops on Earthsaving
Invite local instructors, nursery owners and activists to speak or teach about saving the earth. Subjects could include organic gardening, energy-saving, becoming active in the community or city or composting.

Build a Community Recycling Center
Gather a group together to build a recycling center for the community. Use the previous year's Earth Day festivity funds to pay for the materials.

Invite a Speaker from the Local Recycling Center
Ask them to talk about what strides are being made in recycling. Ask them to bring a film or other material to describe to the children what happens to recyclables after they are collected.

Hold Contests
Have contests for the best earthsaving idea or for the best idea for next year's festivities.

Earth Day Honors

Although Earth Day comes once a year, we can do some things all year round to honor the earth.

- Take a weekend morning with the family to clean up a littered street or nearby forest.
- Write congress about how you and your family feel towards the environment.
- Write or call your local county government and ask them about curb-side recycling.
- Get your club or church group out to pick up litter in a local park.
- Talk to your friends and relatives about saving the earth.
- Put up a poster at work for a carpool.
- Plant a tree in a field or sparsely-wooded area.
- Start a compost and get a neighbor to start one too.
- Read about the advantages of keeping rainforests standing.
- Educate yourself and your neighbors on what organizations pick up discarded furniture, rugs and bicycles in your area.

Earth Day Calendar

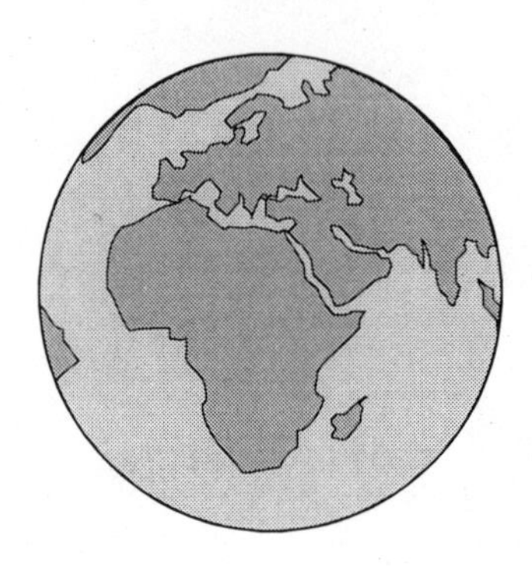

January

As cabin fever begins, spend some time writing local officials about instituting a curbside recycling program; or congress about offering more incentives to Green companies; or companies about reducing product packaging.

February

Work with your children's school or your community to create an environmental newsletter. The newsletter could be as little as one page with tidbits of information to educate and inform.

March

Gather the family together to begin planning and planting a flower, vegetable or herb garden. Assign a plant or plants to each family member. Each would be responsible for caring for her or his assigned plant or plants.

April

Create your own Earth Day Activity by picking up trash and debris around your neighborhood or having an Earth Day Party complete with no paper or plastic.

May

Support organic farmers by asking for organically grown produce at the grocery store. Buy produce at organically grown stands at your local Farmer's Market.

June

Start a *Plant Sharing Club.* People share cuttings and extra plants with one another. The club could also donate some plants to nursing homes or other charities.

July

Plant trees in your yard and community. Transplant seedlings to woods and parks. Ask permission to plant trees on public or private lands.

August

Start a Neighborhood Paint Exchange Program.

September

Campaign for sidewalks and bike paths to be placed in your community.

October

Organize a community or school Yard Sale to help everyone rid themselves of unwanted items. Or organize a community charity collection. All unwanted items will be donated to a charity.

November

Organize a group of relatives and friends to exchange magazines. Decide who subscribes to what magazine and in what order the magazines will be passed on.

December

Give environmentally-conscious gifts. Or give books which educate people on ways to improve our environment.

HALLOWEEN

Halloween Party Cuisine

Halloween Party Cider
10 cups apple cider or apple juice
1 package frozen red raspberries (12 oz.)
5 inches of stick cinnamon

In a large saucepan, combine apple cider or juice, raspberries and cinnamon. Bring to a boil, reduce heat. Cover and simmer for 10 minutes. Remove from heat and strain. Serve warm.

Chocolate-Coated Apples
12 wooden ice cream sticks or popsicle sticks
12 medium apples, stems removed
1 10-oz. package peanut butter chips
1/2 cup vegetable oil
2/3 cup cocoa
2/3 cup powdered sugar
1 cup peanut butter chips chopped finely

Insert wooden stick into stem end of each apple. Cover cookie sheet with wax paper.

Microwave 10-oz. package of peanut butter chips and oil on high for one minute, stir. If necessary, microwave on high at 15 minute intervals stirring after each heating until chips are melted.

In a small bowl, stir together the cocoa and powdered sugar; gradually add to chip mixture, stirring until smooth. Microwave on high 1 minute or until very warm. Dip apples in warm mixture, twirling to remove excess coating.

Place coated apples on wax paper 2 to 3 minutes; sprinkle lower half of each apple with chopped chips. Let cool. Refrigerate until ready to eat.

Spooky Sandwiches
Make peanut butter sandwiches. On the face of the sandwich, use orange marmalade to create a jack-o'-lantern face.

Halloween Cupcakes
Use your favorite cupcake recipe to make cupcakes. Tint cream frosting with orange food coloring and frost cupcakes. Decorate with raisins, nuts or sprinkles to make jack-o'-lantern faces.

Halloween Treats to Make

Halloween is a happy time for children. They can dress like ghosts, goblins or their favorite heroes and receive sweets and snacks. Whether you are having a Halloween party or giving out snacks to the little trick-or-treaters, the candies and snacks can be expensive. You can save $10 to $30 or more by making them yourself.

Brownie Truffles

Make your favorite brownies as usual except bake 5 or 10 minutes less than normal until they are a little doughy, but done.

Roll dough into small balls and roll in cocoa or finely chopped nuts. Put 2 to 3 to a small plastic bag and refrigerate. When the trick-or-treaters arrive, just take them out of the refrigerator and drop in their treat bag.

Popcorn Balls

25 cups popcorn (popped)
1/2 cup mixed nuts
1 lb. marshmallows
1/2 cup butter
1/2 cup oil

Mix popcorn and nuts together. Melt marshmallows and butter with oil in saucepan over medium heat. When melted, pour over popcorn and nuts, and mix together. Wait for a few minutes until mixture has cooled, then with buttered hands make 3-inch balls and place on lightly oiled cookie sheet.

Other Syrups for Popcorn Balls (for 6 cups popped popcorn)

White Sugar Syrup

2/3 cup sugar
1/2 cup water
1 1/2 tablespoons white corn syrup
1/ 8 teaspoon salt
1/3 teaspoon vinegar

Halloween Howls

Halloween lasts one day each year, but it is howling time when it is over and the clean up begins. However, we can find ways to recycle and reduce the garbage created by the festive holiday.

- Instead of giving out paper-wrapped candy to trick-or-treaters, give out fruit. Every bit of the fruit is biodegradable.
- When carving pumpkins, use the pumpkin for pies, cakes and breads instead of throwing it out. Toast the seeds for a nice snack or give the seeds to the birds.
- Do not buy costumes which are made to throw away after use.
- Give small toys instead of candy. These toys can be found grouped in bags in discount stores.
- Discourage *Tricks* on Halloween. Many times these involve wasted paper or eggs and toppled garbage cans.
- Have a Halloween Party with popcorn, fruit and baked goods.
- Ask your children to throw the candy wrappers in their trick-or-treat bags while eating them on the howl instead of throwing them on the ground.

Stir until sugar is dissolved. Bring to a boil. Cook covered for about 3 minutes. Cook uncovered until temperature reaches 290°F or the hard-crack stage.

Molasses Syrup
1 tablespoon butter
1/2 cup molasses
1/4 cup sugar

Melt butter, then add molasses and sugar. Stir until sugar is dissolved. Bring to a boil. Cook covered and uncovered as above recipe.

Caramel Syrup
1 1/2 tablespoons butter
1 1/2 cups brown sugar
6 tablespoons water

Melt butter, then add sugar and water. Stir until sugar is dissolved. Bring to a boil. Cover and cook for about 3 minutes. Cook uncovered until temperature reaches 238°F or soft ball stage.

NOTE: To add variety to the popcorn ball mixture, add chocolate chips or marshmallows to the popcorn mixture. Or dip the balls in melted chocolate or dribble some around the ball.

Earthsaver

Never buy paint brushes meant only for one use. We don't need another thing to add to the landfill.

Spooky Costumes for Less

Recycle old Halloween costumes by handing them down to younger children, giving them to other children, or donating them to charity. Many costumes can be re-designed by making just a few changes.

You don't have to be a seamstress to put together a Halloween Costume. Re-using various things around the house in a creative way can make a nice, but inexpensive, costume for your child or yourself. If you have all these items around the house, your costumes will cost you nothing.

Spooky Black Cat
Black T-shirt or long-sleeved shirt
Black tights or leggings/stirrup pants
Black shoes or boots
Black Gloves (optional)
Embellished black sunglasses
Two Black Belts
Two Black Hair Bows
Bright, shiny necklace

Dress all in black with the shirt, tights, gloves and shoes. Wear black sunglasses or embellish the frames with glitter. The black belts will create the tail. Wear one belt around waist looping the buckle of the other belt through it. Slide the hanging belt to the back. Wear this over shirt or under. Place the two black bows in hair on either side of the head to create ears. Wear a bright necklace around the neck to simulate a shiny collar.

Jack-O'-Lantern
Orange or black tights or leggings/stirrup pants
Orange or black sweat shirt or long-sleeved shirt
One orange jack-o'-lantern leaf bag
2 - 4 pillows
Black scarf or ribbon
Black or orange shoes
Green stocking hat or scarf
Black, orange or white gloves (optional)

Dress in the tights or leggings/stirrup pants, shirt, gloves and

shoes. Wrap pillows length-wise around the waist in front and ba
with a belt or rope. Cut neat holes in the leaf bag for arms and legs.
Pull on leaf bag and tie opening at the neck with scarf or ribbon. Tie into a bow. Pull on stocking hat or tie on scarf so that knot is at the nape of the neck.

Ghost

One white sheet
Black marker
Black or white belt (optional)
White shoes

This is one of the simplest costumes to make. Cut holes just as big as eyes, no larger. With black marker, draw an oval around the cut holes and fill in. Pull sheet over and fasten belt around waste. Put on shoes.

Zombie

Sweats or jeans or long underwear (optional)
Thin and/or cotton shirt and pants (any colors), preferably old and worn
Old black or brown shoes
Old and worn hat or scarf
Multi-colored markers
Black nail polish
Make-up

Pull on sweats or long underwear. Tear or cut holes in old and worn shirt and pants. Good places to create holes are at the knees and elbows. Mark up with markers, preferably red and brown. Make these clothes look as old and dirty as possible. Pull on over sweats or long underwear. Put on shoes. Paint fingernails black or dark red. Use make-up on hands and face to create a dirty and spooky character. Put on hat or tie scarf at nape of neck over mussed hair.

Use your imagination to alter these costumes for your needs or to create new ones.

...ɡiving Hash Mishmash

yo...
at the gr...
a few tips to he...
some of that expense...
some fun too:

- Have the guests all bring a dish for Thanksgiving dinner. This not only saves you money but time too. And your guests will enjoy adding to the festive table.
- Try to make all your dishes from scratch. You always pay more for ready-made items.
- Buy as big a turkey as you can find. You always save money by buying in large quantities. Freeze the leftovers in small portions for future meals. If you tire of eating turkey, skip a week or even a month of eating turkey meals. The turkey will keep in your freezer for up to six months.
- Prepare as many dishes in the microwave as possible. This will not only save money but time as well. Cooking with the range all day or half the day can really add to your electric bill at the end of the month. Save the money instead.

...ɔd to the environment and your health! Buy a free-range ...ıic turkey for your Thanksgiving meal. These are turkeys ...ed where they are free to walk around and are not given ...ıibiotics or hormones.

...Jse fall-colored leaves for table centerpieces or to add to a cornucopia centerpiece.

It is said the pilgrims had popcorn for Thanksgiving. While you are still cooking and the guests are waiting, serve some popcorn. You could spice it up a bit by adding 1 tablespoon of olive oil, 1/4 cup parmesan cheese and 1 tablespoon garlic powder. (Add more for very large quantities.)

- To save time, make some dishes the day before and heat them in the microwave when it is time to eat dinner.
- Serve fruit or a fruit salad for dessert.
- Refrigerate or freeze your Thanksgiving leftovers.

Below are some ideas for your leftovers.

Potato Bake

Use your leftover mashed potatoes for this dish.

3 cups mashed potatoes
1/4 cup finely chopped onion
1 tablespoon Oil
3/4 cup small curd cottage cheese
1 tablespoon parsley, minced
1/2 tsp. salt

Sauté onion in oil until soft. Stir onion, cheese, parsley and salt into mashed potatoes. Spoon mixture into well-greased casserole dish. Bake at 350° F for 20 to 30 minutes.

Turkey & Vegetable Soup

Use leftover turkey and vegetables for this dish.

2 - 3 cups sliced turkey
8 cups water
1 onion, chopped
3 - 4 cups leftover vegetables
Salt, pepper, chopped parsley and other spices to taste

Place turkey in pot with water, onion and vegetables. Bring to a boil, then add salt, pepper and other spices to taste. Lower heat and simmer for 2 hours. Serve.

Countdown to a Fast, Easy and Inexpensive Thanksgiving

- Use a chicken instead of a turkey. Or have guests bring a meat dish instead of only having turkey. Use old bread and corn bread to make stuffing.

- Decorate the table with a vase of cut branches and a few evergreen bush branches. Throw a summer afghan or bedspread over the table instead of a fancy tablecloth.

- Ask everyone who plays an instrument to bring it with them. Have them play before or after dinner for entertainment as well as to create special moments among family and friends.

- Ask everyone to bring the ingredients for apple or pumpkin pies, such as the crust or pastry, apples, sugar, pumpkin or pumpkin puree, spices, etc. After dinner the children or an adult group will prepare the pies.

- While the dinner is still being prepared, send the children outside to gather nature items, such as pine cones or bird feathers from the yard or nearby woods. After dinner all could sit around while each item is shown and discussed.

- Make the Thanksgiving dinner a group effort by assigning different tasks to all guests. One could be responsible for the turkey, one could decorate and set the table, one could be responsible for vegetable dishes, one could be responsible for dessert, one could be responsible for the children and so on.

- To keep children occupied while adults talk and reminisce, have a table ready for them to create Christmas food for the birds. Have pine cones and peanut butter, cranberries and string, popcorn and string, oranges and suet available.

- Turn off the lights during dinner and have many candles burning. Keep them far away from the children, however.

- If Thanksgiving is to be an all day affair, have a room prepared for the children to nap.

Buy your food items on sale even if that means a little earlier than you had planned. The money you save will be worth it.

Homemade Cranberry Sauce

11/2 cups fresh cranberries
1 cup water
1 cup sugar

Wash and drain cranberries. Bring water to a boil. Add cranberries and sugar. Cook for approximately 10 minutes or until skins pop. With a large spoon, skim off the white froth. Let cool. Refrigerate until ready to serve.

NOTE: More sugar may be added to taste.

The Natural Turkey

Definition: Free-range turkeys which are raised on wholesome grains with no artificial ingredients, synthetic herbicides or hormones added, and minimally processed.

Sources: Ask at local health food stores.

Fresh Fields, a national grocery store chain which promises all products are natural with no additives and vegetables are organically grown whenever possible, has a natural meat, poultry and fish section. Call (301) 984-3737 for store locations.
Walnut Acres, a mail order company featuring natural foods, carries organic meats as well as pastas, grains and beans. (800) 433-3998.
Coleman Natural Meats, a company specializing in raising and processing meats naturally, offers poultry as well as other meat. (800) 442-8666.

Local poultry farmers.

For More Information: Contact the Center for Science in the Public Interest for a copy of the July/August 1992 issue of the *Nutrition Action Healthletter* which discusses organic meats. The address is 1875 Connecticut Avenue, NW, Suite 300, Washington, D.C. 20009.

PrairieFire Rural Action is a farm advocacy group for natural meat farmers. The quarterly journal can be obtained by calling (515) 244-5671 or writing 550 Eleventh Street, Des Moines, IA 50309.

Earthsaver

Be more aware when using balloons at parties or for celebrations. Do not let helium balloons fly away. They eventually come back down to wreak havoc among wildlife. Foil balloons are not biodegradable.

CHRISTMAS

Make Your Own Christmas Decorations

Greens, such as pine, juniper and holly, can be used to make wreaths and table decorations.

Table decorations are simple to make. Place a platter in the center of the table with a red candle on a pedestal in the center of the platter. Arrange cut greens around the candle pedestal. Place holly berries on each of two sides. Weave a gold ribbon through and around all the greens.

Other table decorations can be made by tying a bunch of greens with gold, silver, red or blue ribbon. Spread out and place a few on a buffet or coffee table.

Make Your Own Wreath.

If you want a *Wreath of Greens,* buy a wire wreath at your local craft store. Clip small stems of pine, juniper and holly. Tie them onto the wire frame with floral wire (available at floral shops). Tie things close together to make a thick wreath. Spray some water on the wreath and let it sit. Tie a red, blue or gold ribbon at the 12:00 position or the 8:00 position. You can also add dried flowers or ornaments to the wreath.

Wreaths can be made out of almost anything. Buy a straw or foam wreath at you local craft store. Use cut greens 2" to 4" long. With a glue gun, fasten greens onto wreath thickly. Glue greens all in one direction or vary directions. Be sure to cover stems when placing greens on the wreath. Glue a ribbon tied in a bow or a purchased bow on the bottom in the center.

The wreath could hang as is or you could glue on pine cones or nuts in a few places around the wreath.

Ribbon can add color or texture to plain or already decorated items. Tying red bows to outside tree branches adds a festive, yet simple, look.

Inexpensive Tree Decorations

- A box of candy canes.
- Popcorn you make and string for a garland.
- Pine cones threaded with colorful ribbon to hang as ornaments.

Cheap Gift Ideas

- A stamp-collecting kit.
- Tickets to a sporting event.
- Offer to do some gardening for someone.
- Potholders and tea towels.
- Deck of cards, a board game, a globe.
- A Christmas stocking, tree, or ornament.
- Book of movie tickets.
- A book on angels.
- Coloring books, crayons, markers.
- A Christmas wreath.
- Napkins or placemats.
- Paper dolls, child's make-up kit.
- A doormat, door knocker.
- A bottle of wine or other spirit.
- Sweets, fruit, breads.
- A table centerpiece.
- Soaps, bath salts, colognes.
- Pillowcases, pillows, hot water bottles.
- Birdhouse, bird feeder, birdseed.

Homemade Gifts

Food Gifts

Almond Mocha Coffee
2 cups ground coffee
1/2 cup almonds, coarsely chopped
1/2 cup unsweetened cocoa
1 whole vanilla bean

Combine all ingredients and place in a muslin bag. Tie top together with a ribbon.

NOTE: Do not use instant coffee.

Mulled Cider Mix
2 teaspoons dried orange peel
1 tablespoon allspice
1 teaspoon ground cinnamon
1 teaspoon ground cloves
1 teaspoon anise seeds
1 tablespoon dried apple, chopped coarsely
5 whole cinnamon sticks

Mix first five ingredients together well. Add dried apple and mix well. Pour in a small muslin bag. Place four cinnamon sticks carefully on top. Tie bag with a ribbon and one cinnamon stick.

Sage Vinegar
4 cups white wine vinegar
1 cup fresh sage leaves

Combine the vinegar and sage in a bottle, seal and store in a cool, dark place for two weeks. During that time period, shake the bottle every now and then. After the two weeks, strain into clean bottles.

Spicy Pecans
2 cups pecans
2 tablespoons vegetable oil
5 bay leaves
1/2 teaspoon salt
1/2 teaspoon curry powder
1/4 teaspoon chili powder
1/4 teaspoon garlic powder
1/4 teaspoon cinnamon
Dash of hot sauce

A Pioneer's Christmas

Christmas Cards

Christmas cards were made using potatoes to print designs on paper. Cut a potato in half and carve out a design. Apply ink or paint onto design, and then print. Seal the envelopes with candle wax allowed to drip from a lit candle.

Christmas Decorations

- With a sharp knife, punch small holes all over an orange. Place cloves in the holes. Lightly mist the orange with water, and then roll it in spices, such as cinnamon and nutmeg. Place the fruit on a plate to allow it to dry for a few weeks. After the pomander has dried, tie ribbon around it and hang.
- Acorns gathered in the fall can be painted or strung for a garland at holiday time.
- String cookie cutters and hang over doors or cupboards.
- Hang homemade cookies on the tree.
- Place candles in windows and bunched together on tables.

Combine pecans, oil and hot sauce in a bowl. Stir until thoroughly mixed. Add remaining ingredients and mix well. Pour mixture out onto a cookie sheet. Spread out flat. Bake at 325° F for 30 minutes, stirring every 5 to 7 minutes. Let cool. Take out bay leaves and pour in a tin. Wrap tin with ribbon.

Nut-Butters

2 cups roasted, unsalted cashews, peanuts or almonds
1 tablespoon peanut oil
1/2 teaspoon salt (optional)

In food processor using knife blade, add nuts, oil and salt. Process 1 1/2 minutes until mixture forms a ball. Store in refrigerator.

For a more chunky consistency, stir in 1/2 cup chopped nuts when done.

Herb Oil

1 cup fresh basil leaves
1 cup fresh oregano sprigs
2 cups vegetable oil

Pour all ingredients into a blender. Process until all herbs are coarsely chopped. Pour into jar and cover. Let stand in cool, dark place for one week.

Using a sieve with cheesecloth, strain mixture. (Save herbs for later use in cooking.) Store at room temperature.

Herb Vinegar

Use fresh basil, dill or thyme sprigs. Place one herb in jar, such as basil, pour vinegar in jar to cover herb sprigs. Cover tightly and let stand in a bright place for three weeks.

Strain vinegar with sieve and cheesecloth. Store at room temperature.

NOTE: All the previous items can be placed in decorative jars. Place a label on the outside or paint them.

Italian Herb Vinegar

1/4 cup basil
2 tablespoons garlic powder
1/2 cup marjoram
1/4 cup oregano
1/4 cup thyme
1 tablespoon red pepper flakes

Mix ingredients well. Pour into bottle. Pour vinegar over herbs. Use a bottle with a tight-fitting top. Store in refrigerator.

Christmas Gifts to Make

Red Pepper Jelly

1/2 c. hot red peppers, minced
2 c. red bell peppers, minced
1 c. apple cider vinegar
1 1/2 c. sugar
2 oz. liquid pectin

Mix and stir all ingredients in a pan and bring to a boil. Simmer for 5 minutes while stirring. Pour into sterilized jelly jars and seal. Makes 2 pints.

Mustard

1/2 c. mustard powder
1/2 c. sugar
1 tsp. salt
1 tbsp. lemon juice
Boiling water

Combine dry ingredients with lemon juice and enough boiling water to reach a spreadable consistency. Let stand overnight. Pour into jars and store in refrigerator.

Croutons

4 - 5 slices old homemade bread, cubed
2 tbsp. garlic powder
2 tbsp. Parmesan cheese, grated
2 tbsp. basil, finely chopped
2 tbsp. marjoram, finely chopped
1/2 c. olive oil

Place bread on baking sheet and sprinkle with dry herbs and cheese. Drizzle oil over bread. Broil for 30 seconds, then stir. Repeat this process until croutons are lightly browned.

Beef Jerky

Cut lean beef into thin 1-inch strips 4 to 5 inches long. Sprinkle with salt and Worcestershire sauce. Lay flat on wire rack or screen and bake at 140°F. Check often until done.

Fudge

12 oz. semisweet chocolate
12 oz. baking chocolate
1 pint marshmallow creme
1 13.oz can evaporated milk
3 tbsp. butter
4 1/2 c. brown sugar
2 c. nuts

Break up chocolate into small pieces. Combine chocolate and marshmallow and set aside. Mix milk, butter and sugar in saucepan and bring to a boil, stirring often. Simmer for 5 minutes while stirring. Pour over chocolate mixture and stir until well blended. Add nuts and mix well. Pour mixture into 9 x 13-inch buttered pan. Let cool, and then cut into small squares. Wrap in cheesecloth and tie with a ribbon.

Fruit Bon Bons

1 lb. figs, finely chopped
1/4 lb. raisins, finely chopped
1/2 lb. dates, finely chopped
1 lb. nuts, finely chopped
2 tbsp. sugar
1/4 c. rum
1 c. coconut
1/2 c. powdered sugar

Combine all ingredients and mix very well. Add coconut and mix again. Form mixture into balls and roll into powdered sugar.

Walnut Bread

3 cups all-purpose flour
1 cup granulated sugar
4 teaspoons baking powder
1 teaspoon salt
3/4 cup shortening
1 1/2 cups coarsely chopped walnuts
1 egg, beaten
1 1/2 cups milk
1 teaspoon vanilla

Sift flour with sugar, baking powder and salt. Cut in shortening. Stir in 1 1/4 cups walnuts. Add egg, milk and vanilla. Mix by hand until ingredients are blended. Pour into greased and floured 9x5-inch loaf pan. Sprinkle remaining 1/4 cup of walnuts on top. Bake at 350°F for 60 to 70 minutes.

Remove from oven and let stand for 10 minutes. Remove loaf from pan and let cool on wire rack. Makes 1 loaf.

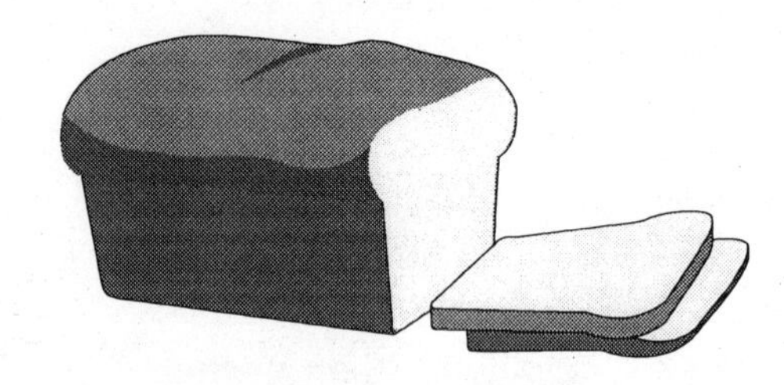

NOTE: Wrap this bread in aluminum foil and then wrap with wrapping paper or just tie a ribbon around it.

Gifts for Children

Bookmarks

2 x 6-inch piece of cardboard
5 x 13-inch piece of wallpaper
3 6-inch pieces of yarn
Hole punch
Scissors

Wet the wallpaper and fold around piece of cardboard so that seam is on one side of cardboard. Smooth out with fingers or popsicle stick. Cut off excess wallpaper. Wait for a few minutes to let wallpaper dry.

At top center of cardboard punch one hole. Thread pieces of yarn through hole and braid. Tie knot at end of braid.

Gifts for Adults

Adorned Gloves

1 pair of plain knit gloves
5 matching buttons

Sew buttons around cuff of gloves.

OR

1 pair of plain knit gloves
½ yard lace trim

Sew trim around cuff of gloves.

Winter Bath

1/2 cup pine needles
1/4 cup juniper berries
1/4 cup coarse sea salt

Pour ingredients in a muslin or silk bag and tie with ribbon.

Sweaters

Female

1 plain sweater
11/2 yards tassel trim
Fabric Glue

Measure collar area, cuffs and bottom of sweater. Cut trim to measure. With fabric glue, press on trim to collar area, cuffs and bottom of sweater.

Male

1 plain sweater
6 gold buttons
Needle and thread

Place buttons on shoulder area from collar to arm seams, evenly spaced, three to a shoulder. Sew in place.

For the Birds

And don't forget the birds. Decorate an evergreen tree in your yard with ornaments of food for the birds.

- Hang net bags of suet on the tree.
- Spread pretzels with peanut butter and cornmeal, then stick on freshly popped popcorn. Hang with a ribbon or string.
- Roll pine cones in peanut butter and suet, then in birdseed. Hang by ribbons on outside trees.
- Cut oranges in half and scoop out pulp. Mix sunflower seeds and raisins with the pulp and fill orange. With a needle thread yarn from one end of the orange to the other and hang outside.
- String freshly popped popcorn on florist wire and decorate a fir tree outside. Be sure to secure the wire onto the tree, so that it doesn't blow away.
- Mix suet and sunflower seeds together. Mold into a large wreath and place in the refrigerator to harden. Tie a ribbon around it and hang outside.

Firestarters

Materials

Pine cones
old candle stubs

Instructions
In a double boiler, melt candle stubs. Take out wicks with a fork and lay on a cloth or wax paper to cool. Dip bottom end of pine cones in melted wax and place on wax paper. Immediately take the wicks and stick each of them to the bottom layer of the pine cones. Let dry. When all are cool and dry, place in a box or basket.

Milk Bath

Materials

A felt, silk or cheesecloth bag
Ribbon (3" - 4" long)
3 cups powdered milk
1 cup ground oatmeal
2 herbal tea bags
1 large spoon or scoop

Instructions
Take tea out of bags and mix with powdered milk and ground oatmeal. Pour into bag and place spoon or scoop on top. Tie with ribbon. Decorate the front of the bag as you wish.

Miscellaneous Gifts

Gift certificates or coupons can be made for personal services, such as making dinner, running errands, baby-sitting, washing the car or pet-sitting. Use nicely colored paper and draw coupons with markers or crayons. Or take your ideas to a printer for more professional looking coupons or certificates.

Example:

Gift Certificate

Good for 10 hours of baby-sitting.

___The Johnsons

Decorate them with stickers, drawings or ink stamps.

- Make hanging planters from gold or silver cord.
- Create a Christmas basket for a newborn in the family by including their first tree ornament, a star or angel for the tree, and a frame for a photograph of the baby enjoying the first Christmas.

Give Homemade Gift Baskets

For a Gardener: A trowel, gloves, seeds, sun hat, knee pads and a gardening book.

For a Cat Lover: A cat book, cat treats and cat toys. Use a cat food dish or a kitty litter box as your basket.
For a Dog Lover: A dog book, dog treats, leash, dog sweater and Frisbee. Use a dog food bowl or a dog bed as the basket.
For a Wine Lover: Wrap up a bottle of wine, cheese, crackers and wine glasses in a small tablecloth.
For a Food Lover: Pasta, canned tomatoes, basil and garlic. Use a colander, saucepan or pot as the basket.
For Someone who Sews: Spools of thread, needles, sewing book and a yard or two of cloth. Use a sewing basket as the basket.

- Carefully thread crackers onto florist wire. When the wire is full, fasten the ends of the wire together over a branch on a tree.
- Thread apple peel and cranberries onto florist wire to form small wreaths. Fasten three together loosely to hang down on the tree.
- Smooth suet on crackers and dip in bird seed. Thread a needle with thin ribbon through the cracker and hang on the tree.

Earthsavers

Grow your own Christmas trees for future cutting. Pick out fast-growing species at the nursery. Douglas firs and Scotch pines can grow up to 2 feet a year. Monterey, Mondell and Aleppo pines can grow up to 8 feet a year.

After the holidays cut off the branches of your holiday tree to make wreaths or table decorations for winter. Use the trunk as firewood. If you do not have a fireplace, give it to someone who does.

Save all those computer paper strips as packing material for sending packages.

Christmas Tree Odds & Ends

Various trees are considered Christmas trees. Artificial trees, live trees and cut trees are all environmental choices. Artificial trees have come a long way since they first appeared. Every year, they seem more like real trees. Choose an artificial tree and you need not take a tree from the environment nor waste the gas of transporting the tree to your home.

Live trees make a great investment. Not only will the tree serve as your Christmas tree, but as a beautiful addition to your yard. If you choose a live tree, dig the hole where you plan to plant the tree before the ground becomes difficult to work—or have a large container ready for planting the tree.

When you bring your live tree home, leave it in the basement or garage for a few days to give it a chance to adjust to indoor temperatures. Repeat this again when you are ready to plant the tree outdoors. Live trees do not do well if they remain in the house for more than two to three weeks, therefore plan your purchase carefully.

Add variety to your holiday by purchasing a small tree and planting it in a container. Leave it outside for several years until it is large enough to use as a Christmas tree. Do this every few years and you could alternate between cut trees and live trees for your holiday enjoyment. You would also save money by purchasing the small trees instead of larger trees.

Cut trees, the most popular Christmas tree choice, offer us the most convenient way to have that festive pine odor of the season. The best place to purchase cut Christmas trees are on Christmas tree farms because you can be relatively assured trees are being replaced with new plantings. Scotch pines, Douglas, balsam or Fraser firs are all good choices for Christmas trees because the needles remain on these trees for the longest period of time.

Christmas Tree Care & Safety

- Once you arrive home with the tree, saw approximately one inch from the base, and then immediately place the base in water.
- Place the tree in a well-ventilated area and away from the fireplace or other source of heat.
- Check the water supply every day. Water your tree frequently. Ice cubes provide an easy way to water the tree.
- If you have a live Christmas tree, you must water it frequently so the root ball does not dry out.
- Never leave the house with the electric lights on.
- Be sure to remove the tree as soon after the holidays as possible. Trees dry out and can become fire safety hazards.
- Plant your living Christmas tree as soon as possible. After filling the hole, anchor the tree with two or three stakes. Then mulch heavily with mulch, pine needles or leaves.

Most environmental problems are created after the holidays when the tree is no longer needed. If you have an old artificial tree, don't throw it away. Instead, give it to a charitable organization.

Cut trees, one of the horrors of the landfill, can be disposed of in many ways. If you happen to have a wood chipper or shredder, you

can use your Christmas tree as mulch for your garden in the spring. Add the tree to your compost pile. Or cut off the branches and protect tender plants in the garden, using the trunk of the tree for firewood.

Christmas trees can be used to create winter shelters for birds. Lean the tree against another tree or against the house or shed. Hang oranges, popcorn and birdseed from the top branches. If you have a pond, tie a large rock to it and drop it in the deep part of the pond. Small fish will use the tree as a shelter from larger fish.

Many communities now have recycling programs which designate a few days for Christmas tree collection. If you do not have such a program, contact a local nursery which has mulching capabilities and ask if they would accept your Christmas tree.

IKEA furniture stores rent Christmas trees for $20.00 plus tax in December. In January, you return the tree and receive mulch, $10 cash or a $20 coupon towards an IKEA purchase, and a coupon for a free tree sapling to be picked up in April. Call (610) 834-0180 for store locations across the country.

Christmas is the time for giving. Don't forget to put the earth on your Christmas list.

Environmental Wrappings

Replace bows and ribbons with yarn, rickrack, old cloth belts, dried flowers or silk flowers.

Decorate presents with candy canes.

Have you ever noticed the pile over in the corner after all the Christmas gifts have been opened? The pile of scrunched up wrapping paper, bows and boxes? Just think, nearly every household in the world has the same pile. And it all goes in the trash. Ugh!

There has to be a better way, right? Well, there are some solutions to this dilemma. Using creativity and some old-fashioned methods, we can reduce, or even eliminate, that pile over in the corner.

Wrap gifts with other gifts, such as tablecloths, towels, sheets, blankets or clothes. You are guaranteed these will not be thrown away.

If you have a person on your list who sews, wrap gifts in fabric. The extra fabric will surely be appreciated, and if you buy it on sale, will cost you no more than wrapping paper.

Use paper bags with handles for wrapping gifts. Place the gifts inside and top with fabric or tissue paper. Another idea would be to tie the top of the paper bag together with ribbon or string.

Wrap gifts in newspaper which then can be recycled. Tie the gift with pretty red ribbon. Or have the children decorate the gifts with stickers or by coloring.

For your own family, hide all the gifts until Christmas, and then bring them all out unwrapped. However, for some, the fun is in the unwrapping, therefore hide some and wrap the remainder.

Some other ideas include:

- Use one large box to place lots of unwrapped gifts, then wrap the box.
- Use Sunday comics to wrap presents for children.
- Use some of the colorful shopping bags which are used at holiday time.

- Decorate small paper bags with stickers, stamps or drawings. At the top of the bag, punch two holes about an inch apart through both sides of the bag. Thread a ribbon through the holes and tie a bow to close the top of the bag.

- Use scraps of wallpaper to wrap gifts.
- For large gifts, stuff in a trash bag. Tie the top with a ribbon, and decorate the bag with stickers or old Christmas cards.
- Wrap gifts in brown shipping paper. Decorate gifts with old Christmas cards.
- Use old calendars or old road maps to wrap gifts.
- Tie a small candle on top of a gift with ribbon.

- Use large 81/2 x 11 envelopes to contain small gifts, then decorate.
- Give grandparents gifts wrapped in drawings from the grandchildren.
- Use natural items from your yard to put on presents, such as holly berries, evergreens, a gnarly twig, a bunch of herbs or a pine cone.
- Place a monetary gift or gift certificate in a book. Tie a ribbon around the book.
- Use brown paper bags decorated with stickers or drawings. Fold the top of the bag once and punch two holes side by side about two inches apart. Thread a small twig through the holes to secure the gift.
- Other gifts with which to wrap gifts could be comforters, pillow cases, napkins, table runners or potholders.
- Use a brand new belt to tie around a gift instead of ribbon.

When opening gifts, open them carefully to keep the wrapping paper from tearing. Wrap the used paper around an old wrapping paper tube to be used next year. Be sure to remove or cut off the tape. If you fold the paper, iron out the creases with an iron on a low setting. If paper has small tears or blemishes, place stickers or bows over these areas.

Always save gift boxes. They can come in handy throughout the year for birthdays, showers or anniversaries.

Bows can be used over and over again. If they become a little crushed, try blowing a little steam over them with an iron. If they are not usable as bows, take them apart and use the ribbon.

Encourage friends and family to reuse gift wrappings. At the very least, ask them to give their wrappings to you for reusing. However, you will impress environmentalism upon others mostly through your example.

Christmas with Earthsaving Products

Finding the perfect gift is difficult enough, especially for those on your list who seem to have everything. Products which help the environment are good choices for anyone on your list, including that person who seems to have everything. I bet he or she does not have chemical-free shoe polish or dioxin-free baby wipes.

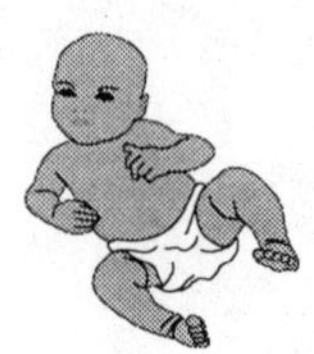

Giving an earthsaving gift, not only is a great idea because the receiver most likely does not have the item, but the gift sends a positive message about the importance of environmental health. If saving and preserving the beauty of the earth is one of your concerns, you can do your small part by sharing that message through your gift-giving.

Small gifts can serve as stocking stuffers, such as cloth shopping bags or earthsaving desk calendars. These types of products are usually found in local bookstores or shopping malls.

Energy-saving products, such as low-flow shower heads, draft guards and window quilts are excellent gifts for those frugal individuals on your list because they also save money. Another energy-saving gift idea is a dimmer switch. Dimmer switches save energy when the light is low.

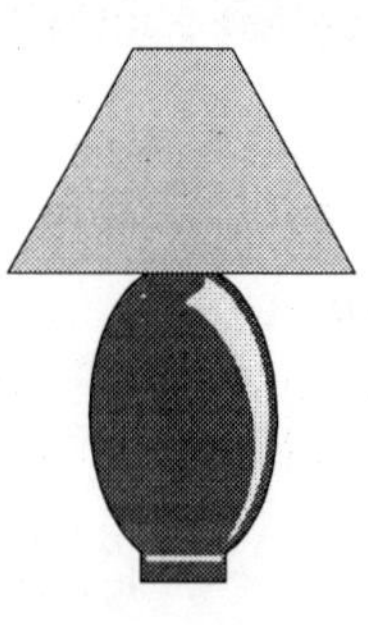
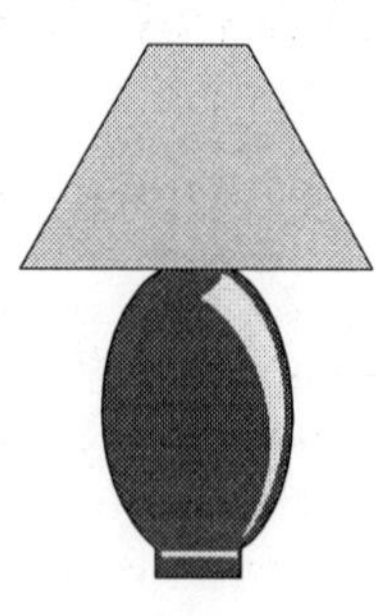

For animal lovers give cruelty-free products, such as makeup or hair care products. These products are usually found in health food stores. Also, some major manufacturers are creating these products which can be found in some department stores. *Aveda, Bare Essentials and Nature Cosmetics* are just a few of the companies using no animal ingredients in their products. Ask the store sales clerk for more companies and products. *The Body Shop* has long sold these types of products. If there is not a store near you, order items from their catalog by calling (800) 541-2535.

Green Mail Order Houses

A Brighter Way, (H. Schacht Electrical Supply, 5214 Burleson Road, #317, Austin, TX 78744. (512) 444-5583. *Lighting supplies and equipment*

Earth Care Paper, Inc., Ukiah, CA 95482-8507, (800) 347-0070. *Recycled paper products including stationery, paper towels, greeting cards, note cards and tissue.*

Gardens Alive!, 5100 Schenley Place, Lawrenceburg, IN 47025. (812) 537-8650. *Organic fertilizers, safe pest control products, and composting equipment.*

For the gardener on your list, give an organic gardening book or a compost bin. Herb, flower and vegetable seeds make great stocking stuffers.

For the new mother, give a year's worth of a diaper service or a box full of organic baby food.

Ecotourism is becoming a helpful and enjoyable way to educate people about the rainforests and eco-systems. Give a gift certificate for a vacation in the Amazon or the plains of Africa. *The Sierra Club* organizes wilderness exploration trips for its members. Contact them at: 730 Polk Street, San Francisco, CA 94109; (415) 776-2211. *International Expeditions, Inc.* is one of many companies providing educational and informative tours with expert

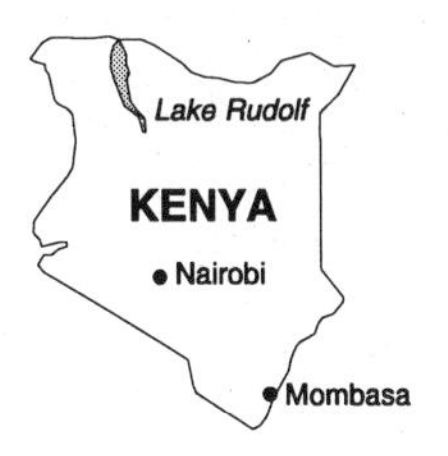

guides—to places all over the world. For more information, call them at (800) 633-4734. One thing to remember before giving this gift—your recipient must be willing and able to camp, hike, and experience the earth and forests firsthand. Ecotourism is more an experience than a vacation.

Seventh Generation, 49 Hercules Dr., Colchester, VT 05446-1672. (800) 456-1177. *Cloth grocery bags, recycled toilet paper and paper towels. Non-toxic animal repellent, non-toxic batteries and organic fruit juices.*
Sunelco, P. O. Box 1499, Hamilton, MT 59840. (406) 363-6924. *Solar equipment and supplies.*

Wouldn't it be wonderful if we all gave earthsaving gifts or stocking stuffers? We would all have the tools to begin or continue saving the earth. And we would have the satisfaction of having shared our concern with others.

EARTHSAVING Ways to Increase Your Savings by $1000 or More This Year

- Make your own votive candleholders by wrapping peat pots in aluminum foil and wrapping a red ribbon around the center. ($5 - $25)
- Use wrapping paper as gift tags. Cut a small rectangle out of your wrapping paper and fold in half. ($5 - $25)
- Use postcards instead of sending holiday cards. ($5 - $25)
- Save wrapping paper in good condition for next year's use. ($5 - $25)
- Use what you have around the house or yard to create holiday decorations. or instance, use ribbon scraps of fabric, fruit or pine cones to create table centerpieces. ($10 - $100)
- If a gift is in an unmarked box, decorate it and wrap around with colorful ribbons. ($5 - $10)
- Use paper clips to hang ornaments instead of buying ornament hangers. ($1 - $5)*

*Figures are estimated for a family of four. Your savings may be more or less.

Earthly Presents

Decorate the house for the holidays with lots of candles. Tie ribbons around them or surround a bunch of them with greens.

Decorate planters with ribbon or yarn.

Give a gift which has meaning or make a contribution to a charity or helpful organization in someone's name. Support organizations, companies and charities which are dedicated to saving the earth, providing alternatives to waste and destruction, or providing recycled products.

The Body Shop, 45 Horsehill Road, Cedar Knolls, New Jersey 07927-2014 or Call 1-800-541-2535. If there is not a shop near you, order items from the catalog. *The Body Shop* makes and sells lots of naturally-based products. Some of their products are made by people in countries, such as India, Brazil and Ghana through their Trade Not Aid program. Products include: handmade writing sets, hand-crafted bracelets, gift baskets and endangered species socks for kids. They also offer refills of their containers to reduce waste.

Other Gifts

50 Simple Things Your Business Can Do To Save The Earth by the Earth Works Group. **Earth Works Press**, 1400 Shattuck Avenue, #25, Berkeley, California 94709.
The Recycler's Handbook, a book offering suggestions on how to recycle. **Earth Works Press**, 1400 Shattuck Avenue, #25, Berkeley, California 94709.
Save our Streams Adoption Kit provides information on organizing a project, recognizing pollution and restoring a stream. **The Izaac Walton League of America**, 707 Conservation Lane, Gaithersburg, Maryland 20878-2983. (301) 548-0150.
Adopt-A-Turtle through the Caribbean Conservation Corporation (CCC) and receive an adoption certificate, newsletter and fact sheet. **CCC**, P. O. Box 2866, Gainesville, FL 32602. (800) 678-7853.

Chapter 8

Moneysavers

All things are artificial, for
nature is the art of God.

- Thomas Browne, *Religio Medici*

Moneysaving Bread Recipes

Market Savings

Saving money at the market seems simple, but can be difficult. Fortunately, there are a multitude of ways to save money at the market.

The first step is to make a firm commitment to stick to the budgeted amount for food each month. Be sure the budgeted amount is realistic.

Next, check your local grocery store ads every week and compare prices. Soon you will come to know which store or stores consistently offer the most savings.

Use coupons, especially at stores offering double coupon savings. And if coupons are used on sale items, the savings can be tripled.

Take advantage of rebate offers. Once in a while, the item will be absolutely free when you receive your rebate.

The taste of bread made at home far surpasses the taste of bread from the store. And making bread at home is inexpensive and usually more nutritious, too.

White Bread

2 tablespoons shortening
2 teaspoons salt
2 tablespoons sugar
1 cup hot milk
1 cup hot water
1 package dry yeast
1/4 cup warm water
6 cups white flour

In a large bowl mix shortening, salt and sugar. Add hot milk and hot water and let cool until lukewarm. In a small bowl mix warm water with yeast. Let stand for 5 minutes. Add yeast mixture and 3 cups of flour to first mixture. Beat until blended. Add 2 more cups of flour and mix. Turn out onto lightly floured surface and knead for 2 minutes and let sit for 10 minutes. Add more flour and knead until dough is elastic and not sticky. Place dough in a large greased bowl, cover and sit in a warm place. Let rise until dough doubles in bulk. (Approximately 1 to 2 hours). Punch down and separate in half for two loaves. Place each half in greased loaf pans, cover and sit in a warm place. Let rise until dough doubles in size again.

Bake bread for 15 minutes at 425°F, reduce heat to 375°F and bake for 30 minutes more. Remove from loaf pan and let cool.

Cost: $.50 - $.70 per loaf (2 loaves)

Whole Wheat Bread

1/2 cup hot water
1 cup milk
1/4 cup sugar
2 teaspoons salt
1/2 cup warm water
1 package dry yeast
2 cups whole-wheat flour
4 cups white flour

In a large bowl mix hot water, milk, sugar and salt. Let cool until lukewarm. In a small bowl mix warm water with yeast. Let stand for 5 minutes. Add yeast mixture, whole-wheat flour and 2 cups of white flour to first mixture. Beat until blended. Turn onto lightly floured surface, knead for 2 minutes, and let sit for 10 minutes. Add remaining white flour as needed while kneading the dough until elastic and not sticky. Place in a large greased bowl, cover, and put in a warm place. Let rise until double in bulk. (Approximately 1 to 2 hours.) Punch down and separate into two loaves. Place in greased loaf pans, cover, and let rise until double in bulk again.

Bake bread for 45 minutes at 375°F. Remove from loaf pans and let cool.

Cost: $.70 - $.90 per loaf (2 loaves)

Rye Bread

1 cup hot water
1 cup milk
2 tablespoons shortening
2 tablespoons brown sugar
1 tablespoon salt
1/2 cup warm water
2 packages dry yeast
3 c rye flour
3 cups white flour

In a large bowl mix hot water, milk, shortening, sugar and salt. Let cool until lukewarm. In a small bowl mix warm water with yeast and let stand for 5 minutes. Add yeast mixture and rye flour to first mixture. Mix thoroughly. Add a little of white flour until dough is easy to handle. Turn out on lightly floured surface and knead for 2 minutes. Let sit for 10 minutes. Add remaining flour while kneading until dough is smooth. (Rye dough will be a little sticky.) Place dough in a greased bowl, cover and sit in a warm place. Let rise until double in bulk. (Approximately 1 to 2 hours.) Punch down and separate in half. Place in greased loaf pans, cover and let rise until double in bulk again.

Bake at 375°F for 45 - 50 minutes. Remove from pans and let cool.

Cost: $.80 - $1.00 per loaf (2 loaves)

Buy generic brands in the grocery stores. They are usually less expensive and offer similar quality compared to other brands.

Buy vegetables and fruits in season.

Buy items in bulk where possible. Some grocery warehouses offer lots of savings through selling bulk items, but if you don't have access to these, buy bigger items in the grocery store. You nearly always get more for you money.

Season Reason

It only stands to reason—you save money if you buy things in season.

Vegetables

January: Broccoli, Brussels Sprouts, Cauliflower, Sweet Potatoes
February: Broccoli, Cabbage, Carrots, Cauliflower, Spinach, Sweet Potatoes
March: Broccoli, Cabbage, Carrots, Cauliflower, Peas, Sweet Potatoes
April: Asparagus, Broccoli, Peas, Sweet Potatoes
May: Asparagus, Beans, Broccoli, Corn, Leeks, Peas, Radishes.
June: Corn, Cucumbers, Green Beans, Peas, Radishes, Summer Squash, Tomatoes
July: Corn, Cucumbers, Green Beans, Leeks, Peppers, Radishes, Tomatoes
August: Corn, Cucumbers, Eggplant, Leeks, Peppers, Squash, Tomatoes, Zucchini
September: Cauliflower, Corn, Peppers, Sweet Potatoes
October: Broccoli, Brussel Sprouts, Cauliflower, Pumpkins, Squash
November: Broccoli, Brussel Sprouts, Cauliflower, Squash
December: Broccoli, Brussel Sprouts, Cauliflower

Dinner for Pennies

Making dinner at home is more inexpensive than ordering out or going out for dinner.

Macaroni & Cheese

2 tablespoons flour
2 1/2 cups milk
2 tablespoons butter or margarine
1/4 teaspoon salt
1 1/2 cups macaroni
1/4 cups shredded cheddar cheese

Start cooking macaroni in hot boiling water. Meanwhile, in large saucepan, melt butter or margarine over medium-high heat. Add flour and salt, stirring for one minute. Pour in milk, stirring constantly, until just boiling. Remove from heat. Stir in cheddar cheese until melted. Add cooked macaroni and transfer to greased baking dish. Bake, covered, in 375°F oven for 15 minutes. Uncover and bake for 5 minutes more. (Serves 2 - 4).

Cost: $1.50 - $3.00*

Variations: For variety and a little more cost, add bread or cracker crumbs or parmesan cheese to the top of the dish before baking. Beef and a little tomato sauce could be added for an entirely different dish.

Tuna Casserole

2 tablespoons butter or margarine
2 tablespoons flour
1 can tuna
2 eggs, hard-boiled and chopped
2 1/2 cups milk
1 small onion, minced
2 cups cooked noodles

In large saucepan, melt butter or margarine over medium-high heat. Add flour, stirring until sauce thickens. Add milk, stirring constantly, until boiling. Remove from heat. Add tuna, noodles, eggs and onion, mix together. Pour in greased baking dish. Bake at 350°F for 20 minutes. (Serves 2 - 4).

Cost: $2.50 - $4.00*

Variations: Top with bread or cracker crumbs before baking. Add mushrooms or green peppers. An even more inexpensive version is to replace the butter, flour and milk with Cream of Mushroom soup and leave out the onion and eggs. ($1.50 - $3.00).

Frankfurter Potato Bake
1 pound frankfurters
1 tablespoon flour
2 cups cheddar cheese, shredded
2/3 cup milk
2 tablespoons onion, minced
8 medium cooked potatoes, peeled, sliced

Slice frankfurters and set aside. In large saucepan, stir milk and flour together over medium-high heat. Add cheese and stir until thick and smooth, then add onion and a pinch of salt. Fold in potatoes and sliced frankfurters, and transfer to greased baking dish.

Bake, covered, at 350°F for 40 minutes. Uncover and bake for 10 minutes more. (Serves 6 - 8).
Cost: $2.00 - $4.00*

NOTE: Replacing milk with nonfat dry milk will decrease the total cost of all dishes even more.

*Figures are estimated. Your savings may be more or less.

Fruits

January: Apples, Grapefruit, Oranges, Tangerines.
February, March, April, May: Grapefruit, Oranges, Pineapple.
June: Apricots, Cantaloupe, Cherries, Oranges, Peaches, Strawberries, Watermelon
July: Apricots, Blueberries, Cantaloupe, Cherries, Honeydew, Nectarines, Oranges, Peaches, Plums, Watermelon
August: Blueberries, Grapes, Honeydew, Oranges, Peaches, Plums, Watermelon
September: Apples, Grapes, Oranges, Peaches, Pears
October: Apples, Coconuts, Cranberries, Grapes, Oranges, Pears
November: Apples, Coconuts, Cranberries, Grapes, Oranges, Pears, Tangelos
December: Coconuts, Cranberries, Oranges, Pineapple, Tangerines, Tangelos

Cheap Things to do to Deter Burglars

1. Have a dog bowl outside on the porch and a "Beware of Dog" sign whether you have a dog or not.
2. Be sure to keep all areas of the outside of your house lighted.
3. Have a tape available of dogs barking loudly.
4. Have a friend house-sit when you are gone.
5. Stop your papers and mail while you are gone.
6. Have inside lights set on a timer to give the appearance that someone is home.

Cheap Pizza Recipes

Wake up those leftover mashed potatoes by mixing with onions, garlic or cheese.

Basic Pizza Dough
(for 2 12-inch pizzas or 1 thick-crusted pizza)
4 cups sifted flour
1 cake yeast
2 tablespoons oil
1 teaspoon salt
1 1/3 cups warm water

In 1/3 cup of the warm water dissolve yeast. Let stand for 5 minutes. Add half of the flour, all of the oil, water and salt. Mix well. Add remaining flour until dough forms a hard mass. Knead dough on floured surface for 10 minutes. Place in a bowl covered with a damp cloth to rise for about two hours. Punch down and divide into two balls of dough.

Oil two 12-inch pizza pans. Place dough in center of pans and flatten by hand. Gently pull and stretch dough to edges. Form crust by pinching up dough around edges.

Vegetarian Cheese Pizza
1 cup tomato sauce
1 clove garlic, minced
1 green pepper, sliced
1 small onion, sliced
1 small tomato, sliced
1/4 cup mushrooms, sliced
1/4 teaspoon basil and oregano
1/4 cup grated parmesan cheese
1/4 to 1/2 cup grated mozzarella cheese

Pour tomato sauce over flattened dough. Sprinkle on parmesan cheese. Spread all other ingredients except mozzarella evenly over entire pizza. Sprinkle mozzarella cheese evenly over other ingredients. Bake at 400°F for 20 to 30 minutes.

Cost: $2.00 - $3.00* (for one 12-inch pizza)

Tortilla Pizza
Two soft corn tortillas
1 cup tomato sauce
1/2 pound ground beef
1 clove garlic, minced
1 small onion, chopped
1/4 teaspoon basil and oregano
1/4 cup shredded cheddar cheese
1 teaspoon olive oil

Sauté garlic and onion in olive oil. Add ground beef. Cook until beef is browned. Add tomato sauce, basil and oregano. Bring to a boil and take off heat. Place tortillas in oiled pizza pans or baking sheets. Divide sauce in half and spread evenly over tortillas. Sprinkle each with cheese. Bake at 300°F for 20 minutes.

Cost: $2.00 - $4.00*

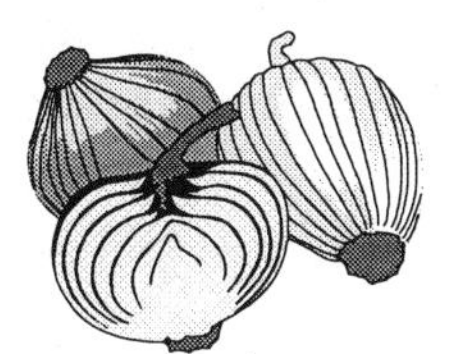

Pita Pizza
4 pita breads
1 cup tomato sauce
1/2 pound sausage, cooked and crumbled
1 onion, sliced
1 clove garlic, minced
1 green pepper, sliced
1/4 teaspoon basil and oregano
1/4 cup shredded mozzarella cheese

Place pita breads on oiled baking sheet. Pour sauce over pita breads. Sprinkle with toppings and then cheese. Bake at 350°F for 10 minutes.

Cost: $2.00 - $4.00*

*Figures are estimated. Your savings may be more or less.

To rid your refrigerator of odors, place crumpled newspaper inside and leave for a few hours.

To decrease waste, leave excess packaging behind in the store. Companies will get the message. Write companies to let them know how you feel.

Earthsavers

At work or school, request that paper towels or hand dryers in the bathroom be replaced with the cotton towel on the roll. The cotton towel saves energy and reduces waste.

Recycle your car tires. Next time your mechanic says you need new tires, ask if you can have your tires recycled.

Moneysaving Househunting

- Decide what your price range is and subtract $5,000 to $20,000. This figure will be your starting price range. If you buy a new house, there may be extras which you will want to purchase with the house. If you buy an existing house, you may need to pay a point or more, make construction or design changes or repairs. Be sure you have a basic idea what your house could sell for. Find out what other houses are going for in your neighborhood. All this will help you to know what you will need to put down on a house, and how much house you can afford to buy.

- Research builders in the area where you are considering moving. Which builders build high quality homes for economical prices? Are there existing homes for sale if you do not want a new home? Find out where these neighborhoods are.

- List the most important features you want in your next home, such as a bigger kitchen, more closet space or more windows. Keep this list with you as you look at homes.

- Consider buying land and then building a house. Build it yourself with different contractors for each construction job or consult a builder for the entire job.

- Consider attending house auctions.

- Consider buying a *Fixer-Upper.* If you have good construction knowledge and skills or know those who can help, this could be a great buy.

- Take your time. Do not be pressured into buying or influenced by short-term deals.

- Search out builders or sellers who are willing to offer buyers help with closing costs or paying points.

- Is the home energy efficient? Is it well-insulated? Are the appliances energy efficient?

- Hire an inspector to inspect the home to ensure there are no structural problems, such as leaky pipes, faulty roofs or poor attic ventilation.

The Economic Move

Moving out of your house and into a new home can be exciting, stressful, and expensive. After the down payment, the closing costs and the Realtor costs, there is not much left. Below are some ideas for saving money and headaches:

- Begin packing boxes a few months before the move. Pack a few boxes a day and when moving day comes you will do a lot less.
- If you are moving across the country or overseas, consider selling some or all of your furniture and large items to save on transporting your household goods.
- If you do not have many items, consider renting a small truck or borrowing a truck from a friend.
- Have a moving party! Invite some friends over for sandwiches and snacks, and they can help you pack and move.
- Use your work and social contacts to find people traveling to your new area. Ask if they would mind traveling with a few of your boxes. Offer them a favor in return.
- Have a yard sale to rid yourself of extra *stuff* which you do not need.
- Pack breakables, such as glassware and dishes in tablecloths and with napkins or clothes.
- Take your plants with you in your car. In a dark and hot truck or moving van, they will die or be highly stressed.
- When packing books, combine them with light items, such as clothes. Boxes filled with books are very heavy and may break.
- A month or two before the move, try to use up as much of the food in the house as possible. Just buy what you absolutely must.
- Ask grocery store chains, retail stores and furniture stores for boxes.
- If you are hiring a moving company, pack and unpack all your items yourself. Companies will charge extra for these services.
- If your new home is so far as to take a two day drive, make a camping trip out of it instead of staying in a hotel.
- If you must store some of your boxes and household items, rent the smallest storage room available and stack your boxes to the ceiling. Ask relatives or friends if they have any available storage space in a basement or garage.
- Since you must keep the house food-free during the move, make some homemade burritos ahead of time and freeze them—instead of eating out. At mealtime pop them in the microwave.
- After everything is out of the house, have each family member go through the house to make sure nothing has been left. Check closets, cabinets, drawers and the attic.

After your move, donate the boxes to local charities who collect donated food or other items. Or recycle the boxes with your local recycling center.

A free booklet with moving tips is available from Ryder Truck Rental at (800) GO-RYDER.

Vacation Moneysavers

Much of our savings goes toward annual vacations. Understandably and most deservedly, we all need the rest and relaxation, not to mention the possible education of visiting new places. However, we need to consider our budget requirements, and then discover areas where we can cut our travel and vacation costs.

Transportation

- Drive to your vacation destination instead of using paid transportation.
- Travel by bus or by train and ask for a family discount.

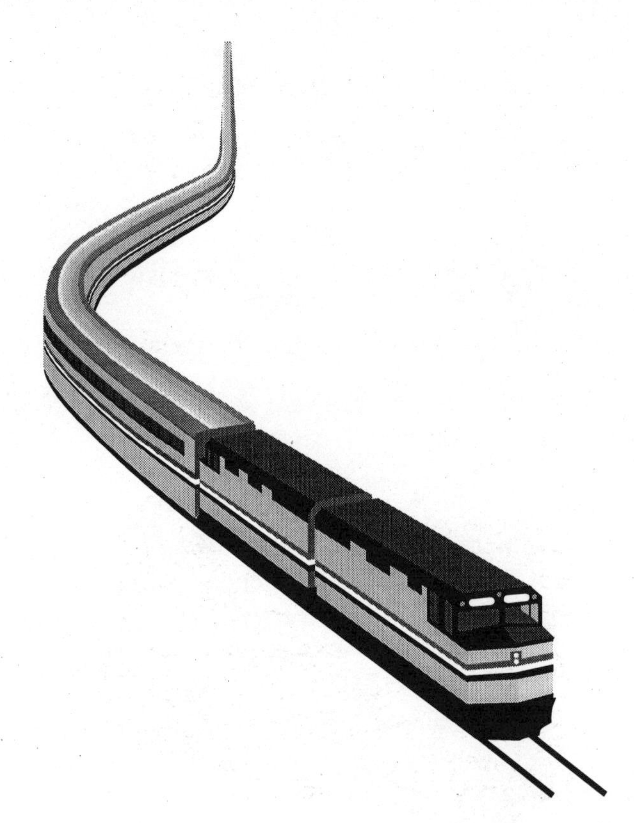

- If traveling long distances or driving is a big part of the vacation, consider renting a travel or tent trailer.
- Consider a cruise for your next vacation. If you call a week to a few days before departure, you may be able to receive great savings. There is always a scramble to completely book the cruise.
- Go on a cruise with a group. Discounts are given for groups of 16 or more.
- Sometimes the best cruise discounts are given very near to the time of departure. Contact the Cruise Line, Inc., at (800) 777-0707 or contact Cruise One at (800) 327-SHIP. Both of these companies offer savings on cruises.

General Tips

- Bring sandwiches, fruit and snacks instead of stopping on the way or buying on the train or at the airport.
- Have someone drop you off at the airport instead of leaving your car in the parking lot. Or consider using a shuttle service which picks you up at your home.
- If you must park at the airport, use satellite parking.
- Stay in accommodations with kitchens and microwave family meals.
- Stay in a bed and breakfast which will allow you to store some food in the refrigerator.
- Join AAA for hotel discounts.
- Travel off-season to receive low rates.
- Make arrangements far in advance to take advantage of early booking rates.
- Call your destination's tourist office or Chamber of Commerce to receive information about activities which are scheduled during your visit. Free activities and sites will also be listed.
- If you are a senior citizen, always ask for senior citizen discounts.

- Try cruising by freighter. For more information contact:

Sea the Difference - (800) 666-9333
Bergen Line - (800) 323-7436

- Enroll in a Frequent Flier Program.
- Use travel agents to find the lowest airfares. They cost nothing and usually have more information to get you the best buy.
- Check with the airline to see if you could fly into another city a little further away from your destination. Sometimes the price difference is considerable.
- Schedule your flight through a firm which buys blocks of unsold seats from airlines. Be sure to ask if the fare is refundable or if there are any additional charges. For more information call:

UniTravel Corp. - (800) 325-2222
TFI Tours International - (800) 745-8000
1-800-FLY-CHEAP - (800) 359-2432

- If traveling by air, have someone drop you off at the airport. Arrange to be picked up when you return. This saves lots on parking fees.
- To schedule low-cost trips on regularly scheduled airlines, call **Airhitch** at (212) 864-2000.

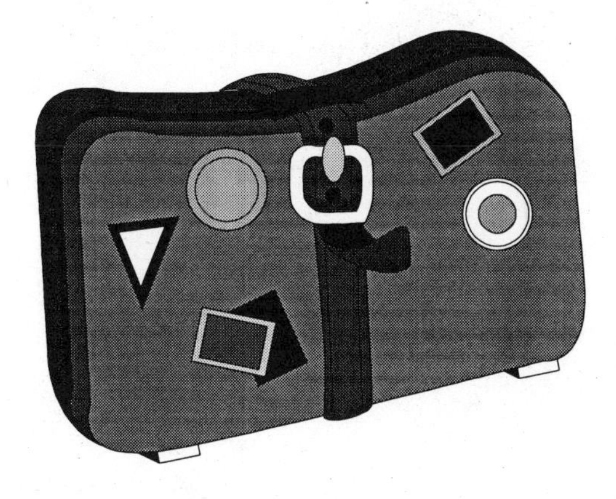

Consider traveling by air with an air courier where you board a cargo flight. Savings can be as high as 75%. Some restrictions apply, such as limited luggage. Courier brokers match passengers with flights and usually require a small fee. Below is one courier broker:

Now Voyager
74 Varick Street, Suite 307
New York, New York 10013
(212) 431-1616

- Take many short vacations throughout the year instead of one long vacation in the middle of summer. You will save by spending some vacations off-season and letting your savings accumulate interest for the next long weekend.
- College dormitories are available for summer lodging at 700 colleges and universities around the world for about $15 to $30 a night.

For more information write to:

The Campus Travel Service
P. O. Box 5486
Fullerton, California 92635

Eco-Boating Tips

If you enjoy boating or fishing, keep in mind these tips to safeguard the environment.

- Be sure to use legal bottom paints.
- Be careful to fuel up without spilling.
- Always pump out at onshore pump out stations.
- Clean your boat with biodegradable cleaners.

Cheap and Exciting Vacations

- Hike the Appalachian Trail
- Camp out in the backyard.
- Swap houses with friends who live out of state or out of the country.
- Drive across country with a tent in the trunk.
- Hike across the state.
- Visit relatives and take day trips from there.

Aruba has embarked on an eco-project to create a national park out of a quarter of the island. Arikok National Park will expand to allow environmental preservation and agricultural research facilities as well as hiking and biking trails.

Accommodations

- Check with relatives, friends or co-workers about condos which may be available for rent. Many times these people will offer a lower rate to you than a stranger. If renting a condo for your vacation, bring as much of your own food as possible. Many times markets in resort areas and beaches are expensive.
- Stay at the Y. YMCA's are located across the United States and provide very inexpensive lodging. For more information write:

The Y's Way
224 E. 47th Street
New York, NY 10017
(212) 308-2899

- Share a condo with relatives or friends.
- Rent a RV or camper.
- Camp for all or some of your vacation. One night can be as low as $10. For more information on camping and locations, write:

National Park Service
P. O. Box 37127
Washington, D.C. 20013-7127

or check your local library or bookstore for *Woodall's Campground Directory.*

- Use a travel agency which rebates some of their commission to clients. One such agency is Travel Avenue of Chicago. Contact them at (800) 333-3335.
- Use a lodging reservation service to book lodgings at reasonable rates. Contact Quikbook at (800) 789-9887 or Hotel Reservations Network at (800) 964-6835 for more information.
- Book rooms in advance. Rates can be up to 50% lower.
- Ask hotels what special discounts they are currently offering. Sometimes if you do not ask, they do not tell.
- Stay outside of large cities or tourist areas. Rates are usually lower.

- Consider staying in a hostel for as low as $10 a night, sometimes lower. There are over 200 in America and over 5,000 in the world.

Write to:

American Youth Hostels
1017 K Street, NW
Washington, D.C. 20001

- Many European villages have private homes which offer a spare bedroom for lodging very inexpensively. Ask around when you arrive in the village.

- Use a home exchange service. Listings are from all over the world. Fees for listing your home range from $25 to $75. Write home exchange services listed below for more information:

Worldwide Home Exchange Club
806 Brantford Avenue
Silver Spring, Maryland 20904

International Home
Exchange Service
P. O. Box 3975
San Francisco, California 94119

Trading Homes International
P. O. Box 787
Hermosa Beach, California 90254

Vacation Exchange Club
P. O. Box 650
Key West, Florida 33041

Intervac Home Exchange
P. O. Box 590504
San Francisco, California 94159

Green Accommodations

Hotels which are going green by offering recycling to guests, saving on water usage, or eliminating the use of non-biodegradable food containers are: Hyatt Regency, Boston Park Plaza in Massachusetts, Marriott, Inter-Continental, Canadian Pacific Hotels.

Look for the *Ecotel* designation which is given to those accommodations which have passed on-site audits for environmental compliance. For more information, contact them at Ecotel, Hospitality Valuation Services, 372 Willis Avenue, Mineola, NY 11501. (516) 248-8828.

One thing *you* can do is to ask not to have linens and towels changed daily.

Do not buy or use disposable cameras. They are unnecessary waste.

A Cheap, Natural Relaxing Bath

Fill tub with warm water. Toss in 5 - 10 chamomile tea bags. Let steep for 5 minutes.

Savvy Cosmetic Cents

Cosmetics can be very expensive. For many of us, we cannot do without them. Below are some tips to reduce costs:

- For men, use witch hazel as an after-shave lotion.
- Mix eye shadow colors instead of buying new colors.
- The last bit of water-based foundation can be salvaged by rinsing out the jar with a little water. Cotton swabs can also be used to scrape the insides of the foundation jars.
- Use cosmetics conservatively.
- Buy at discount stores.
- Use cotton swabs as eye make-up applicators instead of buying applicators separately.
- The last bit of lipstick in the lipstick tube applicators can be used instead of thrown away by using a lip brush to reach the lipstick below the rim.
- Always ask for free samples when you can.
- Use baking soda as an underarm deodorant. Mix with water to make a light paste, and then apply to underarms.
- Use apple cider vinegar as a hair rinse. This rinse adds shine as well as balances hair pH.
- Using a knife or scissors, cut open plastic shampoo and hair rinse bottles and scrape out the remaining with a spatula. Or simply rinse out with water.
- Use baby powder as a face powder.

Sale Days

Each month certain items are on sale by manufacturers and retail stores. If you buy these items during these specific times, you can save a bundle.

January - Appliances, Bicycles, China, Cosmetics, Glassware, Handbags, Luggage, Radios, Stereos, Televisions, White sales.
February - Air conditioners, Dryers, Hosiery, Men's clothing, Silverware, Washers.
March - Coats, Glassware, Humidifiers, Infant clothing, Spring fashion sales, Washers and Dryers, White Sales (Sheets, pillow cases, comforters, etc.) Winter sporting goods.
April - Clothing clearances, Clothes Dryers, Mother's Day gifts, Ranges.
May - Baby products, Blankets, Bridal gowns, Dishwashers, Furniture, Lingerie, Luggage, Memorial Day sales, Microwave ovens, Refrigerators, Sportswear, Tablecloths, Televisions, Towels.
June - Bathing suits, Freezers, Father's Day Gifts.

July - Bathing suits, Handbags, Sound systems, Toiletries.
August - Air conditioners, Automobiles, Bedding, Camping equipment, Curtains, Fans, Furniture, Summer sports equipment, Tires, Towels.
September - Automobiles, Children's clothing, Summer clothes.
October - Bicycles, Fishing equipment.
November - Men's and boys' suits.
December - Blankets, Dishwashers, Holiday clearances, Microwave ovens, Shoes, Televisions.

Free Plants

Avocado
Fill a jar with water. Place two toothpicks in each side of an avocado stone and let it rest in the mouth of a jar with the bottom of the stone touching the water. Place it in an area of low light and keep the water level always touching the bottom of the stone. In a few weeks the stone will develop roots. Plant the stone halfway down the top of the soil. Let the plant dry out before watering.

Date
Date palms are beautiful plants. To force the date stone to germinate, place it in water in a dark warm place. After germination, place the stone in potting soil.

Lemon
Plant a few lemon seeds in potting soil. Place in a warm dark area until germination. Transplant each plant in individual pots when the seedlings are 3 - 4 inches high.

Peach
Slightly crack the stone with a nutcracker and plant in soil. Keep the pot in a warm dark spot. After the seedling appears, bring into the light.

Pineapple
Cut the top off of a pineapple, about one inch down from the bottom of the leaves. Cut out the fruit to the hard center. Let this dry for two to three days. Remove the bottom leaves and plant in potting mix. Place the pot in a light and warm spot. Soon it will develop roots.

Pennysavers

Moneysaving tips are available in a brochure provided by the Consumer Information Center. Send 50¢, your name and address, and request *66 Ways to Save Money* to: Consumer Information Center, Pueblo, CO 81009.

- Keep children occupied on long car trips with games, so their attention will not be focused on where to stop to eat. Bring food packed from home.
- Buy discontinued items. Sometimes you can pay up to half as much for a discontinued item compared to new stock items. Be sure the seller or manufacturer will provide parts, if you may need them in the future.
- Freeze leftover gravy in ice cube trays. Pop out and store in a freezer container. When you need some flavoring for a sauce or soup, add a few cubes.

- If you find you have run out of eggs in the middle of making a cake, use mayonnaise. Use 1 heaping tablespoon of mayonnaise per egg called for in the recipe. (Do not worry about tasting mayonnaise in your cake, however the cake may be more moist.)

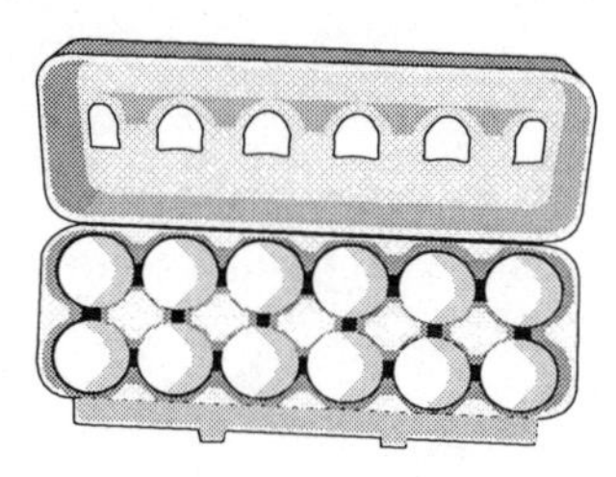

- Think twice about purchasing Service Contracts especially on new items. The likelihood of something happening in one to two years on a new product is very small.
- Buy only generic prescription medicines.
- Cut fabric softener sheets in half.
- Use your address labels on catalogs as return address labels on letters.
- Collect small bath soap pieces and sew into cheesecloth or other fabric to use as drawer sachets.
- Keep cheese fresh longer. Wrap in cheesecloth soaked in vinegar and wrung out. This does not affect the taste of the cheese.
- Rubber gloves will last longer if you stuff the finger ends with cotton. This protects them from the holes poked by fingernails.
- Use old jars to store cotton balls or cotton swabs in the bathroom.

- Prepare meals from scratch instead of buying pre-packaged foods.

- Make your own chicken baking mixture.

2 cups flour
2 cups ground crackers
2 Tbs. salt
1 tsp. onion powder
1 tsp. garlic powder
1 tsp. dry mustard
1 Tbs. paprika
1 Tbs. sugar
1 Tbs. vegetable oil

Mix all ingredients together and store in an airtight container in the refrigerator. The mix will last up to a year or more if it is not contaminated with other food.

- Have the engine rebuilt in your car instead of buying a new car.
- Use a few tablespoons of water instead of oil or butter to sauté vegetables.
- Pick your own produce from vegetable fields or fruit orchards.
- When ordering pizza for home delivery, order a cheese pizza. While waiting for the pizza to arrive, sauté or microwave ground beef and your favorite vegetable toppings, such as green peppers, onions and mushrooms.
- Vacuum carpets often to reduce wear and tear of dirt on fibers.
- Many airlines offer bereavement fares. Ask the airline about your situation.
- Use topstitching thread instead of floss for flossing teeth.
- If you are a heavy coffee or tea drinker, try brewing a lot and storing it in a thermos.

- Use skim milk or powdered milk instead of milk.

Freeze ripe tomatoes off of the vine. Drop the ripe tomatoes in boiling water for a few seconds, then remove and place in a bowl of ice water to release the peel. Dice tomatoes and keep in a container in the freezer. These tomatoes will make an excellent tomato sauce or addition to recipes.

BellSouth Telecommunications recycles old phone books to make their billing envelopes. In 1993, they recycled approximately 8000 tons of phone books and saved about $300,000 on envelopes.

- In the winter when dry skin problems abound, avoid using soap in the shower. Instead, use warm water and a washcloth.
- Dilute your shampoo with equal parts water.
- Sometimes grocery stores will give extra meat fat out just for the asking. Give to the birds.
- Free carpet samples can be used to carpet small closets or as car mats.
- Ask for free calendars from banks or libraries.
- Use powdered milk instead of coffee creamer.
- Call your phone company to report misdialed calls to receive credit.

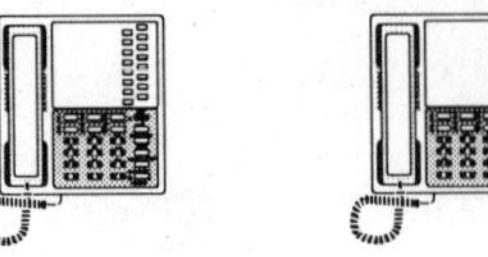

- Always check meats for fat. You will get more for your money if you buy leaner cuts of meat.
- When at the checkout counter, always watch the cash register for mistakes.

- Purchase tinted glasses instead of prescription sunglasses.
- Subscribe to *Consumer Reports* to inform you of what products perform best at a lower price.
- When planning outings to restaurants, try to go when restaurants are offering *All-U-Can-Eat Brunches.*
- Cable television will provide you with entertainment at a fraction of the cost of going to the movies.
- Have your air conditioner checked every few years to ensure it is operating efficiently.
- Use onion mesh bags for hanging suet out for the birds.
- When baking, substitute sugar and water for corn syrup. For 1/2 cup of corn syrup use 3/4 cups sugar and 1/4 cup water.
- Always ask for an estimate from your mechanic before repairs are done.
- Add a few drops of lemon juice to milk when the recipe calls for sour cream.
- If you serve raw vegetables with dip at a party and have leftovers, make a stir fry dish the next day.
- Buy home office furniture at government surplus auctions.

- Use a musical greeting card battery as a replacement for the battery in your wristwatch.
- Buy bird seed in bulk.

- Remove wax from candleholders by placing them in the freezer for a few hours. When you remove them, the wax flakes off easily.
- When the feet in footed pajamas wear out, cut the feet off. Sew on a good pair of socks in their place.
- If you have wood floors, use boiled tea to clean them. Let the tea cool after boiling, then use to clean floors.
- Extend your sour cream by mixing it well with fresh milk. Store in the refrigerator for a day or two and you will have more sour cream.
- Instead of going out for dinner, go out for a cappuccino and dessert.

- Use computers at your local library or at print shops instead of buying one.
- Build your own deck.
- Throw out burned toast or old bread and cookies to the birds.

1095

CHEAP CHECKS ________ 19 _____

PAY TO THE ORDER OF __________

____

FOR __________

Order checks from discount printers instead of from banks. Banks charge $8 to $15, however some discount printing companies charge as little as $4. *Current* is a greeting card company offering high quality cheap checks. Call them at 1-800-426-0822 or call *Checks in the Mail* at 1-800-733-4443.

__________ $ [ ]

__________ DOLLARS

____

Stretching Home Office Dollars

Advertising

Stretch dollars by doing your own advertising. Offer discounts to clients who refer others to you. Circulate posters and fliers around the community about your business. Post your business card on local bulletin boards. Join clubs and groups and share your business skills.

Buy in Bulk

Whether you use paper products, photographic film or food for your business, try finding suppliers who will sell to you in bulk. Office supply stores will usually quote a good price on bulk items. And if you are a frequent customer, you may even get a better price. On a year's budget, you could possibly save up to 50% compared to not buying in bulk.

Phone Service

If you don't need an extra phone line for your business, do not get one. Use your home phone. When you are not available, use an answering machine instead of an answering service. Tape a message which sounds courteous and professional.

Services

Use other small or home businesses for needed services, such as accounting and word processing. They usually provide good service for half the cost of bigger organizations.

Green Office Supplies

Eberhard Faber's EcoWriter pencils are made of graphite and 100% post-consumer newsprint and cardboard.

The John Rossi Company sells journals, address books and desk planners with recycled tire covers, pencils made from recycled newspaper and other eco-products. For more information, contact them at 180 S. Highland Avenue, Ossining, NY 10562, (914) 941-1752.

Chapter 9

Strictly Earthsavers

There is a pleasure in the pathless woods,
There is a rapture on the lonely shore,
There is society, where none intrudes,
By the deep Sea, and music in its roar:
I love not Man the less, but Nature more.

- Lord Byron, *Childe Harold's Pilgrimage, IV*

Earthsaving

Many of us are avid recyclers and devoted environment lovers in our homes, but how can we expand our environmentalism to outside the home. To begin with, many of us are involved in other groups, such as work, community, school, church and clubs. We can affect change in these groups by making suggestions, organizing for change, and creating new programs. Below are a few ideas of how to get other people involved in saving the earth in their homes, in schools and in communities:

Community

Push for a Recycling Program in Your Community

Gather neighbors together to form a committee which circulates a petition for a curbside recycling program. Send the petition to your city council. In the meantime, set up a day in your neighborhood for neighbors to bring their recyclables, such as newspapers, glass and aluminum cans to a nearby central location, preferably on their street. Make a fanfare out of it. Serve snacks and refreshments. Make it as easy for them as possible. Then take turns gathering all the recyclables and taking them to the recycling center.

Educate Your Community on Methods of Organic Gardening

Circulate fliers or newsletters offering information on alternatives to pesticides for lawn and garden care. Most people are simply not aware there are safe and effective alternatives. Hold weekly or monthly meetings to discuss these alternatives with some organic gardening experts. At these meetings display some natural pest deterrents, such as garlic or cayenne pepper as well as some natural commercial products.

Celebrate Earth Day Every Year

Earth Day falls in April. Plan to hold community picnics, clean up days or parties to celebrate. Have educational materials available for people to take home with them. Provide games for children which teach them about the environment, such as environmental quizzes. Ask for donations for environmental community problems.

Have a Neighborhood or Community Yard Sale

A yard sale is a great way to recycle items. Organize the yard sale in the late spring, summer, early fall or on Earth Day. Circulate fliers, advertise in the local paper and set up tables for community members. Charge a small rental fee for the tables to cover costs. Serve snacks and refreshments for yard sale participants and visitors. Invite some neighborhood amateur musicians to play.

Begin a Neighborhood or Community Paint Exchange

Many people have partly filled cans of paint which they are tempted to throw away. To prevent unnecessary waste, start a paint exchange in your neighborhood or community. Find a central location where paints can be stored. Each person is allowed to trade cans of paint for other cans of paint. If a person does not find the color they want, give out vouchers to be used in the future. The Vermont Agency of Natural Resources has published a helpful booklet, *Paint Drop & Swap: Guidelines for Conducting Events.* For more information, contact Vermont Solid Waste Division, 103 S. Main Street, West Building, Waterbury, VT 05676.

School

Voice Your Environmental Concerns at PTA Meetings

Suggest the school be checked for radon, asbestos, water contamination and energy waste.

Set up a committee which looks into instituting school environmental programs or creating an environmental curriculum.

Many nonprofit organizations have developed environmental education materials. See Resources in the back of this book to contact them.

Set out boxes by copiers for employees to place the one-sided copies they do not use. When drafts of reports are needed, these pages could be re-used.

Talk to Your School About Saving Energy
Suggest that low-flow showerheads be installed in showers. Ask for more fluorescent lighting in school buildings. Insist that the school look into the installment of storm windows and increased insulation to lower energy usage during the winter. If the school is planning to renovate or rebuild, ask about using solar energy. Energy conservation in schools is addressed in a booklet, *The Economy of Energy Conservation in Educational Facilities.* The booklet is available from the Academy for Educational Development, 1255 23rd Street, NW, Washington, D.C. 20037.

Office

Suggest the Purchasing of Recycled Products Where Possible
Many office supply companies offer recycled paper in the form of envelopes, bond paper, tissue and paper towels. Some companies offer clocks, desk mats and other products which are recycled from tires or factory waste.

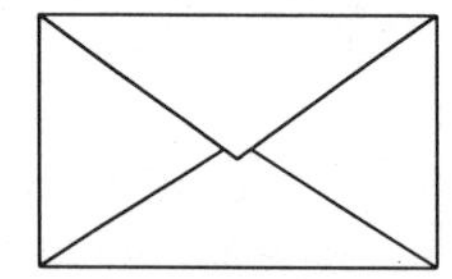

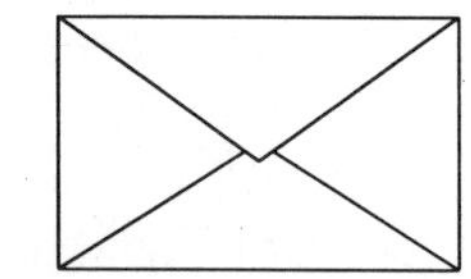

Establish a Waste Evaluation Committee
Start a committee in your department or for the entire company which evaluates whether items should be destroyed or discarded. For instance, the committee would evaluate whether some old typewriters could be used elsewhere in the company, sold or donated to charitable organizations instead of thrown away.

Create More Awareness of Energy Usage
Some companies have their computer systems running 24 hours a day. Have the company look into the installation of systems which automatically fall into a low-power-consumption state when not in use. Often referred to as *green pc's,* these systems wear the *Energy Star Seal*—which is an indicator they comply with the energy-saving guidelines established by the EPA in the Energy Star program.

A source for information on industry energy reduction is the Department of Energy's, *Conservation Plan.* Write U.S. Department of Energy, Office of Conservation, Washington, D.C. 20585.

EARTHSAVING WAYS TO INCREASE YOUR SAVINGS BY $1000 OR MORE THIS YEAR

- Rent large tools and other items instead of buying. ($20 - $200)
- Use old aluminum foil one more time. Scrunch it up and use it to scrub pots and pans. ($5 - $20)
- Make your own ground spices, such as ground pepper, cinnamon, cumin and coriander with a spice mill. ($10 - $25)
- Restore furniture instead of throwing it out. ($100 - $500)
- Barter for goods and services. ($20 - $250)
- Quit smoking! This habit not only drains you of money, but hurts the environment and your health. ($50 - $500)
- Get more out of your broccoli. Use the stems too. Cut off ends, peel stalk, and cut in small strips. Cook with broccoli flowerets. ($10 - $50)
- When cooking pasta, bring water to a boil, add pasta and turn off heat. Let sit for 20 minutes, stirring once or twice. ($5 - $50)
- Never keep heavy items in the trunk or back of the car. It requires more gas to drive the car when it is weighed down by heavy items. ($10 - $50)
- Instead of purchasing over the counter products, buy an aloe vera plant and use it for burns, cuts and scrapes. ($10 -$25)
- Wash your car after a rain storm. Just wipe off with a cloth. ($20 - $100
- Use cornstarch instead of body powder. ($10 - $25)
- Maintain the standard tire inflation on your car. When car tires are underinflated, the miles per gallon is decreased. ($10 - $100)
- Use baking soda to deodorize shoes. ($5 - $20)
- Try hand-washing items instead of dry-cleaning. ($25 - $200)
- Create sachets by putting 1 tsp. potpourri in unused shoulder pads. ($10 - $25)
- Use white vinegar to soak dentures. ($25 - $100)
- Use sweater shavers to make your clothes look like new. ($20 - $200)
- Shine tarnished brass by polishing with half of a lemon dipped in salt. ($5 - $30)
- Use toothpaste to clean crayons off of walls. ($5 - $20)*

*Figures are estimated for a family of four. Your savings may be more or less.

What's New with Food

Over the years the food we eat has been studied and altered to make it grow disease-free and appear blemish-free. Animals for meat products have been confined for a more tender and fatty meat. Pesticides, fungicides and waxes are applied to growing food to protect it from insect and disease. Antibiotics and hormones are given to cows to produce milk at the least possible cost. To think this has no effect on us or our environment is naive. Even though we can sympathize with farmers and ranchers, we must look at the broader picture. Other farmers and ranchers are able to farm or ranch organically. And the demand for their food is growing.

Here's the Beef

Organic ranchers are producing beef and poultry products which are free of antibiotics, pesticides, fertilizers and hormones. One company, Coleman Natural Meats, a major producer of natural beef, claims to give no hormones or antibiotics to cattle. Hundreds of ranchers are seeking admittance into Coleman's natural beef network because of the high popularity. For more information on organic meat, contact the International Alliance for Sustainable Agriculture, 1701 University Ave., SE, Minneapolis, MN 55414, (612)331-1099.

Fish Out of Water

Fish and shellfish are caught wild from lakes, rivers or the ocean, however some come from polluted waters and can carry dangerous chemicals. Buy fish at a familiar market where the source is well known.

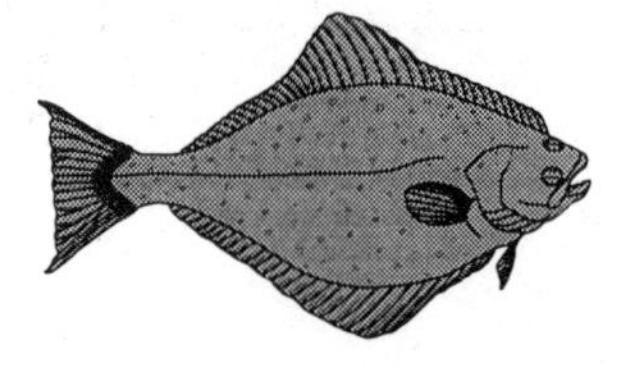

Fish which are caught in deep ocean waters are usually free of contaminants. Some of these are salmon, tuna, red snapper, flounder, cod, halibut and sardines. Freshwater fish are the most vulnerable to contamination from industrial toxins. Since these toxins are stored in fat, choose fish with low fat levels, such as bass, rainbow trout and white or yellow perch.

The Organic Way

Organically grown fruits and vegetables are raised without chemical fertilizers or pesticides. Check your area for grocery stores with organic produce sections; organic produce stalls in farmer's markets; or pick-your-own organic farms. Fresh Fields, a store which boasts all products in the store contain no additives or preservatives has become very popular.

Organically-grown vegetables can be obtained from your own backyard. Starting a small organic garden does not require much and will provide you with fresh organic vegetables at little cost.

If you are not near an organic market or farm and cannot grow your own, order organically grown food through the mail. The

Organic Wholesalers Directory and Yearbook lists over 300 names and addresses of growers and distributors all over the country and can be ordered from CAN, P. O. Box 464, Davis, CA 95617, (916) 756-8518. Or you can ask for a short list of organic food mail order suppliers by writing, Americans for Safe Food, 1501 16th Street, NW, Washington, D.C. 20036.

Water in the Bottle
Bottled water has become extremely popular because of the desire for purity and the convenience of traveling with pure water. Plastic and glass beverage bottles make up the second largest source of solid waste, however glass can be recycled indefinitely, but plastic bottles can be recycled only once. The best thing to do is invest in a water filter and reuse an old bottle for traveling with filtered water.

The Juice Wrap
Juice packages and cartons are made from chlorine-bleached paper coated with wax or plastic to create a moisture barrier. And they cannot be recycled. The small juice packages, popular because they can fit in lunch pails, are a pure waste since they can only end up in the landfill.

Make your own juice. Buy a small juicer and make your own fresh orange or grapefruit juice. Or invest in a large juicer and make everything from carrot juice to tomato juice.

Earthsavers

Save paper by buying loose tea. Teabags are made with formaldehyde and other chemicals. Besides, loose tea usually tastes better.

Use sodium percarbonate instead of bleach when washing. Sodium percarbonate is made from salt, limestone and hydrogen peroxide and works only in high water temperatures.

Musk oil for perfumes and scents is obtained by killing the male musk deer. Buy only synthetic musk oil. Check with your perfume manufacturer to find out what they use.

Greening the Way

Paper made from kenaf, a native plant of Africa, has been researched by the USDA to be the most viable source for paper products. For more information on kenaf: KP Products Inc., P. O. Box 4795, Albuquerque, NM 87196-4795.

More and more companies are changing and creating products to be kinder to the environment. Greening the way, so to speak. Manufacturers are listening to the cries of people to produce products which have less packaging, require less energy to use and produce, and use recycled waste. By our support we can foster the growth of these companies and use our dollars to send a message to other companies about our preferences. Preferences which clearly show our commitment to a cleaner and better environment.

Beauty and Bath Products

Instead of throwing out your entire toothbrush once the bristles wear out, throw out only the head with this ***toothbrush with replaceable heads***. For more information, contact **Seventh Generation,** Colchester, VT 05446-1672, (800) 456-1177. Or **National Wildlife Federation,** 1400 16th Street, NW, Washington, D.C. 20036-2266, (800) 432-6564.

Sappo Hill Soapworks, a company in Oregon, produces ***all-vegetable oil glycerine soaps***. **Sappo Hill Soapworks**, 654 Tolman Creek Road, Ashland, OR 97520, (800) 863-7627.

Use a non-toxic chemical-free deodorant. These ***crystal deodorants*** are available in most health food stores.

GeremyRose Fresh Cosmetics are made using essential oils and herbal extracts. For more information, contact **New Moon Extracts,** P. O. Box 1947, Brattleboro, VT 05301. (800) 543-7279.

Stonybrook Botanicals provide ***shampoos, conditioners and lotions which are not tested on animals and contain no animal ingredients***. For more information, contact **Rainbow,** 170 Wilbur Place, Bohemia, New York, 11716, (800) 722-9595.

Use natural gums and herbal extracts to hold your hair in place. ***Natural Mist Herbal Hairspray*** comes in a non-aerosol pump bottle. For more information, contact **Mountain Ark Trading Co.,** P. O. Box 3170, Fayetteville, AR 72702, (800) 643-8909.

The Whole Earth Catalog has a multitude of earthly products. Check your local library or bookstore.

For a list of products not tested on animals, write:

Beauty Without Cruelty
175 W. 12th Street, #16G
New York, NY 10011-8275

Business Products

Recycled printed circuit boards make great ***clipboards and binders***. For more information, contact **Seventh Generation,** Colchester, VT 05446-1672, (800) 456-1177.

Scissors, rulers and other business supplies are made from recycled materials. For more information, contact **EcoTech Recycled Products**, (800) 780-5353.

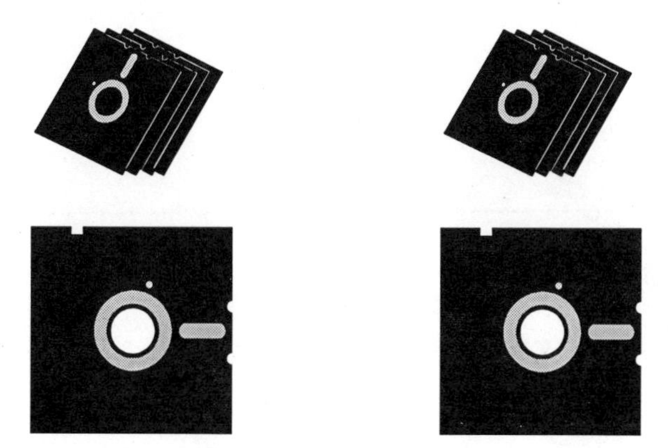

Cut expenses with ***recycled disks***. For more information, contact **GreenDisk** at (800) 305-3475.

Buy ***recycled and remanufactured laser printer toner cartridges***. For more information, contact **RTI Corp.** at (800) 886-6731.

Earth News

Spraying Kills the Good, the Bad and the Ugly!

Using pesticides on the lawn or garden not only kills and deters the bad insects, but also the good insects which could maintain the health of your lawn or garden. Instead, use natural occurring controls. To control grubs (the larvae of Japanese beetles) use milky spore disease. The true name is *Bacillus papillae*, an effective biological control. Bacillus thuringiensis is a bacteria which naturally controls mosquitoes and cabbage worms.

Other controls are mild pesticides (usually from nature) which are not damaging to the environment. Pyrethrum, derived from chrysanthemum plants, is a very effective control against most insects, however the beneficial insects will also be affected. Try to spray only when there is an infestation, and then only once. Insecticidal soap is very effective against aphids, mealybugs and red spider mites.

Ringer Natural Lawn and Garden Products develop and sell organic lawn and garden products. For their catalog, call 1-800-654-1047.

Children

Solar Construction Kit allows children to build solar-powered windmills, helicopters or airplanes. For more information, contact **Real Goods**, 966 Mazzoni Street, Ukiah, CA 95482, (800) 762-7325.

Whether you need art supplies for your children or for your own artwork, there are ***non-toxic art supplies*** available. These art supplies are non-toxic and are mostly made from natural materials. **Karen's Non-Toxic Products,** 1839 Dr. Jack Road, Conowingo, MD 21918, (800) 527-3674. Or **Eco Design, Co.,** 1365 Rufina Circle, Santa Fe, NM 87501, (800) 621-2591.

Clothes

Children's clothes made from organically grown cotton using natural dyes are made in the U.S.A. For more information, contact **Earthlings,** P. O. Box 1055, Ojai, California 93024.

Patagonia's entire ***cotton line has gone organic***. For more information, contact **Patagonia**, 259 W. Santa Clara Street, Ventura, CA 93001, (805) 643-8616.

Clothes made by handicapped people living in India and by Mayan people are available through **Co-op America**, # 600,

1612 K Street, NW, Washington, D.C. 20006. (800) 584-7336.

Organically grown hats and bags from hemp. For more information, contact **Homegrown Hats,** P. O. Box 1083, Redway, CA 95560, (707) 923-5273.

Finally someone has found a use for old worn-out clothing. ***Clothing donated to charities is shredded into fiber and respun into wool-acrylic blend knitting yarn.*** For more information, contact **Seventh Generation,** 49 Hercules Drive, Colchester, VT 05446-1672, (800) 456-1177.

Food Products

Gift Baskets with organic food products make a great gift for the health-conscious individual. For more information, contact **Walnut Acres,** Penns Creek, PA 17862. (800) 433-3998.

Maple Almond Granola made from organic ingredients. For more information, contact **Walnut Acres,** Penns Creek, PA 17862. (800) 433-3998.

Maple granules is a good sugar substitute. Made from organic maple syrup, it can be reconstituted into maple syrup by adding water. For more information, contact **Walnut Acres,** Penns Creek, PA 17862, (800) 433-3998.

Organic unsulphured raisins, naturally dried and unbleached, are a tasty and healthy snack. For more information, contact **Walnut Acres,** Penns Creek, PA 17862, (800) 433-3998.

Organic Coffee made from organic Arabica beans with decaffeinated available, too. For more information, contact **Walnut Acres,** Penns Creek, PA 17862, (800) 433-3998.

They're Bitin' Again

Mosquitoes are one of the most hated insects, and therefore various pesticides exist to spray the backyard or the skin to kill and deter mosquitoes. Electric bug zappers are popular, but unfortunately do not work as effectively as people think. Studies have shown that less than 5% of all the bugs killed by the zappers are mosquitoes.

The best control for mosquitoes is to find and empty sources of water where mosquitoes breed, such as buckets or puddles.

Dolphins Saved

There has been much interest in buying tuna which is *dolphin-safe.* But do you know if your pet food is dolphin-safe? Some pet food companies have adopted a dolphin-safe policy. They are: 9 Lives, Figaro and Safeway Brand.

For Women Only

Tampax Original Regular Tampons are made from cotton. The paper applicator has a food-grade oil coating. All is biodegradable. For more information, contact **Tambrands** at (800) 523-0014.

o.b. tampons are made from cotton and rayon with no applicators. For more information, contact **Personal Products** at (800) 526-3967.

Sanitary pads which are unbleached and made with all-cotton cover sheets are available through **Today's Choice,** Consumer Center, 500 American Avenue, King of Prussia, PA 19406. (800) 262-0042.

Cloth sanitary napkins are made from unbleached cotton and can be reused. For more information, contact **Womankind** at (707) 522-8662 or **Sisterly Works,** RR 3, Box 107, Port Lavaca, TX 77079.

Menstrual cups are made of rubber and are designed to be worn as tampons to catch and hold fluid. For more information, contact **The Keeper,** P. O. Box 22023, Cincinnati, OH 45220.

Sea-sponges are all-natural and can be used as sanitary napkins. Sea-sponges can be found in natural food stores. For more information, contact **InterNatural** at (800) 446-4903.

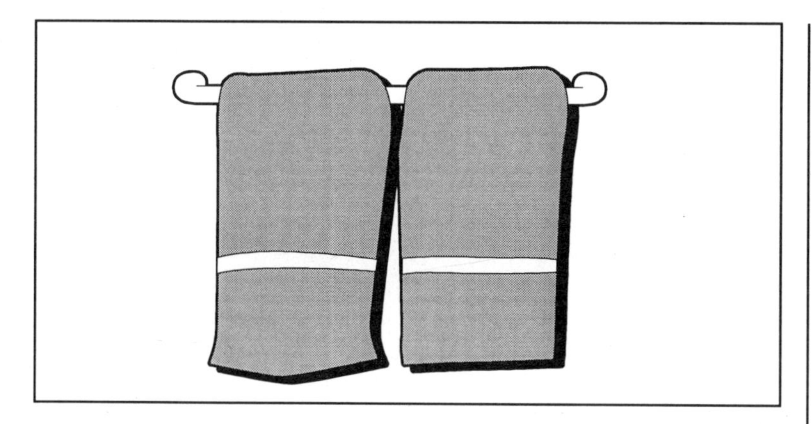

Home

Bag dryers make recycling plastic bags easy. For more information, contact **Seventh Generation,** Colchester, VT 05446-1672, (800) 456-1177.

Organic cotton pajamas, pillows, comforters and mattress pads are undyed and unbleached. The bedding materials are stuffed with untreated wool. **The Natural Bedroom,** P. O. Box 3071, Santa Rosa, CA 95402, (800) 365-6563.

Cleaning products are formulated especially ***for the chemically sensitive***. For more information, contact **Eco Clean**, 3511, N. 70 Street, Scottsdale, AZ 85251, (602) 947-5286.

Natural house paints are created from plant oils and minerals and are easily biodegradable. Varieties include oil- and water-based paints as well as varnishes. Information on these paints can be obtained from the following companies:

Auro-Sinan Co., P. O. Box 857, Davis, CA 95617-0857, (916) 753-3104

Earth Studio, 6761 Sebastopol Avenue, Suite 8, Sebastopol, CA 95472, (707) 823-2569.

Eco Design Co., The Natural Choice, 1365 Rufina Circle, Santa Fe, NM 87501, (800) 621-2591.

If you are unable to grow or find ***organically grown produce***, some companies will send them to you. For more information, contact **Trillium Health Products,** 655 S. Orcas Street, Seattle, WA 98108, (800) 800-8455.

Lemon Oil Furniture Treatment protects and polishes all wood surfaces and is biodegradable and extracted from brazil nuts and lemon rinds. For more information, contact **Home Health,** 1160 Millers Lane, Virginia Beach, VA 23451, (800) 284-9123.

Greening of Television

Our calls have been heard! Several green cable channels have appeared to provide us with greening 24 hours a day. Call your cable operator to ask if they are available or will be available soon. The Ecology Channel, 9171 Victoria Drive, Ellicott City, MD 21042, (410) 750-7291; Earth Television Network, 25-35 23rd Street, Astoria, NY 11102, (718) 721-9536; Planet Central, 1415 Third Street Promenade, Suite 301, Santa Monica, CA 90401, (310) 458-4588.

If you are concerned about pesticides on your vegetables and fruits, use a ***fruit and vegetable wash*** which is non-toxic and biodegradable. This product will remove pesticides, herbicides, fungicides, waxes and oils from the surface of produce. For more information, contact **Mountain Ark Trading Co.,** P. O. Box 3170, Fayetteville, AR 72702, (800) 643-8909.

Scent-free air freshener uses all-natural volcanic material to absorb odors. For more information, contact **National Wildlife Federation,** 1400 16th Street, NW, Washington, D.C. 20036-2266, (800) 432-6564.

Seegreen natural air freshener removes odors from your home with a pump spray and a water-based formula. Available in cinnamon, rose, floral or citrus scents. For more information, contact **Seventh Generation,** Colchester, VT 05446-1672, (800) 456-1177

A biodegradable alternative to disposable paper or plastic plates, ***Botanica LeafWare*** is made from persimmon, orchid and khakhro trees in the tropical forests of India. For more information, contact **Eco Design, Inc.,** 1365 Rufina Circle, Santa Fe, NM 87505, (800) 621-2591.

Thick cotton ***towels*** are free of toxic bleaches and dyes. For more information, contact **Seventh Generation,** Colchester, VT 05446-1672, (800) 456-1177.

The ***BugSweep Vacuum*** disposes of bugs in your home without chemicals. For more information, contact **The Safety Zone,** Hanover, Pennsylvania, (800) 999-3030.

Candleholders recycled from steel are available through **Earth Care Paper,** Ukiah, California 95482-8507, (800) 347-0070.

Composting toilets save the environment and money. No energy is used or water is used. For more information, contact **Sun-Mar Corp.,** 900 Hertel Avenue, Buffalo, New York 14216, (800) 461-2461.

Enviracaire Air Cleaner cleans indoor air of pollutants, tobacco smoke, pollen and bacteria. For more information, contact **The Safety Zone,** Hanover, Pennsylvania, (800) 999-3030.

Environmental Checks print checks with environmental messages and pictures on each check. All checks are printed on recycled paper. For more information, contact **The Styles Company,** 15916 Manufacture Lane, Huntington Beach, California 92649, (800) 356-0353.

Floatron Pool Purifier uses solar panels to convert sunlight into energy releasing ions in the water which kill algae and other microorganisms. For more information, contact **The Safety Zone,** Hanover, Pennsylvania, (800) 999-3030.

Laundry Disks put in your washing machine wash your clothes through electrically charged ceramic chips which break the water molecules up into ions. The disks last for 500 washes. For more information, contact **Real Goods,** 966 Mazzoni Street, Ukiah, California 95482-3471, (800) 762-7325.

Mug rugs are hand-made colorful woven pieces of cloth by New Mexican artisans for resting hot coffee mugs. For more information, contact **Co-op America,** #600, 1612 K Street, NW, Washington, D.C. 20006, (800) 584-7336.

Small compact shopping bags which fit in your purse or pocket are hard to find. ***Pakasac*** unfolds from a small pouch. For more information, contact **Compak Products**, P. O. Box 994, Hermosa Beach, California 90254, (800) 530-3725.

Lead crystal companies find it difficult to dispose of manufacturing leftovers because of lead content. A German company has found a way of making ***crystal glasses without lead***. For more information contact, **Schott-Zwiesel Glass, Inc.,** 3 Odell Plaza, Yonkers, New York 10701, (914) 969-6100.

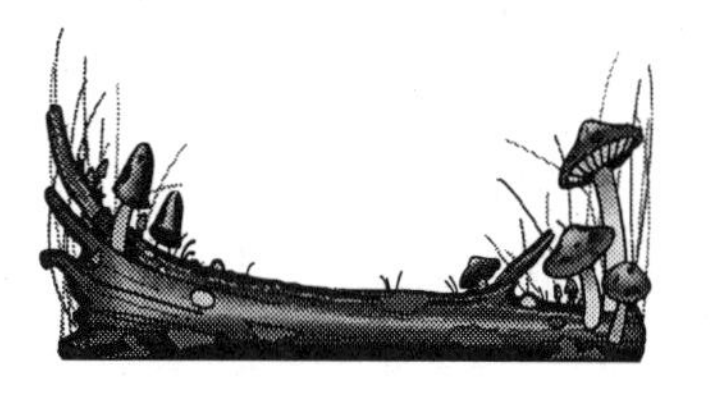

Scotch-Brite Never Rust Wool Soap Pads use a phosphorous-free detergent. For more information contact, **3M** at (800) 362-3456.

Toilet Water-saving Sinks conserve water by using water with which you have washed your hands for the next flush. For more information, contact **Real Goods,** 966 Mazzoni Street, Ukiah, California 95482-3471, (800) 762-7325.

100% biodegradable ***vegetable-based soaps*** are available in oatmeal, seaweed and others. For information contact, **Reviva** at (800) 257-7774.

Miscellaneous

The ***Adopt-a-Whale program*** provides an adoption certificate and a fact sheet. For more information, contact **Tarlton Institute,** Suite 103, 50 Francisco Street, San Francisco, CA 94133, (415) 623-5370.

Plant a tree or more in endangered forests in Costa Rica. For more information, contact **Basic Foundation,** P. O. Box 47012, Saint Petersburg, FL 33743, (813) 526-9562.

Stationery made from government surplus maps is available through **Seventh Generation,** Colchester, VT 05446-1672, (800) 456-1177.

A ***nontoxic antifreeze*** is available which is phosphate-free and performs as well as conventional antifreeze. Many people have lost their cats because they were attracted to the taste, and then died. This antifreeze claims to be perfectly safe for animals and children. *SIERRA* is made by **Safe Brands Corp**. Ask your local auto product store about this antifreeze. **Chief Auto Parts, Inc.,** also has non-toxic antifreeze available. Write or call them at 15303 Dallas Pkwy., Suite 800, Dallas, TX 75248, (214) 404-1114.

Three-Way Recycler allows you to easily sort glass, cans, plastic and paper products. For more information, contact **Solutions,** P. O. Box 6878, Portland, OR 97228, (800) 342-9988.

Use the sun to tell time with a sundial on your wrist. The ***sundial wristwatch*** is available through **Real Goods,** 966 Mazzoni Street, Ukiah, CA 95482, (800) 762-7325.

Zoo Doo is a fertilizer made from manure collected from zoos around the country. The fertilizer has been sanitized. For more information, contact **Plow and Hearth**, (800) 627-1712.

Long distance telephone calls can be green if you sign up with a green company. **Working Assets Long Distance** is a long distance telephone company which gives 1% of all profits to nonprofit groups working for peace, human rights, economic justice and the environment. Each month free long distance time is given to call political and business leaders concerning current issues. For more information, contact **Working Assets** at (800) 788-8588.

Earth Tones, an environmental telephone company, was founded by a coalition of environmental organizations. All profits go to environmental organizations and causes. For more information, contact **Earth Tones** at (800) EARTH-56.

Pets

Pet Powder made of herbs is a way to treat fleas and ticks on your cat or dog naturally without chemicals. For more information contact, **Cat Claws, Inc.,** 1004 W. Broadway, P.O. Box 1001, Morrilton, Arkansas, (800) 783-0977.

Clean animal cages, walls and floors effectively with ***Organic Orange,*** a 100% natural cleaner. **Master Animal Care,** Division of Humboldt Industries, Inc., Lake Road, P. O. Box 3333, Mountaintop, PA 18707-0330, (800) 346-0749.

Travel

Clean Air Cab Company in Washington, D.C. operates taxis with natural gas. For more information, contact them at (202) 667-7000 or (800) 999-8910.

If you are traveling in New York City, use the ***Green Apple Map*** which shows where many environmental sites, such as community gardens, recycling centers, and *great* trees are located. For more information contact, **Modern World Design,** 157 Ludlow Street, #4, New York, New York 10002, (212) 674-1631.

Cedar cat litter is completely biodegradable, is supposed to last longer, and smells fresh naturally. **Cedarific cat litter** is available through **Solutions,** P. O. Box 6878, Portland, OR 97228, (800) 342-9988.

Publications

Energy Efficient and Environmental Landscaping provides information on energy efficiency inside the home through smart landscaping. For more information, contact **Real Goods,** 966 Mazzoni Street, Ukiah, CA 95482-3471, (800) 762-7325.

Reusable News is a quarterly recycling and waste prevention newsletter published by the EPA. For more information, contact **U.S. EPA**, 401 M Street, SW, Washington, D.C. 20460, (202) 260-7751.

Walking Gently on the Earth is a pamphlet on environmentally sensitive living. For more information, contact **Friends Committee on Unity with Nature,** 7700 Clarks Lane Road, Chelsea, MI 48118.

Backyard Composting: Your Complete Guide to Recycling Yard Clippings is a great source for how to compost all that leftover yard debris. For more information contact, **Harmonious Technologies,** P. O. Box 1865, Ojai, California 93024, (805) 646-8030.

If you are looking for an environmental career, ***Green at Work: Finding a Business Career that Works for the Environment by Susan Cohn*** or ***The Complete Guide to Environmental Careers by Bill Sharp*** are books which will help you. For more information contact, **Island Press,** P. O. Box 7, Covelo, California 95428, (800) 828-1302.

Worms Eat My Garbage is all about worm composting. For more information contact, **Flower Press,** 10332 Shaver Road, Kalamazoo, Michigan 49002, (616) 327-0108.

Animal Update

Animals inhabited this earth centuries before we came along. Every species has adapted to a host of changes throughout that time except for the current threats of habitat destruction, toxic chemicals and slaughtering for horns or tusks. Unfortunately, humans are the perpetrators of these attacks on animals. We think we need more space for cattle ranches and land development. We think all our problems will be solved by tossing some chemicals to clear the way for our future. And we think our pockets will be filled if we nab more than a few rhino horns or ivory tusks. Needless to say, all this is very destructive to animals, the earth and eventually, ourselves.

Humans have the potential for great creativity as we have admired in some of our noted scientists, ecologists and leaders. Can we not find a way to exist without destruction or without quick solutions to problems which actually require well-thought out plans? Possibly, we could find a way to co-exist with animals without destroying the whole habitat, without killing *all* the rhinos, and without using toxic chemicals. We certainly do not want to forsake the joy of sighting a blue bird at our backyard feeder, or of snorkeling by a coral reef with multi-colored fish, or of traveling to Africa to watch elephants herding on the plains.

Below is some information on animals and their fight to remain a part of our ecosystem:

The Bad News

- Dolphins and sea birds are caught and die by the thousands in invisible plastic fishnets.
- Elephants are killed for their ivory tusks, depleting the elephant population. There are only a few hundred thousand where there were over a million.
- The survival of owls is threatened by the massive use of pesticides on farms. Owls aid in the control of rodents.
- Some species of animals which may be endangered include the ocelot, jaguar, macaw, cockatoo, iguana and python.

The Good News

- Sea turtles are often caught in shrimp nets. A new regulation issued by the National Marine Fisheries Service requires shrimpers to use turtle-excluder devices year-round instead of only part of the year.
- The Pennsylvania Federation of Sportsmen's Clubs was responsible for convincing power companies to install fish passages along dams so fish could spawn.
- The National Oceanic and Atmospheric Association (NOAA) runs 12 marine sanctuaries along the shores of the United States to preserve and protect sea wildlife.

More About Animals

The black bear has returned to Texas as a result of a 1986 ban on bear hunting in Mexico. The black bear had been depleted in the 1950's from hunting.

Exotic birds are captured, packed tightly into small enclosures, and not given the food and water they require. As a result, over half of them die before they reach here and many others are ill or maimed. If you must have an exotic bird as a pet, try purchasing one which has been raised in the United States.

Poaching of rhinos for their horns has nearly depleted the black rhino population. Approximately 300 are left in Zimbabwe, an area which has the most black rhinos.

Upon request, the U.S. Fish and Wildlife Service will send a brochure listing all the animals considered endangered. Ask for the *Endangered Species* brochure from The U.S. Fish and Wildlife Service, Publications Unit, Mail Stop 130 Webb, 4401 N. Fairfax Drive, U.S. Department of the Interior, Dept. P, Arlington, VA 22203.

Recycling Hazardous Waste

If you need assistance or additional information concerning hazardous waste, contact the Hazardous Waste Ombudsman at (800) 262-7937.

Some items which we throw away are considered hazardous to the environment and should not be allowed in our landfills. Most people throw them away in the everyday trash because they are not aware they are toxic. Items, such as antifreeze, bullets and car batteries contain chemicals which are dangerous to plants, animals and our ground water. Many recycling centers hold "Hazardous Waste" days a few times a year to collect these types of items. They, then, are placed in hazardous waste facilities. Surprisingly enough, many of these items can be recycled which would prevent us from creating large hazardous waste facilities.

Paint
Leftover paint can be traded with friends, relatives or neighbors. Some charities appreciate donations of paint. If you are still left with latex paint, open the can of paint and leave it outside to evaporate. To speed up the evaporation, pour in some plain, unscented kitty litter. Then toss it in the garbage. Never pour paint on the ground or wash brushes outside. The paint could threaten ground water. Oil-based paints, however, must be taken to a Hazardous Waste facility.

Car Batteries
Car batteries can be recycled through service stations. Some offer discounts on trade-ins. Always make sure the old battery will be recycled when you are having your car battery replaced. If, for some reason, this is impossible, contact your local landfill about hazardous waste disposal.

Nail Polish
When nail polish becomes thick, thin it for reuse with a few drops of nail polish remover. Shake well. Use leftover nail polish to secure buttons on clothes. Dab the threads in the center of the button with clear nail polish. Bright colored nail polish could be used to label plastic containers of food or toys. If you must throw away nail polish, open the bottle and let the contents dry for a few days. As a hard mass, nail polish is harmless in the landfill.

Smoke Detectors
Smoke detectors contain radioactive material. Because landfills or hazardous waste facilities do not accept radioactive materials, the

only option is to return smoke detectors to manufacturers. The good news is newer smoke detectors are not being made from radioactive material.

Bullets
Whether you've thought about it or not, bullets are hazardous waste. You can turn in old or unused bullets to your police station or wait for "Hazardous Waste" day in your community.

Antifreeze
Antifreeze is not only hazardous to our environment, but many pets have been killed because they drank it from a puddle under a car. Make sure your service station recycles old antifreeze.

Televisions
Instead of setting your television out by the curb on trash day, try to find a repair shop who would take it for the parts. Some schools and charities will accept broken televisions for teaching purposes.

Some other items which are considered hazardous waste and should be collected for a hazardous waste facility: Bug sprays, turpentine, furniture polish, moth balls, brake fluid, all garden pesticides and herbicides and lighter fluid. Fortunately, many companies are creating new products which contain non-toxic materials and will be a lot easier for us to use, live with and dispose of.

Keep your local landfill's telephone number handy to ask them about the disposal of questionable items.

Paper or Plastic?

A trip to the supermarket inevitably means a decision when confronted by the cashier. Paper or plastic? Should you choose paper because it is easily biodegradable? But what about all those trees? Should you choose plastic because now everywhere plastic is being recycled?

If you grapple with this decision every time you visit your supermarket, you are not alone. Even the experts have not completely figured this one out.

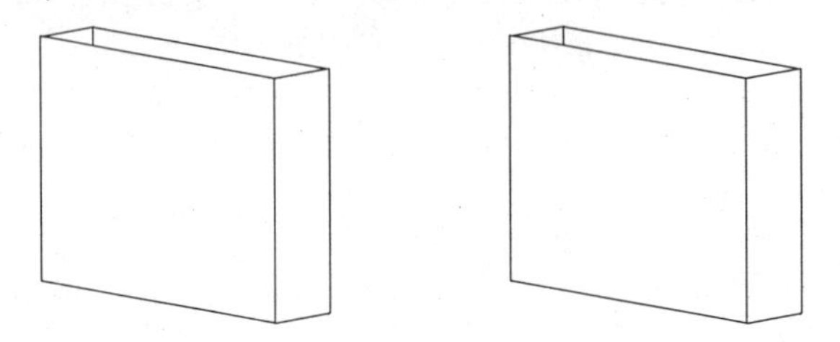

Let's look at the facts! Unfortunately, plastic has not yet been proven to actually biodegrade. The belief is the bags simply break into smaller and smaller pieces but do not actually degrade to a state where nutrients are returned to the soil. However, bags made from LDPE (low-density polyethylene) plastic are easily recycled. Check the bag for the LDPE symbol. Most supermarkets have recycling bins for plastic bags.

Paper bags are biodegradable. In some areas, they are recycled with newspapers. However, paper bags are not made from recycled paper bags. All paper bags are made from scratch, that is, they are made from new trees, new paper.

The important thing to remember is if you do not intend to recycle plastic bags, then choose paper. At least the paper will biodegrade in the landfill.

The best possible choice is a cloth bag which you bring with you whenever you shop at supermarkets, malls or small shops. Cloth bags are re-usable and re-usable and re-usable. You completely rid yourself of the question—paper or plastic?

The hard part is remembering to have them on hand when you go shopping. Below are a few tips:

- Store them in your coat closet. You will see them when you reach for your umbrella or sweater.

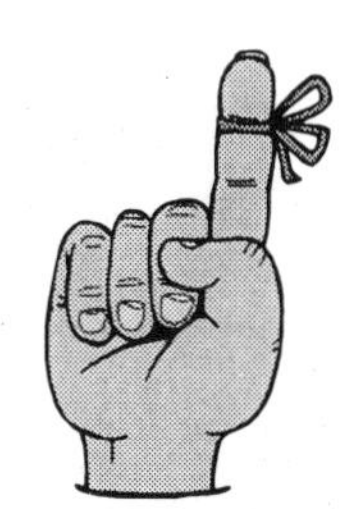

- Keep some in the car. After emptying them of groceries, hang them on the inside of your front door so you do not forget to put them back in the car.
- Fold up a small thin one and put it in your handbag.

Where can you find cloth bags? Cloth bags have become very popular in gift shops, supermarkets and craft stores. You can even make some out of old jeans or curtains.

If you are unable to find any cloth bags, here are a few sources:

Earth Care Paper, Inc., P. O. Box 7070, Madison, WI 53707
Save A Tree, P. O. Box 862, Berkeley, CA 94701
Seventh Generation, 10 Farrell St., Burlington, VT 05403

Now you know what to say when asked, "Paper or plastic?" And you can feel better about your choice knowing the facts.

NOTE: If your area does not have a recycling program call the Plastic Bag Information Clearinghouse at (800) 438-5856 for a location nearest you.

Solar Sense

Make a solar cooker out of cardboard and aluminum foil. For more information, contact Solar Box Cookers International, 1724 11th Street, Sacramento, CA 95814.

At Home with the Sun, a book for children, provides plans for building a Pizza Box Solar Oven as well as many other solar energy activities. Check your local library or bookstore or write Professor Solar Press, RFD #3, Box 627, Putney, VT 05346, (802) 387-2601.

Estimates of only 50 woodland caribou are left in the lower 48 states.

The sun provides an effective and inexpensive energy source for our planet. The energy can be used to heat our homes, heat our water, and run every electrical appliance we own. We can use as much of it as we want without exhausting resources. There are two types of solar energy. One, photovoltaic cells, *active* solar collectors, heat liquid or air and store the heat. Two, strategically placed glass or windows heat the home *passively*. A common passive solar energy use is a greenhouse attached to the house. The warm air collected in the greenhouse is circulated throughout the house. Not only does the room function as part of the heating system, but it can be used as a family room or sunroom.

Manufacturers of these solar greenhouses or sunspaces are:

- Sun Room Company - (800) 426-2737
- Andersen Corporation - (800) 426-4261

Lots of energy can be used in our home for heating water. We wash our clothes, our dishes, and ourselves using hot or warm water. Solar water heaters are efficient and maintenance-free. The energy efficiency of a solar water heater makes up for its initial cost by being 40% less than an electric water heater over a 20-year life span.

Manufacturers of solar water heaters are:

- Alternative Energy Engineering, Inc. - (707) 923-2277
- Solar Development, Inc. - (407) 842-8935
- Sierra Solar Systems - (800) 735-6790

If you have outdoor lighting, you can save lots of energy and money through the use of solar-powered outdoor lights.

Manufacturers of lights are:

- Photocomm - (800) 544-6466
- Jade Mountain - (800) 442-1972
- Real Goods - (800) 762-7325

For more information on solar energy, contact the following:

Solar Energy Industries Association, 122 C Street, NW, 4th Floor, Washington, D.C. 20001, (202) 383-2600.

Conservation and Renewable Energy Inquiry and Referral Service, Box 8900, Silver Spring, MD 20907, (800) 523-2929.

American Solar Energy Society, 2400 Central Avenue, Boulder, CO 80301, (303) 443-3130.

Diaper Rationale

The debate between using disposable diapers and cloth diapers has been going on for a long time and will probably continue for an even longer time. There are advantages and disadvantages to using both. Disposable diapers take up an enormous amount of landfill space, 18 billion are thrown away each year, and do not decompose for hundreds of years. These diapers are usually soiled when thrown away and can contaminate groundwater, even though the manufacturers suggest rinsing the diapers out before discarding. Some disposable diapers are degradable, but because of compacted garbage in landfills, water and oxygen, two requirements for biodegradability, do not reach below the surface of the landfill floor. Therefore, biodegradability does not aid in the quest for the perfect diaper, and the problem of possible groundwater contamination still exists.

Disposable diapers require lots of energy and resources to produce. Tons of wood pulp are used each year. Furthermore, the toxic dioxins, by-products from bleaching wood pulp, have been found in superabsorbent disposable diapers. Not only is this toxic to the environment, but also to the child wearing the diaper.

One advantage to using disposable diapers is, of course, the convenience. Use them and throw them away. This sounded great in 1961 when disposable diapers were introduced, but today we have environmental problems of brimming landfills and toxic chemicals in our air and water. No longer can we afford to use up and contaminate the earth. We have grandchildren and great grandchildren to whom to pass the goods of the earth.

The cloth diaper is not the purest of alternatives. Cloth diapers require an enormous amount of energy to produce, and then consume lots of energy and water for reuse. On the other hand, cloth diapers can be used between 100 and 200 times and cost less to use. Comparably, for one child, disposable diapers cost $50 a month to use, a diaper service costs $30 a month to use, and cloth diapers cost $10 a month to use.

The question whether to use disposable or cloth diapers must come down to personal and environmental considerations. Cloth diapers are by far the best choice when considering biodegradability, reuse and non-toxic choices. Cloth diapers are made from cotton and probably feel best next to your child's skin. The philosophy of reuse definitely supports cloth diapers. They can be reused as diapers and rags.

If you feel you do not have time to wash and disinfect cloth diapers, consider a diaper service instead of disposables. If you know you cannot completely stop using disposables, but you want to do something—use cloth diapers at home and biodegradable disposables when you are away from home. At the very least, this will help reduce the amount of trash going into our landfills.

If you live in an area where landfills have abundant room, but water is not as abundant —use biodegradable disposables. Even though we are aware that most things do not degrade in landfills, it probably is best to choose a biodegradable brand. And always wash out the diaper before throwing it away to prevent groundwater contamination.

Ecotraveling

With the peaked interest in the environment, ecotraveling has become a major industry. People are interested in visiting rainforests, trekking mountain areas, and seeing the plains of wildlife. Many feel they may never have the chance again when considering the bleakest fate of the earth, however with so much interest in this new industry, these ecosystems may be safe from harm. If people will pay money to visit these areas, countries will do all they can to preserve them.

Most touring companies are very careful not to disturb the natural environment of these areas by refusing to use motor transportation, by educating visitors on the regional environmental issues, and by limiting the amount of visits into some areas. And they usually staff their tours with very knowledgeable and committed people. Some companies donate part of their proceeds to conservation groups.

Some ecotraveling experiences include working with a scientist or conservationist. This *working* vacation requires volunteers to aid scientists in research or in restoring habitats. Usually sponsoring organizations will provide food and shelter while only a small registration fee is required for the trip or all the volunteers chip in for the entire cost of the expedition. Some of these types of vacations are physically demanding, however the chance to visit remote areas combined with contributing time and effort towards something worthwhile is, for many, enough reward. In addition, most of the organizations who sponsor these trips are non-profit, therefore expenses are tax-deductible.

Before embarking on one of these adventures, be sure to ask lots of questions. Each company offers various tours at various prices. If you are working through a travel agent, they should be able to answer most or all questions. However, if they are not able to, ask to speak directly to one of the tour companies.

- Ask for a brochure from several tour companies and compare destination packages and prices.
- When deciding on a tour company, be sure to ask about their experience in the area you wish to travel.
- Ask about the experience of guides. Are they able to speak the native languages?
- What are the accommodations? Is camping gear required?
- What are the physical and health requirements?
- Do the tours support the environment by contributing part of the profits to environmental or conservation groups?
- What are the requirements to reduce the tour's impact on the environment?
- Are guides knowledgeable about the current environmental issues in the areas visited?

Responsible Ecotraveling

- Maintain a positive and sensitive attitude. Be considerate of others and the environment. Learn the language and customs.
- Read about the history of your destination prior to arriving.
- Observe and appreciate the cultural differences.
- Do not support the killing of endangered species or the destruction of endangered plants by buying products, such as ivory, tortoise shell, coral, bird feathers or furs. Avoid buying any tropical woods, such as mahogany, purpleheart and cristobal.
- Always observe wildlife quietly and cautiously.

- Are local people hired for tours to benefit the host country?
- Keep in mind some ecotraveling can be done in the United States. For instance, Hawaii contains tropical rainforests and volcanoes. Check with tour companies for U.S. eco-tours.

Below are some organizations to write or call for more information on ecotraveling.

Travel Link, Co-op America
14 Arrow Street
Cambridge, MA 02138
(800) 648-2667

Center for Responsible Tourism
P. O. Box 827
San Anselmo, CA 94979
(415) 258-6594

Earth Watch
P. O. Box 403
Watertown, MA 02272
(617) 926-8200

Many environmental groups, such as the Sierra Club, Audubon Society, U. S. Forest Service, Nature Conservancy and other groups sponsor tours. Call them for more information.

Just Go!, an eco-travel magazine: 544 2nd Street, San Francisco, CA 94107, (415) 255-5951.

Tour Companies

Above the Clouds Trekking
P. O. Box 398
Worcester, MA 01602
(800) 233-4499

Forum Travel Internat'l, Inc.
91 Gregory Lane, Suite 21
Pleasant Hill, CA 94523
(510) 671-2900

Geostar Travel, Inc.
1240 Century Court, Suite C
Santa Rosa, CA 95403
(800) 624-6633

International Expeditions, Inc.
One Environs Park
Helena, AL 35080
(800) 633-4734

Mountain Travel-Sobek
6420 Fairmount Avenue
El Cerrito, CA 94530
(800) 227-2384

Overseas Adventure Travel
349 Broadway
Cambridge, MA 02139
(800) 221-0814

Wildland Adventures
3516 N.E. 155th
Seattle, WA 98155
(800) 345-4453

Defining Terms

Learning about saving the earth sometimes involves terms which are not very clearly defined. For instance, we read about DDT and its negative effects on the environment, but what is DDT? What does it actually do? What particular part of the environment does it affect?

DDT, dichloro-diphenoltrichloroethane, is a toxic pesticide which can be stored in body tissues. DDT affects animals and humans. The use of DDT was banned in the United States in 1972, however levels of DDT can still be measured in some areas. Since DDT has a half-life of 15 years, most levels are declining. Most of Europe banned the use of DDT in the 1970's, however other parts of the world, such as Latin America, have increased their use of DDT.

We hear a lot about wetlands. Why? And what makes them so important? Wetlands include marshes, bogs, ponds and swamps. They are important because they provide food and a home or a breeding ground for many species of birds and fish. Wetlands are homes for approximately one-third of the animals on the threatened and endangered species lists. Besides being a haven for animals, wetlands also aid the environment by preventing floods through the storage of water. Wetlands also maintain soil moisture and groundwater supplies. As important as wetlands are to animals and the environment, threats exist because they have traditionally been seen as eyesores. They are often seen as areas which need cleaning up or filling in. Therefore, they are turned into agricultural or construction areas. We need to realize the importance of leaving wetlands alone.

CFCs, chlorofluorocarbons, are chemical compounds of carbon, chlorine and fluorine atoms. CFCs have been shown to be responsible for the destruction of the earth's ozone layer by breaking it apart. The ozone layer is the protective outer atmosphere which buffers ultraviolet radiation. CFCs were manufactured in hair sprays, deodorants and fast-food packaging. Even though a ban has been agreed upon, the ban is not for all CFCs. Some are still in use because a safe alternative has not been found. If we do not foresee the destruction of the current use of CFCs, we could possibly experience global warming and the greenhouse effect in the near future.

Our technology has afforded us with great knowledge to create new products which make our lives easier. Unfortunately in many cases, the chemicals used in those products will eventually destroy animals, the earth or us. Many challenges exist for us to use technology to benefit us, yet not destroy us.

What are PCBs?

PCBs, polychlorinated biphenyls, are a group of synthetic organic chemicals which were found in paints, dyes, hydraulic fluids and fluids in electrical transformers and capacitors. Wide usage of PCBs were allowed to be used in enclosed electrical equipment. Studies showed PCBs damage the skin, liver and can inhibit the reproductive organs. The EPA estimates that all of the U.S. population has a trace of PCBs in their bodies. In spite of the EPA ban in 1979, PCBs can be found in old, faulty electrical equipment. And the EPA has not developed a fail-safe way of destroying PCBs.

Driving Green

Most of us in the United States own at least one car. We use it to travel to and from work, school, shopping, and for traveling. It would be hard to imagine life without our automobiles.

As much as we depend on our cars, they, unfortunately, are a great contributor to air pollution and ozone destruction. Pollutants, such as carbon monoxide, lead, nitrous oxides and hydrocarbons are emitted by cars, trucks and buses. These pollutants interfere with human and animal health as well as the health of trees and other plants on our earth. CFC's (chlorofluorocarbons) released through our exhaust wreak havoc on our ozone layer. As the ozone layer slowly deteriorates, we are more openly exposed to the sun's direct rays which can cause all sorts of health problems for us and the earth.

In our world, it is impossible at this time to suggest we not use our cars at all. However, we can use them less and more wisely.

The first step in using a car more wisely is to provide regular maintenance. Have the oil changed regularly, and have a tune up once or twice a year, depending on how much you use your car. These small measures will ensure your car runs efficiently, and its emissions will be at a controllable level.

Check your tire pressure regularly. Tires which are underinflated will increase fuel use.

Drive at or below the speed limit, and drive carefully. Speeding and stopping quickly reduce fuel efficiency.

Use the car air conditioner as little as possible. The air conditioner, when in use, emits CFC's into the air and reduces fuel efficiency. You may opt to have your car's air conditioning unit modified to accept an alternative refrigerant, HFC-134a, which is a little kinder to the ozone layer because it does not contain chlorine. Newer cars should already be equipped with these systems.

If you are buying a new car, buy a fuel-efficient car. Consider a car which gets 35 or more miles to the gallon. Or consider an electric car. Solectria manufactures electric cars in Massachusetts. Contact them at 27 Jason Street, Arlington, MA 02174, (508) 658-2231.

Use your car less by carpooling to work or riding a bicycle*. Use public transportation instead of driving. If you can, walk to your destination.

Some states are taking measures to decrease the pollution from automobiles by demanding more fuel-efficient cars be produced. California has declared that at least two percent of new cars on its roads be emission-free by 1998.

*For more information on bicycle commuting, send SASE to League of American Bicyclists, 190 W. Ostend St., Suite 120, Baltimore, MD 21230-3755, (410) 539-3399.

Resources

Electric Auto Association, 2710 St. Giles Lane, Mountain View, CA 94020, (800) 537-2882.

Green Car Journal, 1334-D North Benson Ave., Upland, CA 91786. (909) 985-9700.

Northeast Sustainable Energy Association, 23 Ames Street, Greenfield, MA 01301, (413) 774-6051.

U.S. CALSTART's CITI electric car will be on the market in 1997 for a price of around $10,000.

Several cities around the country have been using *soydiesel*, a fuel which pollutes less and is made from a renewable resource, soybeans. For more information, contact the National Biodiesel Board, 1907 Williams Street, P. O. Box 104898, Jefferson City, MO 65110-4898, (314) 634-3893.

A 15-minute video, "Automobile Care for the Environment," spells out what individuals can do to reduce a car's impact on the environment. Check with your library or local video store or call Environmental Hazards Management Institute at (603) 868-1496.

Easy Recycling Tips

Recycling is easy if you have been doing it for a while. Plastic, metal, paper, glass and cardboard sorting is simple once it becomes a habit. Most of us devise our own methods of making sorting and recycling easier. We place all the newspapers in a chair until the pile gets high, then we take them out to be recycled. Or we throw all the soda cans in a box until the box gets full.

Some of you may have developed some excellent systems and some of you may be looking for some new and efficient ideas. Look at the ideas below and decide if some of them can be incorporated into your system to make recycling easier.

Newspapers
Find a cardboard box approximately one foot high and the size of a newspaper. Lay two pieces of string at the bottom of the box crosswise ensuring they are approximately four to six inches above the top of the box for tying around the newspapers. Let the ends of the string hang out and over the sides of the box. Place the box in a convenient spot for gathering old newspapers. When the box is full, tie the pieces of string around the newspapers. Newspapers are ready to recycle.

Sorting
Under the sink in your kitchen, keep a small bucket or plastic container to gather recyclables, such as plastic, metal and glass. When the bucket or plastic container is full, take it to the garage, shed or basement to put into the sorting bins. Set up three large plastic containers to sort the plastic, metal and glass. If you find it difficult to transport these to the curb or the recycling center, use containers with wheels.

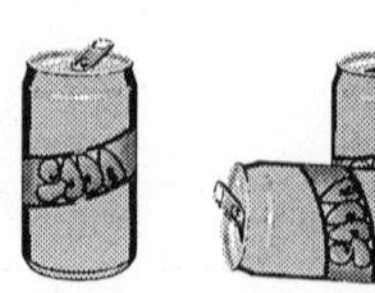

Cans
Invest in a can crusher to make storing them easier. Rinse them out before crushing and storing them, otherwise they may attract unwanted insects.

Recycling Tidbits

- Newspapers are the easiest kind of paper to recycle because they contain no chemicals or fillers.
- In the United States, we use close to 200 pounds of plastic in a year.
- Approximately 3 percent of all trash is disposable diapers.
- Most pet food bags are not recyclable because they are lined with plastic.
- Sweden completely phased out toothpaste boxes.
- Over six billion non-refillable and refillable pens are thrown away each year in the United States.
- Minnesota saves hundreds of thousands of dollars a year through the recycling of tires to produce items, such as garbage containers and doormats.
- Save paper and pay your bills through automatic bank account withdrawal.

Plastics
Check on the bottom of all plastics for a number to identify it as recyclable. Your recycling center should be able to tell you which kinds of plastics they will accept.

#1 = PET (polyethylene terephthalate)
#2 = HDPE (high density polyethylene)
#3 = PVC (polyvinyl chloride)
#4 = LDPE (low-density polyethylene)
#5 = PP (polypropylene)
#6 = PS (polystyrene)

If you are uncertain about what those numbers on the bottom of plastics mean, call the Society of the Plastics Industry, Inc. hotline at 1-800-2-HELP-90. They will also send free information packets on recycling.

Food Scraps
Keep a bowl by the sink for onion skins, banana peels and apple cores. Empty outside in the compost pile every day. Line the bowl with aluminum foil. Decaying food will stain your bowl.

For a no-mess kitchen compost pile, try biodegradable **Food Cycler** bags which are lined with cellulose to prevent leaks and can be tossed in the compost pile as is. Check at your local environmental store or contact the Bio-dynamic Farming and Gardening Association, P. O. Box 550, Kimberton, PA 19442, (800) 516-7797.

Building Materials
If you have leftover building materials, ask your neighbors if they need any of those items. If not, call your local newspaper. Some newspapers will advertise free giveaways in the classified section at no charge. Another option would be to call someone who accepts building materials. Look in the Yellow Pages under "Scrap Dealers."

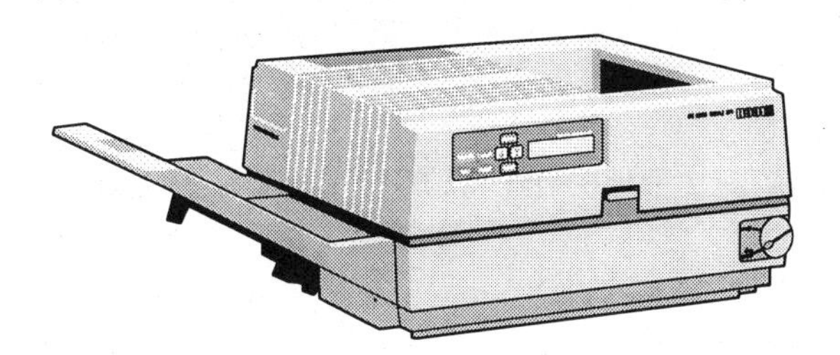

Printer Cartridges
Laser printer cartridges are recyclable. Call local computer dealers for names of cartridge recycling companies. Or contact the American Cartridge Recycling Association at (305) 539-0701, for a list of recyclers in your area. Some companies include a postage paid mailing label in the printer package for it to be returned for recycling.

"One acre of annually grown hemp may spare up to four acres of forest from the current practice of clear-cutting."

- *Industrial Hemp* published by HEMPTECH, Ojai , California

Unfortunately, a hemp ban is in effect in the United States out of fear of hemp being used as a drug. Although hemp cultivated as a fiber and marijuana cultivated as a drug are different varieties, the hemp ban remains.

Besides being grown to make paper, hemp can be used to make clothes, cosmetics and textiles. And a new industry can evolve creating new jobs.

For more information on hemp and hemp products, write to HEMPTECH, P. O. Box 820, Ojai, CA 93024-0820.

Starting a Recycling Business

Recycling has become a big and growing industry. More and more companies and people are recycling. More and more recycling companies are popping up to take advantage of the demand.

If you want a business of your own, you can start small with a recycling pick-up business. This type of business is only profitable when there is no county recycling program in place. You would pick up the recyclables from individual homes to be delivered to companies or recycling centers. Charge the client from whom you are picking up the recyclables or the company who needs particular recyclables.

Your first step is to see if there are companies in your area in need of particular recyclables. Then check to see if you can find a supply, such as individuals who may not want to make the trip to the recycling center.

This type of business could start with very little funds and be profitable immediately if you have a good marketing plan.

Another type of business would be to have a yard or warehouse where recyclables could be stored on a short term basis. You would be a delivery point for recyclables, such as tires or building materials. You would also pick up recyclables from construction sites or other places where recyclables would be found. Companies could pick up recyclables from your place of business or you could deliver them. The key would be to develop a sizable base of recyclable sources and clients.

Yet another type of business would be to propose a recycling program to your local government. You and your company would pick up the recyclables.

Whatever business you begin, be sure to do your research well. It is important to try to be as sure as possible about the potentialities of the business. Talk to people in the community. Ask them if they would be interested in such a service. Would they pay for it? How much? Talk to companies. Ask them if they need such a service? How much would they be willing to pay? Once you are convinced your service could be valuable and profitable, then begin.

Teenagers can start their own recycling business to add a few dollars to their pockets each week. Talk to your neighbors about what you can do for them for a few dollars. Could you collect their recyclables and deliver them to the recycling center once a week? Crush their cans? Flatten their cardboard boxes? Sort?

Once you have built a client base in your neighborhood, branch out to other neighborhoods. Hire some of your friends. This could be a great summer job. And would look good on that college application or resume.

Recycling Jobs

If you desire an environmental career, check with your local government and recycling programs. Some positions require a college degree in fields, such as environmental studies. Go to your local library and find lists of companies which recycle. Some companies may be recycling companies or have a recycling department. Write a letter to these companies telling them of your interest and ask for a list of available positions in recycling.

Check your library or bookstore for *Earth Work: Resource Guide to Nationwide Green Jobs* edited by Joan Moody and Richard Wizansky; HarperCollins San Francisco.

The Alliance for a Global Community has information about *green jobs*, jobs that aid families all over the world to support themselves without endangering the environment. Contact them at 1717 Massachusetts Avenue, NW, Suite 801, Washington, D.C. 20036, (202) 667-8227.

The Complete Guide to Environmental Careers is available through the Environmental Careers Organization, Inc., a national , nonprofit organization, which supports the development of environmental careers. They offer counseling, publications and workshops. Contact them at 286 Congress Street, 3rd Floor, Boston, MA 02210-1038, (617) 426-4375.

The Dollar Power

Even though we are all waking up to the new realities of earth-consciousness, there are still some manufacturers who continue to produce products which do not aid us in the quest for a better environment—free of chemicals and waste. All the blame should not be on the manufacturers, however, since these products are bought by consumers. Therefore, the best way to send messages to manufacturers is through your dollar power. Don't spend your money on items which are harmful to the environment.

The Styrofoam Message
Styrofoam is made of styrene which is made from benzene. CFC's are used to create the foamy texture. Studies have shown benzene to cause cancer, and CFC's wreak havoc on our ozone layer.

The best way to send a message to manufacturers of Styrofoam is to avoid it completely. Bring your own cup to work. If you stop by the fast food restaurant in the morning for that cup of coffee, bring your own cup. Most places will fill it up without a problem.

Many restaurants use Styrofoam containers for take-outs, although just as many have gotten the message and use other containers. Avoid restaurants which use Styrofoam and let them know why you are avoiding them.

Coffee Filter Etiquette
Bleached coffee filters contain TCDD, a toxic dioxin produced as a result of bleaching wood. The Environmental Protection Agency considers TCDD a carcinogen. Additionally, paper coffee filters can only be used once, therefore producing more garbage for the landfill.

With these concerns in mind, many companies have metal or cloth filters on the market. Unbleached filters are also available, however they still contribute to landfill overfill.

Moths Away
Mothballs are very toxic. With chemicals, such as p-dichlorobenzene and napthalene, they pollute the air, irritate our lungs and eyes, and are hazardous to children who may swallow them.

Luckily, there are alternatives. Cedar is a natural moth repellent. Store clothes in cedar chests or place cedar blocks in closets and storage containers. Other natural moth repellents are herbs, such as pennyroyal and lavender. To dispose of existing mothballs, set them out for hazardous waste collection. Do not throw them in with the regular trash.

By supporting those companies which are attempting to preserve and protect the environment, we will increase the availability of products and decrease the costs.

Tropical Wood

The use of tropical woods, such as teak, mahogany and rosewood contributes to the deforestation of tropical rainforests. Rainforests harbor plant life which could help us in curing and controlling many illnesses and diseases. And rainforests produce much of the world's oxygen.

When buying wood or wood products, ask about the wood. What type is it? Where did it come from? Decide whether your purchase could be something other than wood.

Fresh Air

Air fresheners make the air in our homes smell good, but they pollute the air with hydrocarbons. The good news is there are natural alternatives available. Some companies use citrus oils or herbs to create the nice scents and use pump spray bottles which are better on the environment. Examples are Air Therapy and Citrus II.

Green Laundry

Our ancestors stood in the rivers and used sticks and stones to wash their clothes. Today we are inundated with laundry detergent choices, many claiming to be the best stain-fighters or brighteners or whiteners. The problem is most detergents contain phosphates which do not pollute our waters, but do, however, create imbalances in waste water by providing nutrients for algae growth. Unfortunately, as the algae dies, it consumes great amounts of oxygen in the water which is needed by fish to survive. Although many detergents on the market today are low-phosphate or no-phosphate, they still contain unnecessary scents which do pollute our water.

Unscented low-phosphate or no-phosphate detergents are a good environmental choice, however they are more dangerous if swallowed. Better choices for laundry chores include washing soda or borax. Washing soda is made from sodium carbonate and works well to clean clothes. Borax is made from boron, a mineral mined from deep in the earth, and is a disinfectant.

Chlorine bleach contains a toxic chemical, sodium hypochlorite. When mixed with other household cleaners, chlorine bleach can even cause death if the fumes are inhaled. Powdered bleaches are better because they usually do not contain reactive compounds. Some bleaches use hydrogen peroxide as the active ingredient instead of chlorine. Although these are not as effective as chlorine bleaches in removing stains or whitening, they could be alternated from one week to the next with chlorine bleach.

Fabric softeners which are poured in the rinse cycle are biodegradable unless they are scented. An even better choice would be to use white vinegar in the rinse cycle.

Environmental product stores and health food stores sometimes contain laundry products which are friendly to the environment. If you are unable to find these products, ***Real Goods***, a mail order company, carries *Oasis* laundry detergent which is concentrated and biodegradable. ***Real Goods*** claims one gallon of this product can do two washes a week for up to a year.

Seventh Generation carries a concentrated laundry detergent and a chlorine-free bleach which are biodegradable, contain no optical brighteners, and are not tested on animals.

For tips and environmental information, call American PIE (Public Information on the Environment) at (800) 320-2743.

Real Goods
966 Mazzoni Street
Ukiah, CA 95482-3471
(800) 762-7325

Seventh Generation
49 Hercules Drive
Colchester, VT 05446-1672
(800) 456-1177

If you find the *green* products you are using are not as effective as the more toxic counterparts, try pre-soaking your laundry from 30 minutes to an hour. White sheets or clothes which have lost their whiteness, can be spread out on the grass on a warm sunny day straight from the washer. The sun will react to the wet clothes and bleach them naturally.

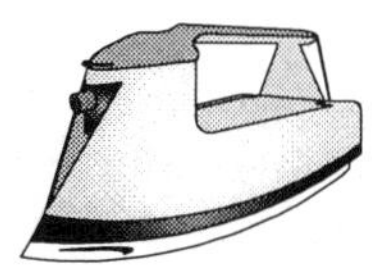

If you starch your clothes often, avoid using commercial starches which usually contain formaldehyde and pentachlorophenol as well as other chemicals. Make your own starch by mixing one tablespoon of cornstarch in two cups of cold water in a pump spray bottle.

Avoid dry-cleaning your clothes. Chemicals, such as perchloroethylene and trichloroethylene contain hydrocarbons which wreak havoc with the ozone layer. Some of these chemicals

are known carcinogens and irritants. Many delicate fabrics can be hand washed in a mild detergent. For instance, silk can be soaked for a few minutes in cold water and a mild dishwashing soap. Rinse with cold water and wrap in a towel. Let air dry on a hanger. Wool can be washed in lukewarm water in your bathtub with a mild dishwashing soap. If stains exist, use a soft bristle brush to gently remove the stain. Rinse thoroughly in lukewarm water. Dry on a towel as you would a sweater. If you do not wish to do this yourself, search out a commercial laundry which will hand wash delicate items.

CAUTION: Pesticides

Children are especially vulnerable to pesticides because their bodies are still in the developmental stages. Furthermore, studies have shown they eat more vegetables and fruits, and drink more juices than do adults. Therefore, their exposure rate and risk are greater.

When we hear the word, *pesticides*, we readily think of the acres and acres of farmland where farmers use pesticides to protect their crops from insect damage. However, pesticides are also used in parks; on areas surrounding businesses, apartment buildings and condos; and private homes.

Most pesticides can disturb the natural balance of the ecosystem by killing insect pests as well as beneficial insects. Beneficial insects include bees which pollinate plants and other insects, such as ladybugs which prey on insect pests.

Groundwater is easily polluted by pesticides, such as malathion and 2,4-D. Just a few years ago, the EPA conducted a study in which they found 74 separate pesticides in wells from 38 states across the country.

Wildlife is greatly affected by the use of pesticides through inhalation of pesticide residue and drinking water polluted with the chemicals. Malathion, Diazinon and Rotenone harm birds and fish. Pyrethrum, Sevin and captan harm fish. And many of these chemicals harm bees—therefore preventing pollination of plants.

Besides threatening water supplies, wildlife and the ecosystem, pesticides also threaten human health. Chemicals such as Diazinon and carbaryl (Sevin) can be toxic if they are swallowed, inhaled or absorbed through the skin. Sevin and malathion can cause birth defects. Many pesticides are thought to cause cancer.

Reduce health risks by washing produce thoroughly if they are not organically grown. Use a little dishwashing soap and water. Peel vegetable and fruit skins where possible. Corn, bananas, grapefruit and oranges are usually eaten with relative safety because the skin is not eaten.

Buy organically grown produce if it is available in your area. Look for a label, *Certified Organic,* which ensures the grower followed strict guidelines for growing the crops in a purely organic atmosphere.

Sometimes buying produce from local growers may reduce exposure to pesticides because the produce does not need to be shipped or stored. Ask the grower what pesticides were used, if any.

Another way to reduce the risk of exposure to harmful pesticides is to reduce or eliminate the use of pesticides in your yard and garden. Use natural and non-toxic insecticides, such as Bacillus thuringiensis (BT) which is a naturally occurring bacteria. BT can be used to control beetles, mosquitoes and corn borers.

Purchase natural products which use herbs to repel insects. Or make your own homemade concoctions. (See Chapter 1)

The Written Word

Sometimes more powerful than the spoken word is the written word. The written word can be reread, pondered and create a visual impression in the reader's mind. In essence, it is possible to make more of an impact through the written word.

Writing letters to our legislative representatives, government agencies and manufacturers can be very effective in expressing exactly what we want from them. Congressional staffers consider each letter a representation of opinions from hundreds of constituents. Manufacturers consider a letter to represent the hundreds or thousands of customers who did not write.

When you feel angry or disappointed about our government or a manufacturer's product, write them a letter. When you are pleased or happy about our government or a manufacturer's product, write them a letter. Let them know how you feel! Your written word counts!

When writing letters be sure to include your name and address. Nine times out of ten you will receive a reply.

Always state your reason for writing and be clear as to what your concerns or complaints are.

Avoid writing long letters. You want your letters to be read and understood.

If you have some solutions or suggestions to particular problems, include them in your letter.

Always be polite. If you are polite in making your point, you most likely will earn respect from those you write. Even if you are angry, give them a chance to respond to your complaint.

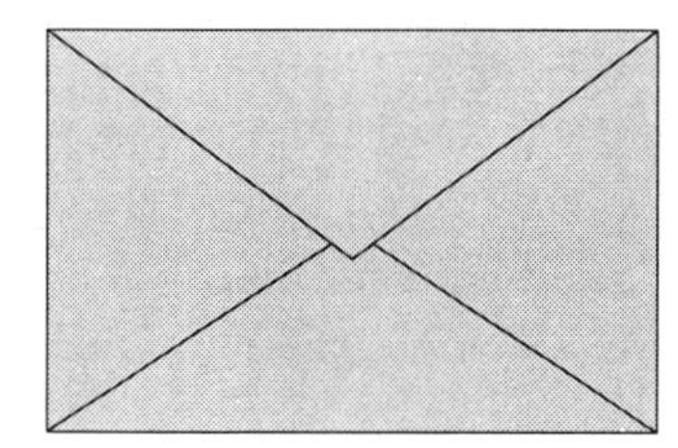

And always offer thanks for positive action. Write a thank you letter if positive action was taken in response to your letter. Next time you have a complaint, they may remember you.

If you wish to write a senator, the address is as follows:

The Honorable (Name)
U. S. Senate
Washington, DC 20510

If you wish to write a House member, the address is as follows:

The Honorable (Name)
U.S. House of Representatives
Washington, D.C. 20515

When you write letters, you are allowing others to hear your concerns which can have a great effect on the future of products and legislation.

If writing is not your thing, you can call the Capitol Switchboard at (202) 225-3121.

Addresses of manufacturers are usually on the product or package. If you are unable to find it, call the 800 number information line, 1-800-555-1212. They can usually give you the number of the manufacturer. You can then call them for their address.

Organizations for the Environment

Many environmental organizations consist of people who work hard and tirelessly to achieve goals which aid in the protection or enhancement of our environment. They educate us on the negative impact we have on the environment as well as what we can do to help the environment. They fund research for solutions to environmental problems, and they seek out policy changes to benefit the environment. For many of us, this is work we wish we could do, but we do not have the time nor the resources.

Many environmental organizations exist to deal with various concerns. Some focus on natural resource protection. Some focus on water pollution. And some others focus on animal protection. These being only a few of the concerns organizations regard as important.

Listed below are only a few environmental organizations and a little information about each:

African Wildlife Foundation works to preserve wildlife and educate people on the value of conservation.

Bat Conservation International is concerned with educating people about the benefits of bat populations on the environment.

Caribbean Conservation Corporation works with the University of Florida to study sea turtles and conserve them.

Clean Water Action is concerned about the cleanliness and safety of water.

Concern, Inc. focuses on educating people on pesticides and water pollution.

Friends of the Sea Otter works to protect the sea otter and its habitats.

National Arbor Day Foundation is concerned with reforestation and tree planting in communities.

National Audubon Society focuses on the conservation and protection of the environment, including native plants and animals.

The Nature Conservancy purchases land in order to preserve ecosystems and threatened habitats.

Rails to Trails Conservancy focuses on converting old railroads to trails.

Rainforest Action Network focuses on protecting rainforests through educating about the benefits of rainforests.

Sierra Club is an old and well-established organization which has a strong reputation for working towards the conservation of the environment.

TreePeople educates individuals and communities on environmental issues, such as how to plant a tree.

United Nations Environment Programme concerns itself with solving international environmental problems.

Worldwatch Institute conducts research on protecting and managing natural resources.

World Wildlife Fund focuses on the protection of wildlife and habitats.

If you are interested in doing more for the environment, contact an organization or two and ask them what you can do to help. Many organizations have a membership fee and send a newsletter to all members to keep them up to date on their activities as well as environmental issues. If an environmental organization is in your area or if they have a branch in your area, ask if you can volunteer some of your time.

For more information on the above organizations, see the Resources section of this book.

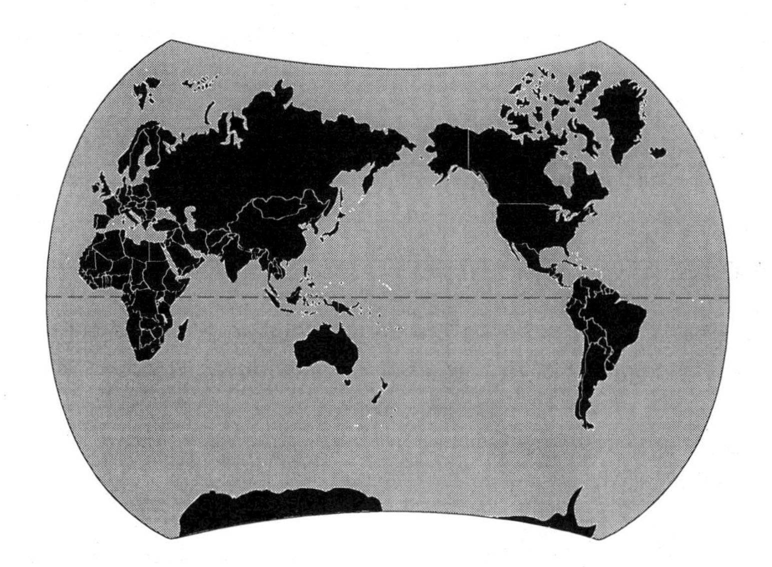

NOTE: See Resources at the back of this book for other organizations of interest.

Mothers & Others

A national nonprofit organization, Mothers & Others focuses on educating individuals and communities on ecological sustainable living, such as healthier and safer food, natural cleaning and other *green* subjects. They publish a newsletter and booklets on living, buying and eating green.

Newsletter - *The Green Guide*

Booklets - 8 Simple Steps to a Green Diet, The Non-Toxic Nursery, The Way We Grow: Good-Sense Solutions for Protecting Our Families from Pesticides

For more information, contact Mothers & Others, 40 West 20th Street, 9th Floor, New York, NY 10011, (212) 242-0010.

Green Money Company List

Aveda Corp.
Bellcomb Technologies, Inc.
Ben & Jerry's Homemade
The Body Shop
Co-op America
Earth Friendly Products, Inc.
Ecoprint
Polaroid Corporation
Real Goods Trading Corp.
Recycled Paper Co.
Tom's of Maine
Walnut Acres

Green Money

Since Earth Day 1990 an increasing number of people have become more environmentally aware, resulting in new companies which serve the environment and existing companies which have changed their operation to be kinder to the environment or have introduced new and more earth-friendly products. Therefore, there is ample opportunity to invest in one or more companies or mutual funds which are environmentally supportive in order to possibly advance their cause as well as your own. Socially responsible investing sends a message to companies and to the world about what concerns you have and what things you deem important. Essentially, you are putting your money where your mouth is.

Together with your investment counselor, choose a few companies and funds which qualify as environmentally responsible. Examine past performance to determine whether they will offer you a good return. Although your desire is to support the environment by supporting companies which are environmentally sound, you, of course, want to establish the return potential of your investment. Create a file for each company, gathering 10K's or 10Q's (SEC disclosure reports), annual reports, company press releases and print media. Study these carefully to learn more about the company's goals, policies and growth.

Use environmental publications and government agency reports to determine the environmental impact or contribution of each company or fund. Particularly examine the impact each company has had on environmental issues, such as waste disposal, ozone depletion, air pollution, global warming, toxic waste, energy efficiency, water contamination, acid rain and environmental damage. For instance, does the company produce CFC's or burn fossil fuels? Does the company produce or dump toxic waste? Does the company recycle? If the answer is yes, has the company created programs which will lessen or halt such activity? Check with the Environmental Protection Agency for reports of violations by companies.

Other things to consider are: what environmental organizations does the company support. Has the company has endorsed The CERES Principles (formerly know as The Valdez Principles). If you are an animal lover, you would also want to consider whether the company treats animals ethically or tests on animals. In addition, a company certainly cannot be considered environmentally responsible if its products are overpackaged. Visit a store to check this out for yourself.

The CERES Principles were created in 1989 by the Coalition for Environmentally Responsible Economics (CERES) after the devastating environmental disaster of the Exxon Valdez oil spill. Primarily, they were created to establish monitoring standards for the behavior of corporations toward the environment.

When deciding what companies to support, keep in mind small companies. Small companies with environmental goals will usually have an easier time of maintaining fervor for the realization of those goals compared to larger, more expansive companies which may have lost sight of the goals within the tangle of their growth web. Additionally, in smaller companies your voice will have a louder resonance as a shareholder and board directors will listen more carefully to your thoughts and ideas.

And lastly, do not ignore your banking institutions for your investments. Do your research on banking institutions in your area to determine which have aided environmental causes by creating loans or programs for companies or communities to advance environmental education or action.

Credit unions traditionally serve a social purpose. Check to see if there is one you can join which serves the environment.

Whatever decisions you make, be sure to consult with an investment counselor to collect additional information and to assess all risks.

GREEN MUTUAL FUNDS

Below is a list of mutual funds holding stock in companies which have a good environmental record:

Calvert-Ariel Appreciation Fund - (800) 368-2748
Calvert Social Investment Fund - (800) 368-2748
Dreyfus Third Century Fund - (800) 782-6620
Green Century Balanced Fund - (800) 934-7336
Kemper Environmental Services - (800) 621-5027
Merrill Lynch Eco-Logical Trust - (800) 422-9001
New Alternatives Fund - (516) 466-0808 (Can call collect)
Parnassus Fund - (800) 999-3505
Pax World Fund - (800) 767-1729

For more information on socially responsible investing or a complete list of companies endorsing the CERES principles, contact CERES, 711 Atlantic Avenue, Boston, MA 02111, (617) 451-0927.

A Socially Responsible Financial Planning Guide is available from Co-op America, 1612 K Street, #600, Washington, D.C. 20036, (800) 584-7336.

The CERES Principles*

1. **Protection of the Biosphere.** We will reduce and make continual progress toward eliminating the release of any substance that may cause environmental damage to the air, water or the earth or its inhabitants. We will safeguard all habitats affected by our operations and will protect open spaces and wilderness, while preserving biodiversity.

2. **Sustainable Use of Natural Resources.** We will make sustainable use of renewable natural resources, such as water, soils and forests. We will conserve nonrenewable natural resources through efficient use and careful planning.

3. **Reduction and Disposal of Wastes.** We will reduce and where possible eliminate waste through source reduction and recycling. All waste will be handled and disposed of through safe and responsible methods.

4. **Energy Conservation.** We will conserve energy and improve the energy efficiency of our internal operations and of the goods and services we sell. We will make every effort to use environmentally safe and sustainable energy sources.

5. **Risk Reduction.** We will strive to minimize the environmental, health and safety risks to our employees and the communities in which we operate through safe technologies, facilities and operating procedures, and by being prepared for emergencies.

6. **Safe Products and Services.** We will reduce and where possible eliminate the use, manufacture or sale of products and services that cause environmental damage or health or safety hazards. We will inform our customers of the environmental impacts of our products or services and try to correct unsafe use.

7. **Environmental Restoration.** We will promptly and responsibly correct conditions we have caused that endanger health, safety or the environment. To the extent feasible, we will redress injuries we have caused to persons or damage we have caused to the environment and will restore the environment.

8. **Informing the Public.** We will inform in a timely manner everyone who may be affected by conditions caused by our company that might endanger health, safety or the environment. We will regularly seek advice and counsel through dialogue with persons in communities near our facilities. We will not take any action against employees for reporting dangerous incidents or conditions to management or to appropriate authorities.

9. **Management Commitment.** We will implement these Principles and sustain a process that ensures that the Board of Directors and Chief Executive Officer are fully informed about pertinent environmental issues and are fully responsible for environmental policy. In selecting our Board of Directors, we will consider demonstrated environmental commitment as a factor.

10. **Audits and Reports.** We will conduct an annual self-evaluation of our progress in implementing these Principles. We will support the timely creation of generally accepted environmental audit procedures. We will annually complete the CERES Report, which will be made available to the public.

*Used with permission from CERES.

A FINAL WORD

This book presents numerous ideas on how you can act upon a desire to be more earth-conscious. You can clean your house using natural methods; garden without the use of chemicals; reuse old things by transforming them into new things; reduce your consumption; make your own gifts; support green companies by buying their products or by buying their stock; use cloth diapers; use cloth shopping bags; make more homemade items instead of using energy and resources to purchase them, and so on. If you were able to do all of this, you would be a Super Green Individual! Ideally, I hope we will all be able to reach that ultimate goal. However, it may not be physically possible for all of us to do everything. Although I think it is seriously important to encourage all people to integrate choices into their lives that support the environment, today's hectic schedules frequently do not allow time for such dedication. In other words, do not judge yourself harshly or compare yourself to more dedicated individuals. The point is to do what you can with fervor and commitment. Believe it or not, you will be able to do more in time. If every person made the commitment to make ecologically sustainable choices every day, however minutely, the world would indeed experience a very large change. The key is to begin. Begin with one act. Next week or month, add one more. The next month, another one. Before you know it, these will be a part of your daily habits, and you will be a part of saving the earth.

RESOURCES

Organizations and Government Agencies

Below is a list of organizations and government agencies. Most will send information, such as newsletters or booklets free or with membership.

Acid Rain Foundation, 1410 Varsity Dr., Raleigh, NC 27606. (919) 515-5290.

African Wildlife Foundation, 1717 Massachusetts Ave. NW, Washington, D.C. 20036. (202) 265-8394.

Alliance to Save Energy, 1925 K St. NW, Washington, D.C. 20006. (202) 857-0666.

America the Beautiful Fund, 219 Shoreham Bldg., Washington, D.C. 20005. (202) 638-1649.

American Cave Conservation Association, P. O. Box 409, Horse Cave, KY 42749. (502) 786-1466.

American Council for an Energy-Efficient Economy, 1001 Connecticut Ave. NW, Washington, D.C. 20036. (202) 429-8873.

American Farmland Trust, 1920 N St. NW, Suite 400, Washington, D.C. 20036. (202) 659-5170.

American Forests (Global Releaf), P. O. Box 2000, Washington, D.C. 20013. (800) 873-5323.

American Forest Council, 1250 Connecticut Ave. NW, Suite 320, Washington, D.C. 20036. (202) 463-2455.

American Forestry Association, P. O. Box 2000, Washington, D.C. 20013. (202) 667-3300.

American Holistic Veterinary Medical Association, 2214 Old Emmorton Road, Bel Air, Maryland 21015. (410) 569-0795.

American Forest and Paper Association, 260 Madison Ave., New York, NY 10016. (212) 340-0600.

American Society for Environmental History, 701 Vickers Avenue, Durham, NC 27701. (919) 682-9319.

American Society for the Prevention of Cruelty to Animals, 441 E. 92nd St., New York, NY 10128. (212) 876-7700.

American Solar Energy Society, 2400 Central Avenue, Boulder, CO 80301. (303) 443-3130.

American Wildlands, 40 East Main St., Suite 2, Bozeman, MT 59715. (406) 586-8175.

The American Wind Energy Association, 122 C Street NW, Washington, D.C. 20001. (202) 383-2500.

Americans for the Environment, 1400 16th St. NW, Box 24, Washington, D.C. 20036. (202) 797-6665.

Americans for Safe Food, Center for Science in the Public Interest, 1501 16th St. NW, Washington, D.C. 20036. (202) 332-9110.

Animal Protection Institute of America, 2831 Fruitridge Rd., Sacramento, CA 95820. (916) 731-5521.

Animal Welfare Institute, P. O. Box 3650, Washington, D.C. 20007. (202) 337-2332.

Appalachian Trail Conference, P. O. Box 807, Harpers Ferry, WV 25425. (304) 535-6331.

Atlantic Center for the Environment, 39 S. Main St., Ipswich, MA 01938. (508) 356-0038.

Basic Foundation, P. O. Box 47012, St. Petersburg, FL 33743. (813) 526-9562.

Bat Conservation International, P. O. Box 162603, Austin, TX 78716-2603. (512) 327-9721.

Bureau of Land Management, 1849 C Street NW, Washington, D.C. 20240. (202) 208-5717.

Caribbean Conservation Corporation, P. O. Box 2866, Gainesville, FL 32602. (904) 373-6441.

Center for Marine Conservation, 1725 DeSales St. NW, Washington, D.C. 20036. (202) 429-5609.

Center for Science in the Public Interest, 1501 16th St. NW, Washington, D.C. 20036. (202) 332-9110.

Clean Sites, 1199 N. Fairfax St., Suite 400, Alexandria, VA 22314. (703) 683-8522.

Clean Water Action, 1320 18th Street, NW, Washington, D.C. 20036. (202) 457-1286.

Clean Water Fund, 1320 18th St. NW, 3rd Floor, Washington, D.C. 20036. (202) 457-0336.

Climate Institute, 316 Pennsylvania Ave. SE, Washington, D.C. 20003. (202) 547-0104.

Concern, Inc., 1794 Columbia Road NW, Washington, D.C. 20009. (202) 328-8160.

Conservation and Renewable Energy Information Service, P. O. Box 8900, Silver Spring, MD 20907. (800) 523-2929.

Conservation International, 1015 18th St. NW, Suite 1000, Washington, D.C. 20036. (202) 429-5660.

Co-op America, 1612 K St. NW, Suite 600, Washington, D.C. 20006. (202) 872-5307.

Council on Economic Priorities, 30 Irving Place, New York, NY 10003. (212) 420-1133.

Desert Fishes Council, 407 W. Line St., Bishop, CA 93514. (619) 872-1171.

Earth First!, P. O. Box 1415, Eugene, OR 97440. (503) 741-9191.

Earth Island Institute, 300 Broadway, Suite 28, San Francisco, CA 94133. (415) 788-3666.

EarthSave, P. O. Box 949, Felton, CA 95018. (408) 423-4069.

Electric Power Research Institute (EPRI), P. O. Box 10412, Palo Alto, CA 94303. (415) 855-2000.

Energy Efficiency Renewable Energy Clearing House (EREC), P. O. Box 3048, Merrifield, VA 22116. (800) 363-3732.

Environmental Action Coalition, 625 Broadway, New York, NY 10012. (212) 677-1601.

Environmental Defense Fund, 257 Park Ave. S, New York, NY 10010. (212) 505-2100.

Environmental and Energy Study Institute, 122 C St. NW, Suite 700, Washington, D.C. 20001. (202) 628-1400.

Environmental Hazards Management Institute, EHMI, 10 Newmarket Rd., P. O. Box 932, Durham, NH 03824. (603) 868-1496.

Environmental Law Institute, 1616 P St. NW, Suite 200, Washington, D.C. 20036. (202) 328-5150.

The Forest Trust, P. O. Box 9238, Santa Fe, NM 87504. (505) 983-8992.

Friends of the River, Inc., Fort Mason Center, Bldg. C, San Francisco, CA 94123. (415) 771-0400.

Friends of the Sea Otter, P. O. Box 221220, Carmel, CA 93922. (408) 625-3290.

Fund for Animals, 200 W 57th St., New York, NY 10019. (212) 246-2096.

Grand Canyon Trust, 1400 16th St. NW, Suite 300, Washington, D.C. 20036. (202) 797-5429.

Greater Yellowstone Coalition, P. O. Box 1874, Bozeman, MT 59715. (406) 586-1593.

Greenpeace USA, 1436 U St. NW, Washington, D.C. 20009. (202) 462-1177.

HEMPTECH, P. O. Box 820, Ojai, CA 93024-0820. (805) 646-HEMP.

Human Ecology Action League, P. O. Box 49126, Atlanta, GA 30359. (404) 248-1898.

Humane Society of the United States, 2100 L St. NW, Washington, D.C. 20037. (202) 452-1100.

Infact, 256 Hanover, Boston, MA 02113. (617) 742-4583.

Institute for Local Self-Reliance, 2425 18th St. NW, Washington, D.C. 20009. (202) 232-4108.

International Alliance for Sustainable Agriculture, Newman Center, University of Minnesota, 1701 University Ave. SE, Room 202, Minneapolis, MN 55414. (612) 331-1099.

International Fund for Animal Welfare, P. O. Box 193, Yarmouth Port, MA 02675. (508) 362-4944.

International Oceanographic Foundation, P. O. Box 499900, Miami, FL 33149. (305) 361-4888.

International Primate Protection League, P. O. Box 766, Sumerville, SC 28484. (803) 871-2280.

International Society of American Foresters, 5400 Grosvenor Lane, Bethesda, MD 20814. (301) 897-8720.

International Wildlife Coalition, 70 E. Falmouth Highway, East Falmouth, MA 02563-5954. (508) 548-8328.

Izaak Walton League of America, 707 Conservation Lane, Gaithersburg, MD 20878-2983. (301) 548-0150.

League of American Bicyclists, 190 W. Ostend Street, Suite 120, Baltimore, MD 21230-3755. (410) 539-3399.

League of Conservation Voters, 320 4th St. NE, Washington, D.C. 20002. (202) 785-8683.

League of Women Voters, 1730 M St. NW, Washington, D.C. 20036. (202) 429-1965.

Marine Mammal Stranding Center, P. O. Box 733, Brigantine, NJ 08203. (609) 266-0538.

Monitor Consortium of Conservation and Animal Welfare Organizations, 1506 19th St. NW, Washington, D.C. 20036. (202) 234-6576.

Mothers & Others, 40 W. 20th Street, New York, NY 10011-4211. (212) 242-0010.

National Anti-Vivisection Society, 53 W. Jackson Blvd., Suite 1550, Chicago, IL 60604. (312) 427-6065.

National Arbor Day Foundation, 100 Arbor Avenue, Nebraska City, NE 68410. (402) 474-5655.

National Audubon Society, 700 Broadway, New York, NY 10003. (212) 979-3000.

National Coalition Against the Misuse of Pesticides, 530 7th St. SE, Washington, D.C. 20003. (202) 543-5450.

National Foundation to Protect America's Eagles, P. O. Box 120206, Nashville, TN 37212. (800) 232-4537.

National Geographic Society, 1145 17th St. NW, Washington, D.C. 20036. (202) 857-7000.

National Parks and Conservation Association, Suite 200, 1776 Massachusetts Ave., NW, Washington, D.C. 20036. (202) 223-6722.

National Tree Trust, 1120 G Street, NW, Suite 770, Washington, D.C. 20005. (800) 846-8733.

National Wildlife Federation, 1400 16th St. NW, Washington, D.C. 20036. (202) 797-6800.

Natural Resources Defense Council, 40 W. 20th St., New York, NY 10011. (212) 727-2700.

The Nature Conservancy, 1815 N. Lynn Street, Arlington, VA 22209. (703) 841-5300.

North American Butterfly Association, 909 Birch Street, Baraboo, WI 53913.

North American Bluebird Society, P. O. Box 6295, Silver Spring, MD 20906. (301) 384-2798.

North American Lake Management Society, P. O. Box 217, Merrifield, VA 22116. (202) 466-8550.

Pacific Whale Foundation, 101 N. Kihei Road, Suite 21, Kihei, Maui, HI 96753. (808) 879-8811.

People for the Ethical Treatment of Animals, P. O. Box 42516, Washington, D.C. 20015. (301) 770-7444.

The Peregrine Fund, 5666 W. Flying Hawk Lane, Boise, ID 83709. (208) 362-3716.

Pesticide Action Network, P. O. Box 610, San Francisco, CA 94101. (415) 541-9140.

Pure Food Campaign, 860 Highway 61, Little Marais, MN 55614. (218) 226-4155.

Rachel Carson Council, 8940 Jones Mill Rd., Chevy Chase, MD 20815. (301) 652-1877.

Rails to Trails Conservancy, 1400 16th Street, #300, Washington, D.C. 20036. (202) 797-5400.

Rainforest Action Network, Suite 700, 450 Sansome Street, San Francisco, CA 94111. (415) 398-4404.

Rainforest Alliance, 65 Bleecker St., New York, NY 10012. (212) 677-1900.

Raptor Education Foundation, 21901 E. Hampden Ave., Aurora, CO 80013. (303) 680-8500.

Raptor Research Foundation, Carpenter Nature Center, 12805 St. Croix Trail, Hastings, MN 55033. (612) 437-4359.

Renew America, 1001 Connecticut Ave. NW, Suite 719, Washington, D.C. 20036. (202) 232-2252.

Resources for the Future, 1616 P St. NW, Washington, D.C. 20036. (202) 328-5000.

Rocky Mountain Institute, 1739 Snowmass Creek Rd., Old Snowmass, CO 81654. (303) 927-3128.

Save the Redwoods League, 114 Sansome St., Room 605, San Francisco, CA 94104-3814. (415) 362-2352.

Sierra Club, 730 Polk Street, San Francisco, CA 94109. (415) 776-2211.

Society for Animal Protective Legislation, P. O. Box 3719, Washington, D.C. 20007. (202) 337-2334.

The Society of Plastics Industry, Inc., 1275 K Street NW, Suite 400, Washington, D.C. 20005. (202) 371-5200.

Soil and Water Conservation Society of America, 7515 NE Ankeny Rd., Ankeny, IA 50021. (515) 289-2331.

Solar Energy Research & Education Foundation (SEREF), 777 North Capitol Street NE, Suite 805, Washington, D.C. 20002. (202) 289-5370.

Toxic Avengers, c/o El Puente, 211 South 4th St., Brooklyn, NY 11211. (718) 387-0404.

TreePeople, 12601 Mulholland Dr., Beverly Hills, CA 90210. (818) 753-4600.

Trees for Life, 1103 Jefferson, Wichita, KS 67203. (316) 263-7294.

Trust for Public Land, 116 New Montgomery St., San Francisco, CA 94105. (415) 495-4014.

Union of Concerned Scientists, 26 Church St., Cambridge, MA 02138. (617) 547-5552.

United Nations Environment Programme, Room DC2-0803, United Nations, New York, NY 10017. (212) 963-8093.

U.S. Department of Energy, 1000 Independence Avenue SW, Washington, D.C. 20585. (202) 586-8086.

U.S. Environmental Protection Agency, 401 M Street SW, Washington, D.C. 20460. (202) 260-2080.

U.S. Fish and Wildlife Service, 4040 N. Fairfax Drive, Arlington, VA 22203. (703) 358-1700.

U.S. Forest Service, 201 14th Street SW, Washington, D.C. 20250. (202) 205-8333.

U.S. Public Interest Research Group, 215 Pennsylvania Ave. SE, Washington, D.C. 20003. (202) 546-9707.

Water Pollution Control Federation, 601 Wythe St., Alexandria, VA 22314. (703) 684-2400.

Wild Canid Survival and Research Center/Wolf Sanctuary, P. O. Box 760, Eureka, MO 63025. (314) 938-5900.

Wild Horse Organized Assistance, P. O. Box 555, Reno, NV 89504. (702) 851-4817.

The Wilderness Society, 900 17th St. NW, Washington, D.C. 20006. (202) 833-2300.

Wildlife Society, 5410 Grosvenor Lane, Bethesda, MD 20814. (301) 897-9770.

Windstar Foundation, 2317 Snowmass Creek Rd., Snowmass, CO 81654. (303) 927-4777.

World Environment Center, 419 Park Ave. S., New York, NY 10016. (212) 683-4700.

World Resources Institute, 1735 New York Ave. NW, Washington, D.C. 20006. (202) 638-6300.

Worldwatch Institute, 1776 Massachusetts Avenue NW, Washington, D.C. 20036. (202) 452-1999.

World Wildlife Foundation, 1250 24th Street NW, Washington, D.C. 20037. (202) 778-9563.

World Wildlife Fund, 1250 24th Street NW, Washington, D.C. 20037. (202) 293-4800.

The Xerces Society, 10 SW Ash St., Portland, OR 97204. (503) 222-2788.

Publications

Below is a list of magazines, newsletters, newspapers and books.

Magazines

The Amicus Journal, Natural Resources Defense Council, 40 West 20th Street, New York, NY 10011. (212) 727-2700.

Animals, Massachusetts Society for the Prevention of Cruelty to Animals, Subscription Services, P. O. Box 581, Mt. Morris, IL 61054. (800) 998-0797.

Audubon, National Audubon Society, Membership Data Center, P. O. Box 52529, Boulder, CO 80322. (800) 274-4201.

Audubon Naturalist, Audubon Naturalist Society, 8940 Jones Mill Road, Chevy Chase, MD 20815. (301) 652-9188.

Consumer Reports, 101 Truman Ave., Yonkers, NY 10703-1057. (800) 234-1645.

E Magazine, P. O. Box 699, Mt. Morris, IL 61054.

EcoTraveler, P. O. Box 469003, Escondido, CA 92046-9850. (800) 334-8152.

FREEBIES Magazine, P. O. Box 5025, Carpinteria, CA 93014. (805) 566-1225.

Green Calendar, Metro DC Environmental Network (MetNet), 645 Morris Place NE, Washington, DC 20002. (202) 544-5125.

New Age Journal Sourcebook, P. O. Box 51162, Boulder, CO 80321-1162. (800) 234-4556.

Organic Gardening, P. O. Box 7304, Red Oak, IA 51591-2304. (800) 666-2206.

Wilderness, The Wilderness Society, 900 17th Street, NW, Washington, D.C. 20006-2596. (202) 833-2300.

Newsletters or Newspapers

Best Fares, P. O. Box 171212, Arlington, TX 76003. (800) 635-3033.

Bottom Line/Personal, Boardroom Reports, P. O. Box 58446, Boulder, CO 80322. (800) 274-5611.

Greenmoney Journal, West 608 Glass Avenue, Spokane, WA 99205. (509) 328-1741.

Marine Conservation News, Center for Marine Conservation, 1725 DeSales Street NW,

Washington, D.C. 20036. (202) 429-5609.

Natural Traveler, P. O. Box 728, Glen Cove, NY 11542-0728. (516)759-4847.

Nutz & Boltz, P.O. Box 123, Butler, MD 21023-0123. (800) 888-0091.

The Planet, The Sierra Club, 730 Polk Street, San Francisco, CA 94109. (415) 923-5653.

Reusable News, U.S. EPA, 401 M Street SW, Washington, D.C. 20460. (202) 260-7751.

Travel Smart, Communications House, Inc., 40 Beechdale Road, Dobbs Ferry, NY 10522. (800) 327-3633.

Books

The Banker's Secret by Marc Eisenson; Villard Books.

The Chemical-Free Lawn by Warren Schultz; Rodale.

Clean & Green: The Complete Guide to Nontoxic and Environmentally Safe Housekeeping by Annie Berthold-Bond; Ceres Press.

The Complete Guide to Green Careers by Bill Sharp; Island Press.

Co-op America's National Green Pages; Co-op America.

Earth Work: Resource Guide to Nationwide Green Jobs edited by Joan Moody and Richard Wizansky; HarperCollins San Francisco.

Eco Vacations: Enjoy Yourself and Save the Earth by Evelyn Kaye; Blue Penguin Publications.

Ecologue: The Environmental Catalogue and Consumer's Guide for a Safe Earth, ed. By Bruce Anderson; Prentice Hall.

Economics as if the Earth Really Mattered: A Catalyst Guide to Socially Conscious Investing by Susan Meeker-Lowry; New Society Publishers.

50 Simple Things You Can Do to Save the Earth by The Earthworks Group; Earthworks Press.

50 Simple Things Your Business Can Do to Save the Earth by The Earthworks Group; Earthworks Press.

Global Network: Computers in a Sustainable Society by John E. Young; WorldWatch Institute.

Green at Work: Finding a Business Career that Works for the Environment by Susan Cohn; Island Press.

The Green Consumer by Joel Makower, John Elkington and Julia Hailes; Viking Penguin.

The Green Travel Sourcebook by Sally Wiener Grotta and Daniel Grotta; John Wiley & Sons.

The Healthy Household: A Complete Guide for Creating a Healthy Indoor Environment by Lynn Marie Bower; The Healthy House Institute.

Home Herbal by Penelope Ody; Dorling Kindersley.

Investing from the Heart by Jack Brill and Alan Reder; Crown.

The New Solar Home Book by Bruce Anderson and Michael Riordon; Brick House.

The New Natural Cat: A Complete Guide for Finicky Owners by Anitra Frazier with Norma Eckroate; Dutton.

The Next Step: 50 More Things You Can Do to Save the Earth by The Earthworks Group; Andrews and McMeel.

Nontoxic, Natural, and Earthwise by Debra Lynn Dadd; Jeremy P. Tarcher.

Office Green Buying Guide by Kathleen Gray; Green Seal.

The Recycler's Handbook: Simple Things You Can Do by The Earthworks Group; Earthworks Press.

Saving Water in the Home & Garden by Jonathan Erickson; TAB Books.

Shopping for a Better Environment by Laurence Tasaday with Katherine Stevenson; Meadowbrook Press.

The Tightwad Gazette, The Tightwad Gazette II by Amy Dacyczyn; Villard Books.

What to do When You Can't Afford Health Care by Matthew Lesko; Information USA, Inc.

The Whole Earth Catalog edited by Howard Rheingold; HarperSanFrancisco.

Internet/Bulletin Boards

Classroom Earth BBS, (517) 797-2737.

Earth Art BBS, (803) 552-4389. (Provides a list of all environmental bulletin boards by logging in and downloading the list.)

EcoNet, (415) 442-0107; E-mail - econet@econet.org; World Wide Web - http://www.econet.org

Environet BBS, (415) 512-9108.

Envirolink, (412) 683-6400; E-mail - admin@envirolink.org; World Wide Web - http://www.envirolink.org

The GreenMoney Online Guide, (410) 573-1595; World Wide Web - http://www.greenmoney.com

HEMPTECH - World Wide Web - http://www.HEMPTECH.com

National Audubon Society - World Wide Web - http://www.audubon.org/audubon/

U.S. Environmental Protection Agency - World Wide Web - http://www.epa.gov/

The Well, (415) 615-7911; E-mail - support@well.com; World Wide Web - http://www.well.com

INDEX

About the Author

Michelle A. Potter, a writer, has written award-winning poetry, environmental articles, and numerous computer software manuals. She began *The SAVing Source* newsletter in 1991. Besides being an avid gardener, she loves quilting, reading, and walking in the woods. She lives in Maryland with Pradeep, her husband of 11 years, and her two cats, Jasmin and Simba. If you would like to contact her with your comments about the environment, the newsletter or this book, write her in care of Rima World Press, P. O. Box 271, Columbia, Maryland 21045.